Dedicated to
Alice Rose Glasser
and Forest Hart Easley

TRANSFORMING
The Difficult Child

The Nurtured Heart Approach

Shifting the intense child to new patterns
of success and strengthening
all children on the inside

Updated
for 2013!

Howard Glasser
and Jennifer Easley

Transforming the Difficult Child

The Nurtured Heart Approach

For information contact: Howard Glasser
4165 West Ironwood Hill Drive
Tucson, Arizona 85745
Email: adhddoc@theriver.com

Cover Art by Alice Rose Glasser. Book production assistance provided by Richard Diffenderfer. Copy editing by Chris Howell, Melissa Block and Barbara Sears. Printed by Vaughan Printing, Nashville, TN.

Library of Congress Card Catalog Number: #99-90249

ISBN-13: 978-0-9670507-0-6

ISBN-10: 0-9670507-0-7

Printed in China

First Edition: 1999
Second Edition: 2005 (not 2002)
Third Edition: 2008
Fourth Edition: 2013

Acknowledgments

I AM DEEPLY GRATEFUL to all those who have supported, encouraged and cheered my development of the Nurtured Heart Approach. It is only because of the many parents who asked "when is your book coming out?" that I finally decided to put this project in motion. Having initially struggled and failed to organize my approach on paper, I am eternally grateful to Jennifer Easley, who agreed to collaborate with me. Jen's skills at relaying my ideas in a cohesive manner and at creating a flow for the written model have been awesome. Thank you. This book would not have happened without your great skill.

I also greatly appreciate the tremendous encouragement from my wonderful colleagues and supporters. My heart goes out to my friends at the many schools in Tucson and around the country, as well as in the many Head Start programs, who have begun the incredible ground-breaking process of integrating the Nurtured Heart Approach into their classrooms and the school environment. I especially wish to thank my dear friend Bob Scheuneman and the many others who have modeled ways to further turn up the dials on these powerful interventions. I am also extremely grateful to Dr. Dennis Embry, the designer of PeaceBuilders and founder of Paxus Institute, for the kind words of his preface and his ongoing support.

My deep appreciation goes to Dr. Patch Adams for initially teaching me the word "Transformation" in 1984 by helping me to understand my own transformative experience.

Recognition is also due those creative souls who joined forces and helped to put the finishing touches on the first edition edition: adept editorial help from Barbara Sears and Chris Howell, and talented book production assistance from Richard Diffenderfer. Great appreciation to Marcia Breitenbach who read and reread the manuscript in the most dedicated and talented efforts to get everything as it needed to be.

Great thanks to Melissa Lynn Block for her magnificent talent and expert editorial support on the 2008 edition and again my great appreciation to Richard Diffenderfer who most wonderfully helped with this 2013 update.

I am forever grateful to the parents and children that I have been fortunate to know and with whom I have been honored to work. You are the heroes of this book.

I am forever grateful to my parents, Nathan and Julia Glasser, and to my brother Joel for their kind encouragement and support.

Acknowledgments

Last, but not least, I am totally indebted to my wonderful and great daughter Alice, who is living proof of the power of the Nurtured Heart Approach. She has shown me how incredible it is to use one's intensity fully. She is a product of the model since birth and I am thrilled that her artwork, which she created at age 7, can grace the cover of this book.

Thank you, too, to the angels who have constantly whispered in my ear sweet words of advice about ways to cultivate and fine-tune this approach.

—Howard Glasser

I T IS IMPOSSIBLE TO ENUMERATE all those who have helped inspire and motivate me in the process of co-authoring this book. There are so many. Primarily, the parents and children I have worked with over the years as a therapist must take the greatest thanks. If not for their experiences, courage and wisdom, the need for birthing this book into the world would not be so clear. It is their contributions and inspiration that have moved my heart and fingers through this project.

Howie Glasser will always be the visionary-warrior, battling on the front lines to bring this magical model into the world—for the far-reaching future changes we need for our children. He was the primary fuel I needed to assist in this momentous undertaking. If not for Howie's undying dedication to change the world and heal the children, I believe I might have given up long ago. It was his fire that spurred me on to the task we needed to do. Thank you Howie.

Thanks must be given to my parents, William and Barbara Stotts—as foundations for my own growth and development, and to my brother, Bill, who impelled me to believe in myself as a writer, or at least behave like one to complete this book. Without the patience and computer tutoring of my nurturing husband Glenn, I believe I would have murdered my computer and possibly the project with it. After months of my whining, computer confusion and repeated mistakes, he was still willing to help us format. Thank you Glenn—for being the stabilizing force I could lean on during those darker hours.

—Jennifer Easley

Table of Contents

Foreword

"Thank you for staying in control when I sent you to time-out. You were frustrated but you didn't throw a tantrum. I appreciate that," encouraged Ann, the playground monitor at one of our local schools.

"Mrs. Willis told me that you used excellent concentration and effort for the last hour. You also chose to keep your cool with Mrs. Willis for her entire class period. I am very proud of you," commented the principal to a child who had a pattern of angry outbursts.

"I see that you're cutting up the green paper and pasting a pattern onto the purple paper. I love that you're focused on your assignment and you're not interrupting my work or annoying the dog," acknowledges a grandparent who has been caring for a severely disturbed granddaughter placed in her custody. She is tuning the child to a new level of success. "Keep up the good work."

THESE COMMENTS MIGHT SOUND ODD to the casual passerby, but as I listen, I know Howard Glasser and his team must be very busy angels touching yet more children's lives in family homes and schools in Tucson, Arizona. The techniques he and his co-workers have refined to a shining brilliance create small, daily miracles in the lives of children and the people who care for them.

The child on the playground now spends much less time angry, upset and making the world an ugly place for himself and others. He is playing more, getting along beautifully and learning the life skills that will continue to extend success everywhere he goes: at school, at home, in relationships and even later in business. That's a lot brighter future for a child who seemed destined to become a life-long bully.

The child in Mrs. Willis' class has started being able to be "in control" for the whole day, instead of disrupting the flow of teaching and learning every few minutes. Now that child is directing his intensity well, opening the door to a whole world of successes.

The grandchild, after three months, now looks and acts like a normal, lovable seven-year-old. Before, the future looked rather bleak for a child who, having grown up with a severely disturbed mother and father under extremely stressful conditions, swore non-stop, acted-out sexually, was destructive and hit others.

All of these children needed some sort of industrial strength intervention at home, at school and in the community to help them have their hearts filled with love rather than hate and to apply their intensity to successes rather than to provoking an ever-growing trail of failures.

These are the children most people have given up on. Not Howie Glasser. He has a rare passion. He truly wants each and every child to succeed. You can see that in the gleam in his eye. He does not give up. So many people do. Therapists and educators in effect give up when they accept some terrible trauma a child has experienced as an etched "circuit board" for the child's life. Parents give up, too, because it's hard to get the right combination of advice and tips that work with intense children.

Howard Glasser struck me as the "Little Engine That Could" from the first moment I met him at a professional meeting of psychologists and counselors. He has kept his eye on the prize— a "nurtured heart" for each and every child.

How has Howard Glasser done this? He's not an academic. He's not a researcher. He is a keen observer. He is a natural scientist. He is always watching to see what works and how he can make it work a bit better the next time. In this sense he is like the founders of our country who were diligent observers of the natural world, such as Franklin and Jefferson. The frontier for the next generation is no longer freedom from an overseas political tyranny, as it was in the founders' time. The frontier now is in creating freedom from the anger, hurt and violence affecting the hearts of our children from nearby, domestic causes. The challenge of today's frontier is to create freedom from the life of failure many children inadvertently experience as a result of a world un-equipped to handle the growing level of intensity with which more and more of our children with the greatest potential are born.

One needs only to read the news, see the headlines about juvenile crime, substance abuse, domestic violence, teenage pregnancy and more to understand that the world needs many nurtured hearts, not injured hearts.

Howard Glasser sees that. More importantly, he has some amazingly simple tools to help anyone who loves children—approaches designed to nurture children with fragile hearts and injured hearts and ultimately all children.

Learning to nurture children's hearts can be a daily habit. Howard Glasser provides us with tools to nurture a child's heart even when the child seems not to want nurturing or acts in a way that makes us want to withdraw or even be angry.

Do the tools of the Nurtured Heart Approach always work? Of course not. However, they work beyond any approach yet designed. They work when many things do not and with both average and special-needs children.

Learning the Nurtured Heart Approach will help any parent, teacher or professional create much greater justice and love in the world. That is all there is in the end, with the great accounting that occurs as we review our time on this planet.

Dennis D. Embry, PhD.
Co-Founder, PeaceBuilders
Founder, Paxus Institute

Introduction

E VERY PARENT WANTS TO SEE HIS OR HER CHILD SUCCEED. Your intention regarding creating success for your child will always be your most powerful ally. It is our intention to give you the tools with which to develop and maintain a way of parenting that creates tremendous success. This book will present strategic ideas and the technology to accomplish this core goal.

In selecting this parenting book, you are a parent already in the process of making a powerful decision to parent more consciously and with more determination. You will be pleasantly surprised to find that you can also parent with much more "peaceful" leverage and results than you would ever imagine.

Not all parenting books and parenting models are the same. Almost all models are designed for the average child. Some work a little bit for the difficult child, but all the methods that we have come across fail to hold up under pressure in the challenging situations in which you most sorely need effective approaches. Traditional methods of parenting and teaching get stretched beyond their capacity when applied to the difficult child. Many approaches will actually backfire and make problem behaviors worse.

This book is about a system designed specifically for the intense, difficult child. We call these methods the Nurtured Heart Approach.

Not only does this approach hold up to extremely challenging behaviors, it works beautifully at the other end of the continuum. It helps the average child to thrive beyond any other style of parenting that we have observed. To withstand the pressures of peers and the stresses of our times, even the average child has to be significantly stronger on the inside than ever before. This model meets that need.

This approach is about strategically creating actual experiences of success for children within the context of their activities and their relationships. Success is powerful medicine. Even limit setting, with the right spin, can become a tremendous source of success.

We intend this guide to be user-friendly. You will find it filled with stories and metaphors from life. It is our objective to make the techniques and the reasons behind them completely understandable.

The sole purpose of this book is to give parents and educators all the skills and knowledge to which we ourselves have had access; and, in that way, **to coach parents toward the ultimate outcome of becoming their child's therapist.**

In the context of our book, "therapist" simply means agent of change. There is no quicker route to having your child live a life of success. You are the most powerful person in your child's life and therefore are in the best position to have a profound effect.

This book is constructed in steps. Each is defined by a recommended strategy and adds to the preceding ones in a way that builds a progressive framework and complete system for parenting even the most challenging child.

Take just one step at a time. Our recommendation is to introduce each new step for a period of a few days to a few weeks before incorporating the next strategy, depending on your child's response and your own comfort level. However, if you are highly motivated and want to move fast, you can initiate all the steps in a matter of a day or two. Either way, make sure to keep the strategies going for the long run.

These strategies are designed specifically for the difficult child. Although they work beautifully for the average child, the techniques need only be applied as intensively as the situation merits. Our rule of thumb in developing these methods over the years has been the more intense the child, the more intense the application required. Normally, this simply translates into performing the techniques more frequently and with more detail, intent and emotion. This will be explained as we go.

Most authors in the field ultimately highlight the limitations and obstacles that form the texture of the life of a difficult child, whether that child is labeled as having Attention Deficit Hyperactivity Disorder, Oppositional Defiant Disorder, Conduct Disorder, Post-Traumatic Stress Disorder, or simply as being "challenging."

Even though most books in the field are loaded with recommendations, the underlying message in most every one that we have seen is ultimately discouraging. A picture is invariably painted of a lifelong dilemma and a lifetime trail of accommodations such as medication, long-term treatment and some level of acceptance of undesirable behaviors.

No one seems to present the possibility of essentially changing the old pattern of challenges and failures to a new pattern of successes. No one seems to believe that a "transformation" is a real possibility: that a challenging child can have an essential change of nature and can begin to consistently use his intensity in remarkably positive ways.

The Nurtured Heart Approach, however, has helped thousands of families have an amazingly successful effect on their child in lasting and powerful ways.

Best of all, parents who had previously felt as if their relationship with their child was hopelessly stuck in the deepening muck and mire of problems wound up feeling like they had a heroic influence in turning their child around.

Changing the pattern to success is much easier than people think. You simply need to believe it can be done; you need to have a plan, the right techniques and the drive and resolve to follow through. Enjoy the journey.

Chapter One
How Quickly Things Can Change
Matthew, Brandon and Monique

Matthew, age 7, pushes his sister to the ground after she tells him to leave her alone. He had been taunting her. His mother, angry and frustrated, lectures him on right and wrong, sends him to his room and promises that if he does it again he'll have no TV for the next two days. Does it work? It would have worked on an average child. It doesn't work on Matthew. He is back at it at the first opportunity. His mother feels betrayed and exhausted. She's run out of tricks. She's tried everything she has read in books and magazines. She worries about what her son will be like in six months and in six years if his seeming addiction to pushing the limits doesn't stop. Mother and child both deeply feel the pain of what has been happening at home and at school. She is a very well-intentioned mom with a bright and well-intentioned child who just can't seem to control himself.

Brandon, age 4, will not take "no" for an answer. He tantrums at the least bit of disappointment, whether in the form of a "no" to his demand for more sweets, or a "stop that, please!" to his efforts to explore the family stereo system. Everyone has been saying that he'd outgrow it, but the tantrums are getting worse… and everyone didn't have to live with him! The tantrums are embarrassing in public and scary at home because he has started to break things and to be mean to pets. Nothing his parents try or read about seems to work for more than a short while. His parents had even visited a psychologist a few times a year earlier for some consultations. They are beginning to feel as if people are staring at them—as if they are being seen as "parents from Hell." They are terrified of how Brandon will fit in at school. As things are going, the situation appears destined for disaster.

Monique, age 13, has habitually under-functioned for as long as her parents remember. She is a smart child who has been failing most of her classes and who would rather argue about homework or chores than ever just do them, no matter how simple they are. Her parents divorced when she was 11. They are tense all the time, largely over their distinctly differing opinions on how to deal with Monique. Her dad feels that she gets away with murder with her mom, and her mom feels that Monique's father is much too strict. Besides, neither style seems to work. Monique's defiance has brought her to the edge of growing up too fast. She wants to pile on the makeup and hang out with older kids with questionable lifestyles. Her mom is positive Monique will find a way to get pregnant before too long. Monique knows exactly how to push her mom's buttons. The arguments, warnings and lectures that follow her defiance have become a way of life.

All three children had several things in common. They had become stuck in patterns of negativity from which they could not extricate themselves, no matter how much individual advice they received. All three children had the impression that they got more interesting reactions and larger responses from the adults in their lives as a result of their negativity than for positive behaviors. And all three children were very smart young people who were seriously under-functioning, primarily because they expended the greater part of their intensity and intelligence in the unproductive endeavor of trying to get strong reactions to their problem behaviors.

All the parents of these children also had several things in common. They were trying extremely hard to be good parents. In fact, they were trying every trick that they could mobilize. They had sought advice, read books and magazines, watched videos and observed the world around them for solutions. They basically had tried every reasonable traditional parenting possibility they could get their hands on. Not only that, but they tried things over and over, with as much conviction as they could muster. Despite their excellent intentions, nothing was working.

Although some might have judged them to be bad parents based on the behaviors of their children, in actuality, just about everything they tried would have worked just fine with easier children. They had already reached their own conclusions that normal methods did not work with their child. They were also beginning to suspect that something was dreadfully wrong with their child. To say the least, they were not enjoying parenting, and they were half-crazed with thoughts of where this all was leading.

What these parents wound up doing, in each case, turned things completely around in only a month. They applied a wonderful combination of techniques designed specifically for the intense and challenging child. These simple but unusual methods created the changes that quickly and surely drew the child into a completely new focus on being successful.

Here's a glimpse of what these families wound up doing:

In all three families, the parents took a four-part class that explained how intense and difficult children really operate. Each class gave them theories and techniques to carry them along the way toward reversing the pattern of problems and toward shifting the child to a new pattern of successes.

After the first class, the parents were clear that they no longer wanted to accidentally fall into the trap of feeding a pattern of negativity by

having a response that was not a true consequence. They were beginning to realize that some of the conventional tactics for parenting a child with problem behaviors—tactics such as reprimands, words of concern, lectures, redirections, threats, discussions, yelling and other ways of making a big deal about negativity—were actually rewards rather than consequences, however unintended that result. They also left the class conscious of different ways they could make a big deal over several different kinds of successes that had been going unnoticed. They were ready to apply some magic and "trick" their child into a world of successes.

All three parents began by briefly visiting their child several times a day—*before* the predictable behavior glitches occurred and applying three techniques. They did **a form of recognition in which they verbally described what they saw the child doing.** They also gave their child **increased acknowledgment for skills, values and attributes that they wanted to see more often, and they consciously gave recognition for qualities like showing a good attitude, using self-control, being respectful, getting along with others, being cooperative and so forth.** The parents needed to be very diligent and creative to ensure that this appreciation occurred whenever possible, at the slightest glimpse of the desired trait.

They also left the class ready and willing to give their child compliments throughout the day for instances when rules were not being broken. In this way they were **teaching the rules by actually creating positive experiences through pointing out when their child was not fighting, not whining, not arguing or not being disrespectful.** They were realizing that, inadvertently, they had always made it more interesting for their child to break rules by reacting more strongly when the rules were broken and, in effect, rewarding disrespect and bad attitude by giving energy to the problem.

Now they were having more animated responses when things were going right, and they were using new techniques and creativity to make it happen. All this added up to *five minutes of intervention a day*—a far cry from the hours it typically took to discuss and solve problems.

By the end of the second week, though for most parents this was not even necessary, some had devised and implemented a way to give their children credit when rules were not being broken; credit for performing chores and responsibilities; and credit and recognition for a host of other desirable behaviors. They had linked this with a clever way to exchange these credits for privileges, and they were quickly seeing how the children were buying in, despite their initial reluctance.

Each child was making considerably more effort to follow the rules, to be cooperative and helpful, and to meet his or her responsibilities. Each child seemed pleased to have acquired a newfound ability to get back old privileges and some new ones in a predictable and straightforward way.

By the third week, the stage was set to have consequences really work. The children now really knew what the rules were and really knew what happened when the rules *weren't* broken. They were beginning to trust that they would be noticed for not breaking rules, and this both felt good and benefited their new economy of credits.

Since the parents were no longer inadvertently feeding the negative behavior, they could now deliver a simple but effective consequence each and every time a rule was broken. After initial testing, each child quickly reassessed his or her new circumstances and realized that all the interesting reactions happened when things were going well and when rules were NOT being broken. And **they also realized that all that happened when a rule was broken was a consequence, without the reward of a reaction.** The children began to deepen their investment in successes.

By the fourth week, the parents were able to extend these beneficial strategies to school. They were now able to have their child succeed, regardless of whether the teacher was skillful or not, and without having to actually spend time there themselves. This made an enormous difference in their ability to go through the workday without fear of being called or remanded to the principal's office for a conference.

Miracles happen. What's more, miracles such as these are driven by tactics that add up to a fraction of the time it ordinarily takes to handle problems. Such tactics ultimately gave these parents the satisfaction of feeling like they had turned things around and that they were indeed gifted and talented parents.

The parents of these children, like many others who have come across the Nurtured Heart Approach, have simply realized that **it's all about how and when we choose to give our energy and that the parenting and education of intense children simply requires a slightly different spin.**

As for Matthew, Brandon and Monique, they are all doing great, living out new scripts of success. And as for their parents, they are savoring both their own accomplishments and that of each of their children.

Chapter Two
A New Primer
Understanding the Difficult Child

I N ORDER TO BEST TEACH YOU THE TECHNIQUES that make up the Nurtured Heart Approach, we'd like to introduce you to the basic premises that explain the thinking behind the techniques. This will greatly increase your therapeutic impact by helping you deeply understand what you are doing and why you are doing it.

This chapter is not about *how*—not about the techniques themselves—but the *why* that underlies and motivates the techniques. Even if you can't stand the suspense and want to jump ahead, hang in there for the next 35 pages. The techniques will follow. These first chapters will keep you briefly on hold while we explain the pieces of the puzzle that we think are crucial.

Keep one more thing in mind as you start reading. When we were bright young therapists fresh out of school, like many other bright young therapists our theories were complex and complicated. Now that we are older and much more direct, our theories are much simpler in nature. Fortunately, simplicity turns out to be far more powerful. What follows are a few of our core ideas:

Playthings 'R Us

Think about your child's favorite toys. How many features do they have? Do they have five, 10 or even 100? Even if they had 1,000 features, they wouldn't come close to approaching the number of amazing features we people have.

Simply translated: **we are, by far, our child's favorite "toys."**

We have many more features than any other toy. We are much more animated, reactive and interactive than other toys. We also have the best remote control ever made.

We can walk and talk and do virtually anything under the sun. In addition to an endless array of actions, we can display a multitude of interesting emotions and moods in an infinite number of combinations, subtleties and gradations.

The other toys can't compete. It isn't even close to a level playing field. **To our children, we are the closest things to a personal entertainment center imaginable.**

We can combine our actions and feelings into seemingly limitless interactive pairings. We can wash the dishes in a flourishing blend of glory, song and dance on one day, and the very next day we can be doing the dishes in an utterly foul mood.

The volume buttons on this superior toy are readily and handsomely displayed, as are all the other buttons that, when pushed, really get the show going.

These buttons are fascinating to the sensibilities of a child in the throes of forming opinions of how the world works, along with opinions of his or her effect on the world.

Here's an illustration. When a child is slow to get ready for school, especially when his parent is in a rush to leave the house, what occurs? The parent, with the best of intentions and simply using mainstream methods of parenting, might express some annoyance or frustration. The parent might then give a few warnings or issue a few mild threats in attempts to move the situation along. If the situation continues, the parent could easily show some anger, give a stern lecture or fire off a reprimand or two. This would all be quite within the norm and might well have the desired effect on the average child.

In any case, the child gets a firsthand glimpse of one of many ways to get the "toy" to have a more animated reaction. This toy is simply more reactive and more energized under these adverse circumstances.

With this in mind, consider how easy it is for a child who is a bit more needy, or a bit more sensitive or intense, to reach a simple conclusion that can come to govern his life, albeit in a most unfortunate way.

The conclusion, again, is that we are by far their most fascinating toys; and that **these toys operate in much more interesting ways when things are going wrong.**

Unfortunately, given the traditional methods of parenting at our disposal, an intense child can have this perception despite our very best intentions.

The Flatliners

The energy, reactivity and animation that we radiate when we are pleased is relatively flat compared to our verbal and nonverbal responses to behaviors that cause us displeasure, frustration or anger.

Get out your Geiger counters.

Our cultural ways of saying "Thank you" and "Good job" pale in comparison to the sharper tones we display even in simple redirections such as "Leave your brother alone" or stronger reminders such as "Get your shoes on, the bus will be here in two minutes."

As a culture, we amp up the "nos," but give little to no juice to the "yeses."

Traditional parenting approaches do not lend themselves to showing much excitement for positive behaviors or smaller successes. Our normal tendency is to deliver a relatively neutral level of acknowledgment.

However, as a culture, we jump all over every level of failure. Non-success captivates us and draws our focused attention and our bigger reactions.

Children have what amounts to built-in energy detectors. They can easily sense when we become more animated. And their impressions stay on file. If you need an image to help hone in on just how judicious children can be in weighing when and how more can be had, just watch the next time your child splits hairs over which serving of dessert is bigger.

If a child perceives that mom or dad gives a bigger reaction to poor grades or annoying behavior, the child absorbs and measures this experience, and other like experiences, as part of her impression of the world and of how we operate. **The basic equation goes something like this: misbehavior or poor achievement plus parent equals lots and lots of energy and lively connection from parent to child.**

Similarly, if a child sees that doing the chores, or doing homework, or having a good attitude or not breaking the rules nets *less* response, that child begins forming an operational view of reality that the greatest payoff lies in *not* doing what the parents want.

In light of experiences like these, the sensitive, needy or intense child is especially likely to become convinced that the payoff for *not* doing what a parent wants is much greater than the payoff for complying or behaving nicely.

It's much more about reaction than attention. In a way, the "toy's" responses are much juicier and far more present when things are going wrong. **Children are drawn in when we show up in more energized ways, whether that energy is positive or negative.**

"Payoff" is used here to refer to the level of energy or level of response that the child comes to believe is available in relation to every event that comprises his or her life. Many children will simply go for the bigger slice of life every time.

The question then becomes: "If we truly are in some fashion our child's interactive, virtual reality toy, then just what kind of toy are we going to choose to be?"

Can we regulate the flow of payoff, or the way we choose to radiate energy, to the advantage of our child and our family?

Fortunately, you can make great choices here—choices that make a world of difference.

Video Game Therapy

Have you ever noticed how many intense and challenging children are drawn to video games?

For the time they are playing, they are captivated, content, focused and alive. The reason is that their lives make total sense while they are engaged in the game.

While they are avoiding dangers or attaining goals, they are constantly being acknowledged and recognized with landmarks of success. When they break a rule of the game, they get a clear and immediate consequence. The timing is always perfect.

Children figure out in no time flat that the game is totally consistent and predictable. There's no getting around the program. It's unflappable. It can't be bullied or manipulated. No amount of tantrums or pleading or nagging can change the format.

They not only come to accept the realities of the game very quickly, on their own, but they also figure out new games in the time it would take the average adult to locate the manual. And once they size the game up and assess that there's plenty of excitement and recognition for their wise and skillful actions and only a consequence for crossing the line, they throw themselves into performing at their top level. They typically don't waste their time trying to manipulate or bully the game. They direct their intelligence exclusively into doing well.

They seem to love video games, and well they should. Children typically throw themselves into the game with great zeal, and that feels good. They get to experience what it feels like to use their intensity in a successful manner. They constantly try to attain new levels and outdo their personal best and the personal best of friends and family members. They can both sense and see their attainment: the game provides evidence of their attainment and the excitement that is associated with success, every time, at every turn.

How many parents would give anything to see their children involve themselves in school life and home life in the same manner… investing and focusing their energies in increasingly successful ways?

The secret is simple. **Video games have the structure that more and more children need and demand.** Think about it. In a video game:

- Acknowledgment and consequences are reflected in completely straight-forward ways. **There's no wiggle room, no unclear line to dance over, no inconsistency in terms of whether the child has overstepped.**

- **Frequent audible "bells and whistles" and discernible continuous scoring reward the child's positive accomplishments as well as steps in the right direction.**

- **Conversely, clear and immediate consequences mark actions that are unacceptable. When the consequence is over, it's right back to scoring.**

Athletic events are similarly structured. There, the lines defining a consequence are perfectly clear, and goals are achieved in clearly delineated ways. The cheering, encouragement and scoring always happen in-bounds, while simultaneously the knowledge exists that every transgression, no matter how slight, carries with it a consequence. The referee doesn't yell or scream at a player, but states the consequence neutrally while still holding the player fully accountable. **No excitement or energy is given to the broken rule—just a result.**

This structure consistently brings out the best that athletes have to give. Even athletes who lack internal structure and who can barely conduct themselves off the playing field without creating havoc seem to thrive within the structured parameters of the game.

The basic translation is: energy, reaction and payoff for the good stuff and "Oops, broke a rule—here's your consequence—no energy, reaction and payoff for violations." The accountability is clean; then, it's right back to the excitement of participation and success. The outcome is predictable and consistent every time the game is played.

It's the same in the venue of the video game. The essential feature is that the excitement and fireworks occur when the child is on track, busily attaining the goals and avoiding the obstacles. "Scoring" equals recognition and emotional nutrition. When things go awry, the game's response is straightforward. The consequence occurs in a simple, unceremonious fashion, and when it's over, it's right back to successes.

The structure is brilliant and simple. It's a beautiful blend of recognition and limits and a beautiful outcome of mastery and accomplishment for the child.

We've never seen a child play these games to lose. That quality of attainment, carried over to important areas of functioning, can have delightful meaning in the life of a difficult child and family members.

We are not enamored by the subject matter of most video games that we've seen on the market. The gratuitous violence and frequently inane content are unwelcome guests in our homes. However, the crucial question is: can we observe, learn and apply these principles to parenting our challenging children away from failures and toward new patterns of success?

The Big Bang Theory

Children are attracted to energy. Very early in their lives, they become sensitized to the energy of interaction with other people, and they quickly perceive what it is that produces fireworks.

When July 4th comes around every year, if fireworks displays are available and in the plans, chances are we'd rather see a significant display than just a few firecrackers. Does a child want to see a few sparklers in the back yard or get to a real show? And does a child want to see the first few minutes of the show and leave or stick around for the grand finale?

Let's return to the video game analogy for a second. Players are quick to determine that flashing lights and high scores are more exciting. It is easy to see that the energy of success has the bigger payoff.

How does this affect a child's view of his or her parent as a personal entertainment center?

Unfortunately, when a child perceives that far more energy and animation are available for negative behavior, he or she quickly becomes fascinated, and mounts repeated attempts to light up all the lights. If the bigger fireworks best capture the child's interest, then he or she might just discover a few circumstances under which this favorite toy tends to have some pretty interesting reactions. Many intense, intelligent children have fixated the greater part of their wits and intelligence on figuring out just how to elicit the strongest possible reactions from adults in their worlds.

Of course, this represents a horrible waste for the child and a miserable state of day-to-day warfare for the parent. However, the child feels, at some level, as if he has hit the jackpot. This is why these situations tend to escalate until and beyond the point where the parents are tearing their hair out, wondering where they've gone wrong and why their child is *out to get them.*

The risk of this phenomenon increases when the child has a high level of energy and sensitivity, along with a heightened need for attention. When the child figures out that negativity is the best or only way to get the bells, lights and whistles really going, he or she will weather the content of the lecture, warning, or reprimand just to get that heady hit of adult energy…as long as there's *more*, that's motivation enough. Under these conditions, the child quickly figures out the "video game" and realizes that *not* doing what the parent wants essentially gets far more reaction and emotion.

Many parents aptly describe this experience in video game-friendly terms: "He really knows how to *push my buttons.*" We all have particular behaviors that are especially frustrating or especially annoying to us. Some of us openly advertise where those buttons are and exactly what it takes to push them. Most of us do this to one extent or another without realizing it. We all have buttons, and this isn't going to change. You aren't going to turn into a saint who isn't bothered by anything. The good news is that you can create better buttons!

When our children are feeling especially needy, sensitive, or energized, they are expert at dialing into our reactions by manifesting particular behaviors that will draw us into the trap. We are particularly vulnerable when we are stressed or distracted and our child takes note that we are otherwise unavailable. We might as well wear neon signs declaring that the only way our attention is available is to push a button and extract a reaction, albeit negative in nature. To a child who is feeling needy, certainly no crime in itself, **any** response is better than no response at all.

It is a trap…unless we can demonstrate, to the child's satisfaction, that the payoffs—the ways in which we choose to give our energies—are substantially greater for the good stuff.

We must create a new perception: that **in our roles as "toys" or "entertainment centers," we radiate greater responses when the challenging behaviors are *not* happening and when successful behaviors *are* happening.**

And we have to be convincing. We cannot just give lip service to this idea. We have to demonstrate that we truly radiate more excitement, animation and energy to everything that is not a problem.

Our challenging children are not out to get us. They are simply going for the best level of connectivity to our energy.

Chapter Three
Patterns
Moving Mountains

Parents who seek help because of a difficult child are truly caught between a rock and a hard place. They are almost always doing something amazing: they are invariably doing the very best job they can with the tools they have. It may not appear that way to an outsider and it may not feel that way to them. However, without a doubt, when examined closely, *most parents of difficult children are using highly acceptable, well-researched, standard methods of parenting that would have an excellent chance of working well with a child with an easier temperament.*

The problem is that traditional and conventional forms of parenting—the kinds that we are surrounded by on television, in film, books and magazines, as well as in our extended families of relatives, friends and acquaintances—invariably fall short of the mark when applied to children with strong needs and stronger manifestations of temperament. It's also virtually impossible to avoid the influence of the most formidable part of our personal parenting training: having been a child in an environment where we were liberally exposed to conventional techniques and philosophy.

Conventional methods of parenting, unlike video games, respond in a low-key way to everyday events that are going well, but as soon as something goes wrong, the energy tends to really explode in the form of lectures, warnings, consequences, and punishments. These are more energetic and emotional responses than those the child gets from "being good."

Despite the best of intentions, attempts to apply conventional parenting or teaching techniques to the difficult child are doomed to failure. Most frequently, the situation worsens because conventional methods put the payoffs in the wrong place. These methods are, energetically, *upside down.* A child can quickly but subtly form a pattern of negative behavior in exchange for that payoff—and this can become a significant disruptor of family life before parents even have a chance to figure out what hit them.

Imagine

Imagine your child playing a video game that had upside-down payoffs, with more points and bigger rewards for doing the wrong things, but minimal recognition for avoiding obstacles and achieving the goals of the game. If scoring and level of excitement were the most important thing, which to children's perceptions they most often are, you'd probably see players becoming adept at "doing the wrong things."

The parents and the teachers we meet are, without a doubt, trying as hard as they can with the tools they have. But these tools are like that fantasy upside-down video game: they accentuate the negative and fail to acknowledge success with the same vivid detail and enthusiasm.

If you were asked to knock down a brick wall and given a rubber mallet to perform the job, you could be wailing away for an eternity and not accomplish the task. No matter how hard you tried, you would not get the job done. Pretty soon, you would begin to feel self-conscious. People might walk by and roll their eyes and look at you as if you were dysfunctional. You might even begin to doubt yourself and wonder if it were true.

Not the right tool for the job.

However, if you were then given tools with more power, such as a sledge-hammer, a jackhammer or a bulldozer, you'd have the job done in a flash. "What's next?" you'd say, pumped with your accomplishment.

The Right Tools For the Job

The job of parenting a difficult child is exactly the same. The more intense the child, the more intense the intervention needed, and the more dramatically conventional methods fall short of the mark.

The same applies to teaching methods. We can't tell you how many times we've heard teachers say they're overwhelmed because they have a handful of difficult kids in a class. They are absolutely trying as hard as they can with the tools they have.

When these same teachers are given stronger and more encompassing strategies and a new slant on how to proceed, things change quickly and dramatically.

Have you ever noticed how technology has evolved in virtually every area of our lives, with many generations of change occurring in a relatively short period of time? Look at computers and the information industry or think about all the advances in the areas of transportation and communications. The progress is phenomenal. Quantum leaps in technology unfold in orchestrated response to the heightening needs and intensities of our ever-expanding lives.

This has distinctly *not* occurred in the field of working with children. Without doubt, new and interesting approaches to working with kids continue to be developed; however, on a level of structural properties—the components of approaches relevant to working with children who are more intense—existing approaches are more or less the same as in years past: the equivalent of trying to knock down a brick wall with a rubber mallet. It just will not work.

Balloons... Balloons For Sale

Imagine putting air into a balloon. It's pretty much a perfect fit and a perfect container. You can tie a knot and bat it around the room and it will essentially hold up. If you substitute water in the balloon, the fit is compromised. The structural properties of the water exceed those of the balloon in a precarious manner. A balloon usually will hold water under non-stressful conditions, but if the container is bumped, bruised or dropped, it's likely to explode.

If you substitute a substance like liquid metal or another denser substance for the air, the container will quickly show itself to be flawed, even though it may hold small amounts at a time. It really doesn't matter whether the balloon is red, yellow, green or blue. The more intense substances will inevitably not be contained.

The very same is true for parenting methods. Even though numerous approaches have been developed that all work to varying degrees with easier children, they are unable to deal with the intensity of the more challenging child. Hailed as fancy new approaches, they are structurally the same yellow, green or blue balloons.

So many parents we have met have gone the extra mile to study this, that and the other thing in attempts to help their child. They sense that their children are stuck in a pattern that they cannot escape on their own. They desperately search for new methods in books, magazines and parenting classes. Many parents of difficult children have other, easier children, and see for themselves that what works for that easier child is not going to cut it with this more demanding child. Frustration grows as method after method fails, and the intense child continues his reign of terror.

Structure

Intense children need to perceive that the container that is each new environment can hold them safely, competently and fearlessly. In a child's eyes, every new milieu is orchestrated by the adult in charge, whether or not the adult is present. A difficult child, in particular, must test every new adult he or she meets to see if that person can handle him or her. If it is determined that the adult can adequately create a positive structure and therefore a suitable container, the child settles down fairly quickly. If not, the testing continues.

Children cannot conceptualize or verbalize what is going on inside them, but they certainly can sense their own needs. Acting-out is their way of expressing this. If additional structure is not forthcoming in positive ways, then the acting-out typically escalates as the child pushes to have his need met. **Any consequent acting-out is a way of saying, "I need more structure. I need more structure!"**

Unfortunately, what many parents worry about is true. Children with a high need for structure will continue their quest, finding themselves attracted to the alternative forms of structure available in the community. Numerous forms of positively structured experiences are available in most towns and cities—like team sports, scouting and various interest groups. Unfortunately, children with high needs for structure and tendencies to get attention in negative ways more often seek out the menu of negative types of structure that seem to be found everywhere.

What drugs, alcohol, gangs, involvement with the juvenile justice system and getting pregnant as a teen have in common is that they are all highly structured experiences. They take over one's life and dictate the course of the day. They all distinctly limit one's freedom.

However, when we intervene with structure in a positive way, the new behaviors from the difficult child begin to fall into new patterns of successful endeavors. Success can become second nature, like breathing, and can take over one's life as well… in expansive and healthy ways.

Across The Great Divide

All parenting can roughly be divided into two general categories:

- *All that we do in the way of being positive:* all the acknowledgment, recognition, affection, loving remarks and gestures, as well as the support, encouragement, modeling and education we offer daily.

- *All that we do in the way of setting limits*: coaching, instructing, warning, admonishing, redirecting and administering consequences.

Every parenting paradigm that we have come across—from formal approaches to very informal approaches—have these two elements in common. Even families that appear to have no approach whatsoever, when examined by way of these categories, will almost certainly be making at least rudimentary attempts to provide positives and to set limits.

Conventional parenting and teaching approaches consistently fail with the difficult child for two main reasons:

1. **Efforts to provide positives and set limits are not well enough coordinated.**

2. **These efforts do not possess the intensity required for the job.**

Most parenting and teaching approaches also have the energetic payoffs in the wrong places. **While excitement may be generated by high-level events like great grades or special achievement, most everyday responses to positives are low-key, vague and infrequent.**

21

Even parents and teachers who are under the impression that they take a strong view on limit setting typically let things go by giving warnings or ignoring incidents. When the limits continue to be pushed, dramatically stronger emotional reactions to problem behaviors occur, either verbally or non-verbally.

These are the straws that break the camel's back, because a child who senses she can get more out of negativity will perceive these bigger reactions as rewards—the very opposite of what was intended. **Some children even think that the only time they receive focused, quality time is when they've broken a rule and they get a lecture or a reprimand.**

In many ways, typical parenting wisdom is upside down. We try to teach delicious qualities like good attitude, responsibility and self-control when those qualities are not being used. An example is having a strong emotional reaction to a child's bad attitude. Energy given to the bad attitude actually *reinforces* the very thing we want to see happening *less often*.

In effect, as a culture, **we try to teach the rules and limits when they are being broken. But there's a backlash: the energy given to the broken rules actually reinforces the undesirable behavior.**

Not only is the time when transgressions have just occurred one of poor receptivity to learning, but the structure also is inverted. With conventional methods of parenting, corrective pressure ends up making things worse by making the payoffs for problem behaviors bigger than they already are.

Imagine being a chiropractor, ushering a new client into your office. Your first glance was shocking. You noticed that his hips were where the shoulders should be and vice versa. You might quickly conclude that this inversion of structure couldn't possibly work. You first need to get things in their right order structurally. A great degree of basic successful functioning will fall into place right away when this occurs.

Some "enlightened" approaches recommend explicitly telling your children how you feel when they act-out. "It hurts my feelings when you annoy your sister." "It makes me sad when your teacher tells me you were not paying attention in school." These approaches, although potentially effective for the average child, backfire with the intense child.

Not only are you explicitly displaying where the buttons are for future use by the difficult child, but you wind up giving payoff, in the form of your energy and relationship, to the problem behavior.

Other approaches call for other kinds of lengthy discussions or discourses in relation to the problem behaviors. Any way you slice it, it adds up to *more energetic payoffs for exactly the behaviors that you least want to reinforce*. Why water weeds?

Patterns, Patterns, Patterns...

Children figure out where the greatest available parental energies exist and gravitate toward whatever it takes to obtain the highest volume of response. This pattern is hard to prevent unless we are extremely skillful, careful and in possession of techniques that work in the right direction. Inadvertent patterns form all too easily.

If, for example, your child is under the impression that the only time he sees you animated, emotional and excited is when he is being demanding or rude or interrupting your phone calls, he will dial this excitement up when he desires a connection or some refueling. Although this is far from a subversive plot, patterns can easily form around such a perception.

The pattern has nothing to do with a particular problem behavior. Its essence has to do with obtaining a connection with you and your intense reactions. Although the pattern may make you feel that your child is out to make your life miserable, the attraction is simply to your energy; the behaviors that follow are mostly subconscious.

This is actually excellent news in that what may appear to be a deep-seated psychological problem is far more likely to be simply a habit. Habits can be changed.

For intense, high-energy children, the tendency to stumble into a pattern of pulling for negative attention is significantly stronger than for children with an even temperament. Their need for relationship, connection and response is profound. At various times during the day, it becomes their be-all, end-all, driving force. If adults are available, it typically is then that their energies are in highest demand. Reactions of other children also can figure importantly in the equation.

It's almost as if these children were desperately seeking a million-dollar check. It is far more captivating than a one-dollar check. They don't quite register that it has a negative sign in front of it. They are just riveted on what they perceive to be a big payoff.

Fuzzy: Was He?

Our children cannot live their lives with clear knowledge of who they are unless we construct their environments in clear ways. The more complex and confusing the world gets, the more evident it is that we require a clear inner guiding voice to keep us sane in an often insane world.

Intense children, who have a proclivity for impulsiveness and lack of inhibition, have a strong tendency to lead confusing lives because they often get more out of the world by acting out than by using good control. What could be more confusing? They very well know that we want them to be well behaved. They see and feel the resulting distress in the lives of everyone concerned when they aren't. We give them strong messages along those lines. In effect, however, we pay them more for the very opposite of what we want.

Children who lead confusing lives proliferate confusion wherever they go. This does not stop when childhood ends. Adults who emerge from childhood with this pattern have to work extremely hard to pull themselves out of this constant tailspin. They lead guarded lives, forever regretting their intensity and forever fighting their tendency to be drawn to chaotic situations, thereby subconsciously sabotaging potential successes.

If we use new technology to reverse the confusion, we effectively make these children's lives clearer. Then, their energies get realigned in new habits of success and they emerge from childhood with a clear inner compass.

They consequently can be drawn to clearer relationships with other people in their careers and in other endeavors. They comee to possess the ability to give *themselves* relationship and recognition for both the small and large successes in their lives.

This minimizes their need to attract attention and gain a reaction for extraneous matters such as doing poorly, acting out, arguing, getting sick or having an outrageous appearance.

They become invested in *not* pushing the limits. They can then also apply control and bring themselves to a halt before they cross the line, despite their intense feelings and intense energies. Rather, they get to a place where they can apply their intense energies to healthy endeavors.

If difficult children experience and integrate clarity early in their lives, they undoubtedly will be better able to provide the same for their own children later on. This in itself is worth the parenting work required now. It certainly beats dreading that our difficult children will bring us difficult grandchildren.

Clarity now makes all the difference in the world later.

Junk Food

As you read the rest of this first section describing the thinking behind our techniques, keep the following in mind:

A difficult child can be getting a tremendous amount of negative attention throughout the course of a day and still be literally starving to be noticed. Some children actually remain restless at bedtime or have poor sleeping patterns because their intense hunger for psychological nutrition remains unmet, despite having had an amazing amount of negative attention. Just as it's hard to fall asleep when you're hungry for food, it's hard to fall asleep when you're hungry for emotional nutrition.

We know this from working with hundreds of children who had sleep issues among their presenting problems and who spontaneously and remarkably changed for the better when their parents were able to deliver a higher grade of nurturing attention.

The salient feature here is that **negative attention is like junk food. You can get it all day long and still be hungry. It has no nutritional value.**

Even worse than the low level of nutrition, however, is the fact that negative attention gets encoded by the child as failure.

Children do not necessarily know how to decipher their experiences, just as a letter entering the post office doesn't know which bin to go into to get to its destination. It is by observing the way we value an experience that our children sort experiences in their memory banks.

If we observe our challenging child testing a limit and we blurt out some version of "Cut it out," "Stop it," or "Quit it," or anything else that is perceived to be tinged with a tone of criticism, it is very likely the experience will be sorted psychologically into the bin intuited as "FAILURE."

Of course, this is far from the intention of the parent, who is trying to do good parenting. Every parent wants to create a successful child. **However, as the child continues to amass experiences intuited as failures, the critical mass of messages downloaded as representing it begin to have a life of their own.** The child's feelings of worth falter because his or her sense of self-esteem is centered around and tied to the experiences for which he or she is noticed most intently.

For the challenging child, unfortunately, these are experiences connected with poor behaviors. **Poor behaviors thus lead to poor self-esteem.** Experience has taught the child that he or she is most worthy of a parent's time and energy when using poor behaviors.

Ordinary Compliments Fall Short

And so, what happens when we try to tell these children that they are really wonderful or tell them that they have done a good job?

Often at these moments we can discern the effects of poor self-esteem and poor self-worth. All too often, these children may reject ordinary positive comments because inside they are doubtful at their very core that anything positive could possibly be true. They are basing this on their primary experiences of themselves, which are their frequent actual experiences and confirmations of negativity and failure.

Inside, these children are combating the attempted nurturing with an inner, subconscious monologue along the lines of "I am *not* a good kid. I'm always getting in trouble."

Their cumulative experience of themselves becomes hinged on their perceived experiences of failure. Ordinary positive remarks like "Good job!" or

"Thank you" thus often backfire and play right into the child's self-confirmation that everything is *not* good.

This is a major source of frustration for the parent of a difficult child, who is often desperately trying to be positive but who cannot quite get under the child's radar of low self-esteem.

We cannot make that "FAILURE" tape magically disappear. However, we can loosen its hold and create a new and healthier tape of substantially more power.

Flying Under the Radar: Digestible Emotional Nutrition

If you were working with a person who had had a stroke and lost the ability to swallow, you would have to evaluate whether you were going to attempt to feed her solid food and weigh the serious side-effects you might encounter. Most likely you would arrive at any number of solutions that involve advances in technology, from simply introducing nutrition through a feeding tube into the bloodstream, to more complex but advantageous methods of pumping nutrition directly into the stomach. In any case, you would be able to circum-navigate the problem.

The same is true for our work with the difficult child. Is there a version of technology that will allow us to deliver powerful and nutritious emotional attention such that the child cannot block, defend against or "choke" on it?

What will follow in subsequent chapters is just that technology. For now, though, a bit more explanation will provide the necessary jumping-off point.

Finding the Right Blend of Structure

If you asked a difficult child to be kind to himself *and* to set limits on his impulses when necessary, he probably would have little or no idea what you meant because he lacks the internal experiences and reference points through which to make the vital connections. Any attempt to comply would, without a doubt, be short-lived.

Challenging children need a level of structure that gets past the defenses—a blend of recognition and limits that matches their level of intensity and consistently envelops their lives. Over time, the child integrates the process: becomes able to give himself recognition and appreciation and at the same time to set inner limits. How many adults can do that? If this were a universal set of skills, the self-help books that line the shelves of every bookstore would quickly become obsolete.

Therapeutic Tension

Imagine having a nagging back problem that brings you to the point of needing help. A friend points you to the orthopedic section of your local drug store. For starters, you get one of those banded elastic braces that the folks in lumberyards use. After a few days you decide that you need added support. So you bite the bullet and visit your doctor, who recommends a more sophisticated orthopedic support.

It turns out to be a brace that comes in two sections. It has two molded sides that fit the contours of your sides. It hooks together in the back and is then cinched up in the front by a series of connectors from the top to the bottom. The more you cinch in just the right places, the more the dynamic tension. When you get the tension just right, your back feels some blessed relief.

One morning, you wake up and cannot find one side of the brace. The dog has dragged it somewhere and hidden it. At some point you realize that it can't be found and that you're running late for work, so you start getting ready for the day. Your back hurts. Out of frustration, you put the one remaining side up to your back and try to attach it. No matter which way you try, half of the brace lends no support.

This is very similar to attempts to parent by either being positive or by setting limits. It also is all too easy to flip-flop from one approach to the other without ever working the two elements in combination.

You can truly be the world's best limit setter and not achieve the necessary level of dynamic tension or "therapeutic physics" unless the limits are used in combination with strong positives.

Or you can be the world's most positive person and still be compromised in working with a difficult child unless the positives are used in conjunction with excellent limit setting.

It is only through working both sides of the bracing, in union, that the right therapeutic physics occurs. By combining limit setting and positives interactively, and turning up the dial, the required dynamic tension is achieved.

Taking the Necessary Stands

If we are going to produce a strong structure based on the components of 1.) effective limit setting and 2.) being positive in a new and effective way, then it is absolutely imperative that we take three very distinct **stands.**

For our purposes, the definition of a stand is a consistent, resolved and committed position based on specific and targeted strategies. Taking a stand also involves elements of being *immovable, relentless* and *unflappable.*

The three stands are as follows:

Stand I:

- Absolutely No! I refuse to get drawn into giving my child greater responses, more animation and other unintended "payoffs" for negative behaviors. I won't accidentally foster failures and reward problems with my energy. There will be consequences for negative choices, but all my energy will go toward energizing successes.

Stand II:

- Absolutely Yes! I resolve to purposefully create and nurture successes. I will relentlessly and strategically pull my child into a new pattern of success.

Stand III:

- Absolute Clarity! I will maintain total clarity about the rules that demonstrate fair and consistent boundaries and consequences. When a rule is broken I resolve to give a true and effective consequence that will quickly lead once again to energizing success.

The Big Mistake

A tremendous mistake that many well-intentioned people make when viewing the family of a difficult child is to walk in and declare that what needs to happen to get things back in order is really very simple.

Typically, the family feature that jumps out for the observer is that something is *very wrong* here. "How can you let that child get away with murder? If only you had stronger rules and stronger consequences. That would fix him." In reality, the family has already intuitively sensed that and has been trying every version of stronger consequences they could imagine.

The reason this is a mistake is: **If a child has a pre-existing perception that she gets more out of life for acting negatively, and we take only the stand of intensifying the rules or the harshness of the consequences, we will actually make things worse.**

A child in this situation will size up the new circumstances and conclude that by breaking the new rules, she can now get a new array of reactions and payoffs. This may pique her interest, and **she will often surmise that she and her parents now are simply playing for bigger and more interesting stakes**.

She will not be doing this on purpose, but the addictive side of the habit will draw her toward the prospect of a larger response. The tougher rules and consequences will only add incentive to act out further. No matter how good the rules and no matter how substantial the consequences, the child's intensity will continue to be centered on pushing the limits. **If the third stand is taken alone, it will simply be a new video game...**

That is, unless the other stands are taken first.

Many family therapists make this same mistake, regardless of their level of experience. We ourselves have certainly had this experience until we woke up, smelled the coffee, and took note of the damaging effects of first intervening with stronger limit setting.

It's much akin to conducting individual treatment with difficult children by dealing directly with the problems. These are children who are already out of control in connection with getting much too much secondary gain and too many benefits from their negative actions…and *here we are, giving their negativity additional response, energy and relationship!*

It is not an accident that these children do not readily progress in individual treatment or that they progress temporarily and then slide back. They quickly assess that all the special connection and relationship they desperately seek would cease if they were to do more than give lip service to improvements. More typically, they keep up a steady stream of juicy incidents to fuel the engaging nature of the therapy. **It's not that they don't wish to change, but they cannot as long as we accidentally play into the very addiction that we wish to alter.**

Before we can effectively take a stand with limits and introduce consequences in a way that will finally have the desired result of breaking the child's habit of pushing the limits, we must first establish, to the satisfaction of the child's perceptions, that there are indeed viable alternatives to getting responses in negative ways.

We must establish trust that nutritious attention and gratifying responses for their successes are abundantly available. That, in fact, a minefield of potential successes awaits them; and that it is virtually impossible to avoid the excitement for all the things that are going right.

Starting with a stronger version of limit setting would be like trying to put the second story on a house before the first floor is in place. It simply wouldn't work, no matter how desperately one wanted the master bath with the jacuzzi tub before anything went in on the ground floor. However, **the more carefully one prepares the groundwork and the first essential steps, the better the second phase will proceed.**

The Nature of Healing

We want to call to your attention two aspects of healing that apply to our methods.

Have you ever noticed how a wound heals? This occurs when new tissue forms and attaches to existing healthy tissue, eventually expanding to the point where the damaged tissue is minimized or dissolved.

This is, in effect, comparable to our view of the healing of the damaged sensibilities of the difficult child. Week by week, as the parents of the child expand their new repertoire of tools and strategies, the healthy aspects of the child's behavior that have always existed but resided in the shadows of negativity become increasingly prominent and override the problem areas. Farfetched? Wait until you see the results. Once you apply the approach, you'll see firsthand that this is true.

This is not unlike another aspect of healing shared by holistic approaches. Instead of dealing directly with the symptom as is common in allopathic Western medicine, many alternative medicine practices respect the connected, systemic and miraculous nature of the human being and conduct treatments that strengthen the inner sanctums of the body—the spirit and the heart, the mind, natural resilience, and the immune system. When these vital energies are restored or bolstered, many health issues are resolved and the person frequently comes through the therapy into a higher level of functioning.

This is nothing less than the path that you are embarking on in this journey to transform your difficult child. As the child's energy is shifted from failure to success externally, via your efforts, his inner world takes on a new and healthier focus. Behavioral issues that once seemed disconnected from one another and from the influences of the environment disappear as the child's inner wealth increases.

Difficult children simply are stuck in patterns from which they cannot extricate themselves without skillful help from the parent/therapist. If seeing yourself as a therapist seems scary, consider that parent as therapist is not entirely a new concept. Therapist simply means agent of change. Change occurs simply and smoothly with a new set of tools that fit the task and a new approach that makes the process doable and understandable.

No one is as well suited for the job of therapist as the primary caregivers, who spend infinitely more time with the child than anyone whose office might be visited now and then for help. Your child will always seek the domain of your relatedness anyway. You might as well take full benefit of its healing advantages.

Caregivers are optimally influential because they exist in context with the child, and their roles in this context have purpose and meaning. The child relies on caregivers for his or her basic needs.

Parents and teachers and other important adults are the central figures in the child's life. They have the most power to make crucial changes toward inner strengthening occur in the quickest and most decisive manner. With your strategic help, your child's intensity will move to a higher level of functioning and acquire new and welcome patterns of success.

Chapter Four
The Energy-Challenged Child
A New Perspective

A LTHOUGH WE HAVE ALREADY DESCRIBED THE DIFFICULT CHILD from a variety of angles, we have conspicuously avoided what most authors on the subjects of Attention Deficit Hyperactivity Disorder (ADHD) and other diagnostic categories of behavioral disorders typically start out with front and center.

This is because we wish to de-emphasize jargon and labels, which have gotten out of hand—in case you haven't noticed.

The difficult child may be assigned one of many labels. Current symptoms, current fads in diagnostic thinking, who is doing the labeling and the labeler's frustration with the child all influence which label the child is given. Schools have become famous for rendering opinions on diagnosis, mostly out of frustration with the task of managing many challenging children.

Attention Deficit Hyperactivity Disorder (ADHD), Attention Deficit Disorder (ADD), Oppositional Defiant Disorder, Emotionally Disturbed, Behavior Disorder, Depressed, Conduct-Disorder, Incorrigible, Anxiety Disorder, Post-Traumatic Stress Disorder and Adjustment Disorder are just a few of the many terms that can be attached to a difficult child. Many more children have avoided formal labels but pose difficulties to their caregivers just the same.

We prefer to describe difficult children as being *energy-challenged*. They are consistently unable to handle or effectively control their physical, cognitive and intensity and emotional energy. Children do not come off an assembly line with evenly regulated energy systems.

Often these children are like a Mercedes Benz with the brakes of a Model T. They are blessed with abundant energy, great potential, strong intelligence, and curious and creative natures, but they have limited internal patterning and limited tools and skills to manage their incredible flow of energy, emotion and thought. Dr. Russell Barkley[1] aptly describes children who have been labeled as ADHD as having a *disorder of self-control.* They often are gifted intellectually, artistically or with special sensitivities but at the same time are overwhelmed by their intensity.

---

1. Barkley, Russell A., PhD., *Taking Charge of ADHD: The Complete Authoritative Guide for Parents,* Guilford Publications, Inc., New York, 1995.

They may actually have a normal or superior amount of control but a far greater than normal amount of physical, emotional, temperamental or neuro-logical intensity.

To characterize the quality of being over-energized is to describe children who are struggling frequently to control or maintain appropriate behavior. These children require much greater effort, focus, inner guidance and self-control than the average child to achieve and maintain success. **Just as you have to work harder to meet the real demands of parenting such a child, an intense child has to work much harder than the average child to appropriately control and channel his intensity.**

Over-energized children struggle with lack of inhibition. There are times when they cannot conjure up the inner control required to override their impulses to do the inappropriate. As a result, they end up behaving in ways that place them in extreme conflict with their environment or the people close to them.

These may become children who are kicked out of school or childcare when adult frustrations accelerate, or who find themselves in out-of-home place-ments. Without tools to deal with their intensity, these children are prone to failure in most conventional support systems.

Under-energized children can also be energy-challenged and difficult, but in different ways. They may be children who are so sensitive or reactive that they often function in an overly passive, depressed, withdrawn or shut-down state. They are often overlooked in a busy classroom or family and do not actively seek to have their needs met in positive ways. They may also turn to misbehav-ior for attention, but usually in obtuse or inconspicuous and less pronounced ways. In some instances, this type of child is the "daydreamer," "doodler" or "worrier" who fails to finish or undertake required work and responsibilities. In other instances the child is quietly defiant.

Difficult or energy-challenged children are often recognizable by the frustrations of those who love and work with them and their own frustration in failing to get in gear more than sporadically. The children we are referring to here invariably are not exercising the potential of their true worth and abilities. These children often defy treatment and educational techniques and are not being adequately served by the current school, home, juvenile and mental health programs.

Energy Is A Gift: The Other Side of ADHD

Anyone who has experienced the glory of focusing his energies to accom-plish a goal or a project or master a skill knows that energy is a gift. The problems occur when energy is disorganized and unstructured. Although energy-challenged children manifest malfunctions of control in pronounced ways, at one time or another we all are flawed in our ability to control our energies.

How many of us can stick to a diet for more than a short period, despite our knowledge of the consequences of yo-yo diets? How many of us properly avoid ultraviolet rays or the intake of foods that can lead to disastrous effects? How many of us are self-disciplined enough to exercise daily or build the inner controls and skills necessary to overcome our fears or to handle our strong feelings or negative thoughts?

The truth seems to be that we are all compromised, at least occasionally, in our healthy ability to apply self-control. Hyper-energized and hypersensitive children are at a serious disadvantage when it comes to applying the brakes because they have so much more to overcome. The brakes on a cement truck have to work much harder to stop the vehicle at 10 miles per hour than do those on a little Honda going the same speed.

Another important thing to keep in mind when dealing with children is that they are still learning to apply the brakes in general. This is a major part of the developmental overlay of childhood. They aren't even close to our mature development in this department, and they certainly weren't born with any ability to control. Babies have virtually no control at all. If they did, there wouldn't be a diaper industry. Control is a process mastered through evolution and development.

As things stand, very few people envy anyone with ADHD (Attention Deficit Hyperactivity Disorder). An ADHD child's inability to control his intensity and impulses is mainly looked upon as a curse. Children who are bouncing off the walls in over-energized fashions are considered by some to be a blight on society.

Having a lot of energy is not a crime. Anyone, though, who has experienced either unharnessed energies in themselves or in another knows that it can seem overwhelming. Just think of the last time you had too much caffeine or were extremely nervous or excited about an upcoming event.

Energy is something that we all have in common, however. It is absolutely essential to every aspect of our endeavors. Without energy, it would be hard to accomplish anything, as is evident when we are feeling run down.

In a like manner, managing our energies is another task we all have in common. It seems that a lot of what we do is a matter of self-regulating our energy systems. When our energies are on an even keel, the management requirements are usually simple.

When our energies drop or explode, the job of managing them becomes much more complex and difficult. Let's say, for example, that you or I feel nervous, angry or just plain excited about something we just heard about. We are now in the position of having to handle an extra boost of energy within the bounds of what is okay. If we are angry and we handle our anger inappropriately, then we often may be judged on the basis of an impaired level of skillfulness and the choices we have made under stressful conditions.

We all have been overwhelmed by our energy at one time or another and we all know the feeling of having our brakes, or our ability to control our energy, falter from time to time. The key is, you wouldn't throw away a Mercedes Benz if the brakes weren't up to snuff. You'd find a brake specialist, and if they were scarce, you'd probably insist that the one you located teach you the tricks of the trade in case the problem ever crops up again. There are too many treasured features of the car to abandon it, but it sure could underfunction if the brakes were on the skids, so to speak.

Most ADHD children simply have underdeveloped abilities to apply the brakes and to contain their strong feelings and impulses. Their energies periodically or even frequently overwhelm them.

They do not consistently get to enjoy the positive impact their energy can have on a project or personal endeavor. If they do, it only happens on and off, seemingly with no rhyme or reason.

What's the difference between a highly efficient, energetic, successful child and a hyperactive child whose behaviors have fallen into patterns of impulsiveness, distractibility, poor response to directions, school failures, poor self-esteem, anxiety, anger, poor peer relationships or more?

The only difference is in *how the child harnesses and directs his or her energy.* It's the same energy with different manifestations.

It's hard to throw yourself fully into any endeavor successfully unless you feel self-assured. Take, for instance, a job situation that at first glance was new and confusing. One who knew exactly what was going on could approach the required tasks with absolute confidence. The ability to apply one's energies fruitfully is diminished to a large degree when there is anything less than clear understanding and a reasonable hope for success.

Like the rest of us, energy-challenged children require clarity of expectations and experiences of successfulness. Success leads to being self-assured in managing one's energy in a positive, confident and competent manner.

Getting A "Brake"

So, can we reach down deeper into the tool kit to see if there is a brake application to match the energy level of the modern high-powered, deluxe model vehicle? Can self-control be developed and augmented to match the intensity of the energy-challenged child? Absolutely!

We can moan and groan about the Model T brakes all day long, but it won't change anything. The brakes cannot change themselves. Likewise, **no amount of urging the challenging child to apply the brakes will work for more**

than a couple of minutes, hours or days at best.

If the brakes on my car weren't working, how much would be achieved by standing by the car and demanding improvement? "When I come back in five minutes, I want you to be working." Fat chance. Even if a miracle occurred and they worked again temporarily, the likelihood of long-term functioning is remote. The situation requires a mechanical solution: an intervention through action.

The Legacy of TV Parenting

While growing up, most of us watched our fair share of family television programming in the *Ozzie and Harriet* genre. Shows like *The Cosby Show, The Waltons*, and *Father Knows Best* have had a strong influence on our collective psyches by depicting an idealized version of family life in which every problem gets solved in 30 minutes and everyone comes out smelling like a rose. It made for great TV. Situations or conflicts were invariably solved with a discussion, a warning, a reprimand or a lecture, and life then proceeded smoothly.

TV versions of parenting easily get co-mingled with our own idealized versions of what a family should look like. This gets in the way, especially when parenting a difficult child. Difficult children need crystal clear and predictable limits. We throw them a curve when we give warnings, look the other way or use fuzzy consequences that seem natural and logical and might work with children of easier temperaments.

For the difficult child—who is literally addicted to negative reaction— lectures, warnings, and reprimands are actually rewards of our attention and energy. The reprimand or sermon that worked on Theo, the teenaged son on *The Cosby Show*, backfires with the difficult child.

The idealized textbook of television parenting to which we've been exposed doesn't come close to meeting the intensity required by the difficult child. Parents instinctively raise the intensity of their interventions with the challenging child, but more intense versions of conventional parenting only wind up reinforcing the child's impression that more reaction can be gained from negativity. What looks good on TV backfires in real life.

So many parents that we see are at their wit's end because the behaviors of their child have escalated beyond their own abilities to help. Ninety-nine percent of the time, these are people who deeply care and who have gone to great lengths to apply the methods at their disposal. Unfortunately, they are also frequently condemned because schools, neighbors and extended families often attribute the continuing behavior problems to inadequate parenting.

No Blame

It is so easy for the parent of a difficult child to feel blamed. Teachers, principals, other school personnel, and significant others in the family or the neighborhood are notorious for assigning blame, unintentionally or intentionally. Even therapists do it. The use of the term *dysfunctional family* has reached nauseating proportions.

Telling a family that their child must be on medications to remain in school is yet another way of communicating to the parents that they are having no impact and there is no hope of their having an impact.

In our experience, blame is almost entirely unwarranted. We know this because **when we give parents who have been so accused different and stronger methods, not only does everything fall into place behaviorally for the child, but the parents come out shining and rightfully feeling great about the changes they have fostered.**

The irony is that they usually have to expend a lot *less* effort using the new techniques. Handling problems on a frequent basis consumes a lot of energy.

Although many societal factors would have us believe that these families of difficult children are dysfunctional, they are far from dysfunctional when they have the right tools for the job.

It's the tools that are culpable, not the parents. It's the tools that are the problem, not the teachers or the child. Culpability rests with the methods we have at our disposal.

Taking the Dive

This book is about the steps necessary to build success and competency for both you and your child. It will involve some effort, as does anything involving change and energy. However, it will be surprisingly simple and the rewards will be enormous.

It should be heartening to know that these strategies are designed to empower parents with powerful, non-conventional tools that work in a short period of time, even with very difficult children. **In essence, you will be given all the tools necessary to become your child's therapist.**

If your child is currently undergoing counseling or psychotherapy, please discuss these techniques with your child's (other) therapist. They are not meant to take the place of therapy, but you may be among the many parents who discover that therapy is no longer necessary once the entire regimen of strategies has been implemented.

You ultimately must be the judge as to what is most beneficial for your child. Some parents may hope an outside therapist can make the desired changes for their child by uncovering some hidden dilemma or by giving the child some new keys to life. However, most parents innately sense that some changes in the home and classroom are the key. Most experts would agree. **For a child who already believes that he gets more close relationship by way of** negative issues, the mere act of talking about problems in treatment stands to deepen that very impression. Most therapists are trained to work with problems and many fall into this trap.

Most benefits or positive changes arising from outside treatment will be short-lived without the environmental shifts that support the child and the parent over the long run.

Committing yourself to all this book's steps in sequence, despite the level of challenge, will sharply increase your chances of a successful outcome. In our experience of bringing this treatment to thousands of families with difficult children, those who follow through with commitment invariably have excellent results.

A basic rule of thumb is this: **the more intense the child, the more intense the intervention.** Our system allows for higher levels of application when necessary. Conventional parenting systems would falter and make things worse when "amping up" the strategies for an extremely intense child. Our system is designed to meet this need.

Many parents are already spending the better part of their mornings or evenings being drawn into time-consuming conflict with their child. Dealing with problems can take hours of your time. The methods described in the following steps will altogether require a small fraction of that time.

Some families certainly will have to work at this with more resolve than others. Families with older children, who have had longer experiences of entrenched negative patterning, will frequently have to intensify the latter stages of this sequence. So will parents of children who have witnessed domestic violence.

Foster and adoptive parents often have children who have had unusually chaotic early lives, and will need to employ more vigorously the steps that we are going to prescribe.

If the challenge of changing your approach with your child concerns you, consider your frustrations up to this point and your worries about the future. You may know the territory of hopelessness and helplessness that often comes from parenting a child with whom little works for very long, if at all. All parents of difficult children have experienced this to a certain degree. To persist in this situation is infinitely harder than undertaking anything you will read in this book.

Frustration is excellent fuel to inspire change. It shows how much you care. These techniques are new ways of putting caring into action.

Chapter Five
Step 1
Windows of Opportunity

B EFORE WE START DESCRIBING OUR FIRST TECHNIQUE, take a few seconds
to contemplate the following two short stories. They embody two important attitudes that will form the thrust of our approach.

Shamu's Secret

One of the many in the delicious series of *Chicken Soup for the Soul* books,
At Work[2], features a fantastic story describing the truth about how Shamu, the
talented 19,000 pound whale, was trained to jump over a rope 22 feet in the
air above the tank.

Shamu may well have been an incredible jumper before he arrived at Sea
World. However, it is unlikely that this whale, weighing nearly 10 tons, could
have jumped over a rope stretched high over the water on command. He
wouldn't draw the big crowds week after week if his trainers gave the signal and
Shamu jumped an hour later or on the other side of the tank, away from the
rope.

Shamu was not with the Peking Acrobats prior to coming to Sea World.
Shamu's secret is his trainers and their approach to accomplishing their goals.

They have the intelligence and the skill to know that you can't start the
training by hanging a bucket of fish 22 feet high and commanding Shamu to
jump. Even though Shamu may want the fish, the proper connections have not
yet been linked up with the sequence of development of Shamu's natural
talents. These connections are not automatic. They evolve and they are developed.

Most people guess that the rope was lower in the training process, but very
few people figure out that **the trainers start out with the rope actually under
the water, at the bottom of the tank.**

Shamu was appreciated, patted, loved and rewarded when he first happened
to cruise over the rope accidentally. More than likely, Shamu didn't even know
what a rope was when he first arrived at Sea World. He just moved randomly
about in the tank.

Once Shamu had repeatedly experienced rewards every time he passed over

---

2. Canfield, Jack et al, *Chicken Soup for the Soul at Work,* Health Communications, Inc.,
   Deerfield, FL, 1996. Story told by Charles A. Coonradt.

the rope, he began to make the connection: *if I swim over this twisted thing, I get a snack and lots of love.* At that point, the trainers could begin, slowly and incrementally, to raise the rope. Hallelujah! The willingness of the trainers to start with the rope at the bottom, creating successes that would not otherwise exist, directly leads to a faster path of learning and a level of attainment well beyond what would normally occur.

You are setting out to build a very similar connection for your child. Once your child finally understands the link between the internal feeling of success and your response in terms of the energy and emotional reaction you have to give, she will begin to seek and integrate success into every aspect of life. A pail of fish is not required. The best part of working with children, in contrast to whales, is that the child will know when to help you raise the rope.

The Dance of the Tollbooth Attendant

The story of the Oakland-Bay Bridge tollbooth attendant has come our way through several different respected sources. One person, a college professor[3], recalls an early morning trip from San Francisco to Berkeley involving a most interesting journey over the Bay Bridge. No other cars were on the road. As he approached the tollbooths, he rolled down the window and heard the glorious sounds of old rock and roll dance music blaring away from a nearby radio.

In a quick scan of the area, he noticed that the tollbooth attendant several lanes away was out there grooving to the beat and having a great time. The driver quickly made his way over to the dancing attendant's lane and commented, "It looks like you're having the time of your life."

The tollbooth attendant's response was, "Of course. I have the best job in the world and the best office in the world."

The driver asked him what he meant and the attendant replied: "Well, I get to be out here listening to my favorite tunes, doing my own thing and meeting nice people.

"Besides, what executive do you know who has an office with four glass walls and a view that comes even close to this one. I can look west and just about see the ocean. I can look north and south and see beautiful views of the bay, and I can look east and see the mainland. If I work the early shift, I can see the sunrise. And if I work later, I can see the sunset. With all these clouds, the view is different everyday. Nothing can compare to this. Besides, I'm going to be a dancer, and I'm getting paid to practice."

The professor then pointed to the other tollbooths and said "What about the other attendants? They don't seem to be having the time of their lives."

The tollbooth attendant replied, "Oh, those guys in the stand-up coffins! They're no fun."

---

3. David C. Morrison, PhD. Grant Writers' Seminars and Workshops, Taos, New Mexico.

Obviously, everything is subject to how we choose to view it. How easy it is to forget that we hold that option card. Is the cup half-full or half-empty? It's our call. We can easily imagine ourselves in both situations: with the incredible attitude of the tollbooth attendant as well as without this vantage point of awe, dreading another day of annoying pollution, noise, traffic and headaches.

It's not only our choice, but we get to choose at *any given moment*. How are we going to view the world and the everyday events that comprise our lives and the life of our child?

The techniques that follow will supply you with practical ways of putting both these lessons into action.

Video Moments

If you're going to change the wiring you need to get to the wire box.

Here is the initial hurdle. How are we going to initiate taking the first stand, pulling our child toward successes, while avoiding the traps of giving energy to negative behaviors?

Say in your mind to your child: "We are not going to let you pull us into giving more response for your negative behaviors. We are not going to fall into the trap of fostering more experiences of failure. We are going to pull you into a new pattern of successes."

Remember, **conventional ways of being positive hit the radar and activate defenses**. Whatever tactic we use must come in under the radar in a way that will really be felt as emotional and psychological nutrition and be encoded as success.

The most efficient way that we have found to get this process underway is through the use of an **active form of verbal recognition**.

This strategy involves describing back to the child what the child is doing, saying or presenting. We call this method *Video Moments* because of its play-back-like quality.

These recognitions are like verbal snapshots of what the child is doing or how he may be feeling, almost as if you had an imaginary blind companion for whom you were describing your child's actions out loud. Video Moments need to be actively and generously given throughout the child's day. These will establish a process of profound acknowledgment, as these positive statements are felt in the child's heart as successes.

"I notice that you're working hard on your drawing. It looks like a fancy car with green stripes and a red top."

"I saw you dribbling the ball up to the hoop. You looked disap-pointed when your shot bounced off the rim."

Being noticed or recognized is much more powerful than one may initially imagine. It offers significant opportunities to account for life events that might otherwise pass by your screen as unworthy of comment. They are every bit as important to your child's feeling worthy of your esteem—and, eventually, her own—as are other more recognizable high-water marks of achievement.

In a way, they are *more* meaningful. How many adults enter therapy at some point, sick of perpetuating a pattern of trying to please their parents, spouses or associates? Typically, these people were only noticed in their childhood for the home runs and the high grades on the report card, if that. They have been forever hooked into seeking their parents' (and now others') mostly unavailable approval.

This technique is a remarkable way of showing your child that you notice and care about many aspects of her life. The moments to choose to describe are exactly those everyday moments that tend to be ignored. **Video Moments provide a powerful way of underlining and documenting that you really value the child for who she is.** It is not only a way of feeding her emotional reservoir, but of proving that she is not invisible. Indeed, many children feel they *are* invisible unless they are either going to the trouble of acting-out or doing something exceptionally well.

Video Moments call for describing what the child is doing, saying or presenting in an active, in-the-moment way. It simply involves feeding back to the child what you see her doing or saying at that moment, *without any kind of evaluation of what you see, or as little evaluation as possible.* Here are some examples of this way of conveying to your child they are being profoundly seen:

"I notice you're using many thick, curving lines in your design. Now it looks like you're coloring the bottom section with your brown crayon."

"I see that you have the first six math problems completed and now you look like you're busy thinking. I see the effort you've made."

In many ways, the moment is all we really have. In our hurried lives, it is oh so easy to become consumed with the past or the future. The magic, however, is in the moment. The moment is proof positive that we really exist. For the child who is desperate to be noticed, recognition of his everyday actions, expressions and feelings is an anchor to his spirit that needs to believe his life really matters.

Think of this like giving the child a **verbal "Kodak Moment"** or verbalizing for the child your awareness of her feelings, behaviors or wishes in a kind of **verbal video playback.** The practical application of this technique requires several unconventional communication dynamics on the part of the parent.

1. Use *non-judgmental language* when describing what you see. It is the neutrality of the message that allows the child to digest the recognition without feeling prickled by criticism or having to brace against praise.

Over time, this type of communication provides a foundation for the development of basic trust. The basic trust is derived from the child's feeling convinced that she is "seen" for who she is…and that this kind of validation is real and here to stay.

Psychotherapists use similar techniques, at times, to build children's trust, ego strength and ability to take in information about themselves and their behavior. Your use of this technique expands its power because a parent has so much more healing influence. Being noticed when things are not going wrong becomes a daily anchor for the child and solidifies the enormously important dynamic of the parent as nurturing and supportive rather than adversarial and critical.

This technique is also a jumping-off point from which the techniques that follow move to step up the child's sense of excitement in relation to positive behaviors as well as her sense of competency in moment-to-moment choices.

2. Be *very* specific. This is a second key quality of Video Moments. General or global statements like "that's great" or "good job" or "wow, that's beautiful" often do not contain enough information for the intense child. They can easily be ignored or distrusted by the child as untrue. For this reason, specific recognition has much more impact.

It is the detail that is convincing to the child. This kind of feedback becomes the child's positive proof of having been witnessed or seen:

> "You have a very proud expression on your face. It seems like you are excited about the tower you are building."

> "I heard you asking for an extra treat… I can see that you were disappointed when you were told 'no' and I sense by your tears that you are sad. I also notice that you're using your control to handle your strong feelings. Keep up the good work."

The true power of these Video Moments is in their ability to create recognition and success messages that the child can take in and metabolize. By "freeze-framing" what you notice and by verbalizing this back to the child, a new flow of energy is catalyzed. The child feels noticed and perceives this recognition from the parent as a success.

It's the neutrality of the message that gets under the child's radar, because it simply describes the reality of the moment and is perceived by the child as undeniably true. The child cannot refute the documented evidence of having been seen.

Circumventing the child's sensitivities about criticism allows the success message to flow right to the heart, the emotional "wire box" where messages about one's self resonate. By expanding the detail of the description, the child feels the certainty of being truly appreciated, which all children seem to need. It is the *details* that make this intervention hard for children to reject or defend against. Instead, they feel cherished and validated.

This intervention also gives the parent an opportunity to expand his or her repertoire of positive attention enormously. Many parents have said at our initial meeting that they saw few, if any, positive things about their child presently to get excited about. This may be true from a traditional point of reference. However, from our non-conventional vantage point, an infinite variety of potentially powerful positive events exists at any moment. Video Moments energize everyday, ordinary events. Remember the tollbooth attendant's beautiful way of seeing things.

"The color you chose for your project is very bright and glittery. I see you combined the purple with some orange."

"I can tell you are hungry. You ate your potatoes in a hurry!"

"I enjoyed seeing you ride your bike. You really seem to have the hang of making those quick figure-eight turns and those fancy stops."

All it takes is a visit to your child's room. Instead of getting caught up in the past (the storehouse of shortcomings and resentments) or the future (what isn't complete and needs to be done), you simply stay in the moment and describe exactly what it is that you see.

"Jason, I notice that you are trying to get the battery cover off your radio. You look very focused."

"Alex, I see that you are stacking the wood blocks and trying to make them balance. It looks like you're trying to straighten out the ones that are wobbly."

These parents have simply described the truth. Such comments cannot be blocked. Ten to 20 seconds total: a great utilization of their time. And they resisted the tendency to tack on remarks that Jason or Alex would absorb as representing failure (such as, "If you would work a little harder, Jason, you could figure that battery cover out," or "When you're done with your blocks, you really ought to clean up this room—it's a shambles"). Instead they creatively downloaded successes.

If a Jason or an Alex were intensely habituated to negative attention and strongly refused positive attention, he may tell you to stop the comments and take a hike. This occasionally occurs as a form of temporary resistance. You can simply *continue your stand* by refusing to get drawn in and thereby provide another success:

> "I can tell by your voice that you are annoyed and that you want me to leave. See you later."

You've generated even more success simply by describing the truth of the moment. Another tactic in meeting resistance is to use humor or a light touch:

> "I don't know what has gotten into me. I can't seem to stop making these comments. I'll try to stop, but I don't think I can. I just enjoy noticing you. Anyway, I can tell by your tone that you want me to stop."

Or, you can just be completely straight and meet your child's resistance or inquiry head-on:

> "I can tell you're thrown by the comments I've been making. You're right, I am being different. I realized that I mostly notice all the things that I think you do wrong. From now on I'm going to notice a lot of the good things you do. It's only fair. I'm liking it and you'll get used to it."

Although a difficult or over-energized child typically has a very high need for recognition, the application or timing of this strategy can be challenging. Some high-needs children fend off or challenge *any* positive response, even when they are starving for it. Although this technique is simple in its form, a powerful and effective application requires that the parent take the following committed positions:

1. I'm committed to doing what it takes to create a sense of success and competency for my child. This position involves a pervasive viewpoint that one of the greatest gifts and responsibilities of parenting is to help create a sense of success and competency. This committed stance energizes an ongoing opportunistic outlook: finding situations for taking actions and creating experiences to make this come about.

2. I'm not going to let my child pull me into a pattern of failure. This position refers to a parent's absolute, immovable resolve to refuse to revert to nonproductive, failure-laden responses—such as criticism, lecturing, admonitions, yelling or other ways of inadvertently energizing negative behaviors. This position's core involves maintaining acknowledgments and energized interest when rules are not being broken.

Determination is the key. Some children will challenge your determination. They need to see for themselves whether you will stick to your guns. **For some children, testing your resolve by sending challenges your way, and seeing** that they cannot derail you, is the only way they can arrive at the important conclusion that you will not revert back to giving a "payoff" for their negativity.

The Flow of Successes

Children who feel successful think and act successfully. Success is something that needs to be nurtured. It is an *active, intentional* stance. Video Moments begin the flow of successes to the child via nontraditional levels of appreciation and recognition. These comments can reflect any combination of physical actions and feelings. In addition to heightening the sense of acknowledgment, this combination helps to create a sense of positive self-awareness for your child. A few more examples:

> "I see your excitement about the car you're building with your Legos. You're using mostly yellow and blue for the bottom and red and green for the top."

> "I notice that you are flipping through your comic with a grumpy look on your face. You look upset."

> "You have amazing control of your video game. You managed to avoid all the trouble. And I notice you have a proud expression on your face."

Judgments, interpretations and interrogations of the child's emotional state may hit the child's radar and may serve to close the child off from further receptivity. However well-intentioned any statements, all of us have observed a child shut down when what we have said has been perceived as criticism. It's clear when the child's information receiver short-circuits… lights out and nobody's home, so to speak.

Without overstating or interpreting, you can, however, simply *document your child's emotional status:*

> "It looks as though your feelings are hurt by what your sister said."

> "It seems like you feel disappointed about not hearing from Sally."

> "You look very angry. I appreciate the effort you're making to control your strong feelings. You're being successful."

If you have missed the mark, your child may give you the correct information; or, having had his or her feelings acknowledged without judgment, may well discuss the situation further… the stuff of which excellent parent-child relationships are made.

Some parents have viewed Video Moments as containers that they attempt to fill with a little extra dash of excitement. This is purposefully done so that the child can begin to feel that it may not be necessary to go to all the trouble of acting out to get the fireworks. This is accomplished by modulating your voice or by putting more heart and enjoyment into your commentary.

The beauty of this method is that every element of a verbal Video Moment is encoded into your child's psyche as a success—a short, sweet snapshot for the child that is easily absorbed. The speed of delivery also makes this strategy one for which there will always be time, despite the busiest schedule. Being noticed and recognized, at no matter how basic a level, is a powerful acknowledgment. It is exquisite emotional food every child needs for a fully balanced diet.

Any Given Moment

A great advantage of this method is that you can imbue successes in your child at any given moment. You don't have to wait until something spectacular happens. The basic idea is that your child begins to form a new experience: your energy is available when things are going well in an everyday sense. The child feels your interest and thus feels held in esteem. This is, of course, how self-esteem begins to take shape.

The objective is to have your child begin to acclimate toward success until the feeling becomes second nature, like breathing. This forms the beginning of a new comfort zone around being successful.

Recognition becomes like a soft pillow for the child. Pushing against it is soft. It feels good; it is not a battle.

Practice will give you your own style and words with your child. Using non-evaluating, neutral statements may feel strange at first. Many of us grew up with models of parenting and education that were based on judgments, defining behavior as right or wrong, good or bad.

Also, **if you were not noticed particularly often as child, especially under positive circumstances, you may well come up against your own sensitivities in using this technique with your child.** At the very least, it may feel awkward and you also may find it hard for your brain to register the recognition and for the words to exit your mouth. Stay determined and clear about your purpose.

The shift to therapeutic parenting involves a conscious shift from the familiar or habitual to the non-conventional. You must trust your resolve to move away from ways that accidentally reward problem behaviors and toward methods that support and encourage your child at the core.

Video Moments begin to give you empowerment as you see yourself as the relentless opportunist, both as you give Active Recognitions throughout the day and as you begin to observe their effect on your child. The flow should be short and sweet. **Keep it simple.** Being specific and being active will help you experience the power of this kind of validation. Imagine walking in to comment on your child's artwork.

Rather than saying "Good job! That's such a neat picture." (evaluation mixed with praise that's too general), try this:

> "I see the effort you are making to keep the colors in the lines. You seem to be going around the border first and then filling in the inside. You've made the animals very bright colors!"

In a short time, even the most defensive, provocative child begins to absorb the magic and intention these words convey. They basically communicate: "You are seen. You are worthy of recognition. I value, appreciate and enjoy who you are."

It is also a wonderful experience for a parent to be in this position of benevolence. Some children become affectionate to a parent after years of holding back. Our interpretation: **as children begin to feel deeply nurtured through this powerfully nutritious recognition, they quickly have more to give back to others.**

Some parents will report that this first step was hard for them because there was nothing good to describe or because the acting-out was so frequent. If this feels like the case in your situation, the stand you must take on behalf of your child and yourself will require even more determination. You will have to be even more opportunistic between incidents and more willing to take advantage of relatively neutral and quiet moments, however few. You'd be surprised how quickly these times can multiply as you begin to lend these moments your energy and withdraw your energy from the negative behaviors.

NOT *Kojak Moments*

Anyone who has ever seen Telly Savalas in his well-known role as Kojak, the New York City cop, may recall that he clearly stood out as very verbal, persistently giving an ongoing commentary to his colleagues and criminal associates. Although this kind of commentary is definitely a sort of Kodak Moment, we advise you to avoid giving your commentary and recognition (your energy) to events that are going awry.

You most certainly can use Video Moments to accomplish redirection through anticipation *before* a rule is broken, but **we do not recommend giving any kind of attention and reaction once the child crosses the line by breaking a rule.**

Redirection through anticipation may involve a situation in which you see the early signs of your child's getting angry or frustrated for one reason or another. **By anticipating a potential problem and catching the situation *before it actually occurs,* you can proactively turn the situation into a success.**

"I notice that you look angry because your baby brother took your toy. I also see that you've managed to control your temper even though you look like you would have wanted to grab it back. I appreciate the self-control that you're using."

"I see you handling your frustration as best you can. The math is hard and you're hanging in there and trying. I see your effort and appreciate it."

Other options are to notice the good choice the child made not to take the anger out on his brother, or to otherwise comment on how he is handling his anger well at this moment in time. Strong feelings are hard for any of us to handle, and children can very well be applauded for smaller amounts of self-control used on their way toward being more skillful. Children are certainly not born with any self-control and need all the encouragement they can get toward increasing their ever-expanding repertoire of responses. Keep in mind Shamu and his trainer's creative use of expectations.

We cannot expect children always to use words and express their feelings early in life when we know full well how hard it is for us as adults both to contain and to express strong feelings.

We can help encourage alternatives like walking away, ignoring or withdrawing from problem situations as successful choices and responsible ways of handling strong feelings. We will go into detail about this type of behavior in a subsequent chapter.

The Letter

A letter does not arrive at the post office and automatically sort itself into the proper bin for the proper destination. Some external process has to help that letter get headed in the right direction.

In the same way, children do not automatically sort their experiences and know what to make of them. They crucially require guidance to nurture inner wisdom.

We especially have to keep in mind that the traditional models for working with children tend to sort experiences in a negative direction.

For example, imagine a group of little kids sitting in a circle taking part in story time at a local childcare center or older children taking part in a math lesson. Now, picture several children losing focus and starting side conversations or beginning to fool around. The norm in such scenarios is for the eye to be drawn to the disruption and for the comments that follow to consist of admonishments in some way, shape or form.

The children who are the recipients of those warnings and comments have acquired two important and depressing pieces of information. First, the leader's attention is available on the basis of unacceptable behaviors. They file that away for when attention is needed…a definite button to make the "toy" work.

Second, warnings or comments construct an actual, in-the-moment experience for the child. But the essence of the experience is failure.

Each failure experience accumulates in the psyche of a child. If these experiences occur frequently enough and begin to have critical mass, then the child's opinions of himself take shape around the feature of failure. And there's no arguing with experience. Try telling these children that they are wonderful, using conventional ways of conveying that message, and you will see a defensive child who *inside* is reacting to the comment with rejection:

"I'm not wonderful. I'm always getting in trouble."

Despite being very bright and perhaps knowing better intellectually, intense children all too frequently fall prey to this phenomenon emotionally.

Since we have the crucial role of sorting and helping our children attach meaning to their experiences, this phenomenon can consciously be shifted to everyone's advantage.

Noticing elements of success—"viewing the cup as half-full" and anticipating problems before they happen—can give parents and teachers the crucial edge they need to aid children in translating experiences to successes.

What we see time and time again is that, if we can convince children via their actual experiences that they are indeed successful, they begin to expand on success and act and think as successful children.

Some encouraging perceptions of mastery can simply be achieved through Video Moments such as:

"Margo, I see that you are focused and paying close attention."

"I notice that you are not losing interest even though the lesson is not very exciting."

We lend the lesson excitement by momentarily breaking away before disruption and breathing life into the driest material through nurturing attention. Ironically, when children begin feeling accomplished on the inside, they can weather experiences that are not highly exciting… even those that are mundane and boring. These non-highlight film times are certainly part of life's journey.

Great teachers do this beautifully by firing off nurturing responses at regular intervals. Children in classroom environments that are fully nurturing through the use of clear limits and energized positive responses are far better learners, regardless of how exciting the subject matter is.

More "advanced" versions of Video Moments—such as noticing effort, self-control, good choice, responsibility, good manners and good attitude—give parents and teachers an expanded repertoire of success-laden responses for any given situation. We call this *Experiential Recognition,* and we will enhance this concept in the next step. Getting a feel for them now, however, will be useful to distinguish them from Step One Video Moments. Examples of Experiential Recognition are:

> "Anthony, I notice your good attitude right now. You are listening carefully to what Dana is saying."

> "Alex, I see the extra effort you are making right now. It looked like you knew the answer and you had to work extra hard to not interrupt Joanne."

> "Sarah, I see the good choice you are making to give Ramone the space he needs. That shows good judgment and thoughtfulness."

> "Billy, you are waiting so patiently. I appreciate the good manners you are using. You are being respectful."

These kinds of comments really help children sort out their experiences. Without them a child might not realize that he or she indeed is being successful. **Why wait for the wheels to come off to interact with our children?**

After all, even if we have just finished handling a problem behavior, and we anticipate several more before the day is done, in a broader context we must remember that *all we really have at our disposal is THIS MOMENT.* Parenting and working with our children in any capacity occurs at its best **when we dispose of the burdens of the past and the future and attend to and take full advantage of what actually exists in the present.**

Receptivity to learning is heightened when lessons are contained in the context of successful here-and-now experiences. And so is joy.

By telling Billy, who is patiently waiting his turn, that he is showing respect *right now*, or using control *right now*, or being responsible *right now*, we are choosing an instance of successfully demonstrating his competence. We not only share our esteem and enjoyment with Billy, we are teaching him an important element of respect, control or responsibility in the all-important context of an actual experience. This experience is very different from reading a story or viewing a film about any of these desirable qualities.

Contrary to commonly held belief and practice, **lessons are not taught by waiting to catch Billy in an act of *not* being respectful.** If he gets anything but a consequence when he breaks a rule, he is actually learning that he can capture our energy and relationship through adversity. In addition, children are not particularly receptive to lessons about values that occur in the context of a problem behavior.

If Billy has a pre-existing habit of getting attention for negative antics, then there is a high risk of his forming lasting opinions based on his observations of what circumstances can produce the greatest payoffs. The lecture after the rule is broken not only does not accomplish its purpose of teaching about respect, it becomes a reward of energy or payoff for disrespect.

By giving your lecture on a desirable and valued quality *before* the wheels fall off, you give it at a time when the lesson is going to be best absorbed.

Active Recognition: Points to Remember

- Video Moments are the foundation strategy on which the subsequent strategies are built. These moments **acknowledge, recognize and describe the child's behavior, actions, demeanor or possible feelings right then or describe the recent past.** The purpose is to start and maintain a flow of successes and encouragement to the child. Video Moments are perceived by the child as successes.

- **Video Moments are neutral in that they suspend value statements or judgments like "Great job!"** They are specific in describing to the child observations about a particular happening. They are not used to influence, coerce or manage behaviors. They simply reflect the behavior that you see.

- An *active stance* will produce the best results of using this strategy. Take advantage of all opportunities, relying on your best conscious determination of what they are. Each application will help the child foster a new succession of impressions that successes are readily available in every corner of his or her life.

- Active Recognition deepens your child's feeling and experience of being *seen* and *held in esteem*. She can then begin to reinforce the all-important new impression that your energy is available for positive rather than for negative behavior. She will begin to feel that she does not have to go to all the trouble of acting out.

Active Recognition: Prescription

- Plan to give your child between 10 and 20 Video Moments per day, or at least one every 10-20 minutes you are together throughout the day. Especially at the very beginning of this intervention, fairly frequent recognition sets up a workable foundation for progress. **Powerful times to use this strategy are first thing in the morning and when the child is at play or relaxing.** This technique is *not* to be used during times when consequences need to be delivered. Find creative ways to cue yourself to remember to use this technique.

- **Keep the Active Recognition straightforward and simple, and persist even if the child reacts negatively.** This reaction is not unusual, especially in the beginning.

- If your child acts out after you attempt a Video Moment, keep in mind that, until her underlying pattern is changed to key into successes, she may still feel that the best way to keep you with her is to pursue negativity. Therefore, continued acting out may be a sign to you that she liked the recognition and wants you to stay awhile. If this is the case, then *more* recognition, not less, is what will eventually contribute to loosening the hold of the old pattern. Remember that you are taking a stand.

- Resist adding on requests to finish tasks, references to the past, subtle threats, judgments, guilt or other critical measures. Use Video Moments in as pure a form as possible for the time being.

- Resist asking questions or making general remarks such as "Good job," "Oh wow," or "That's great"—*unless* additional detail is supplied to expand your observation. It is the detail of the description that really provides the recognition. It is the specificity that is really convincing and supportive to the child… because it is felt as nurturing acknowledgment.

Try Video Moments on yourself or with parenting partners. It keeps humor flowing. It's not only children who love recognition. You might be pleasantly surprised to find that it expands your own base of success.

Practice! Practice! Practice! This is your foundation strategy, so being accomplished at it will pay off in the long run. If you've already been making similar comments, try expanding your repertoire by adding more detail, frequency and intensity to your recognition.

Words Of Encouragement

Negative attention of any kind is like junk food. It has no nutritional value. Video Moments are a form of attention that is highly nutritious. Think of it as invisibly massaging your child's heart. Also, just in case your child is defensive when you first begin using Video Moments, go with the flow of objections and continue by doing more of the same recognition.

Do not let your child derail you. You are the one who is frustrated and therefore motivated. You have the bigger picture. Even if your child very much wants to change, it is virtually impossible for him to make changes on his own for more than a few days at a time.

Your child desperately needs you to begin the process externally. He will internalize his own ability to give himself recognition over time. He may challenge you in various ways to see if you will abandon your new plan or challenge you to see if these new methods will be strong enough to withstand his resistance. The challenge is desirable. You must retain the stands you've set in motion: *Absolutely No — I refuse to energize your negativity. I will strategically energize your successes.* Seeing you not back down is for many children a crucial aspect of the process of transformation.

Some authors recommend similar interventions in context of a "special time." That's fine if you have longer periods of time available. However, with our busy lives, we often must capture just a few seconds here and there with our children. That will work. Half-minute visits using Video Moments are all that are required. Do as many as you can per day, whether they are between tasks or during commercials. Twenty visits a day would be incredible. However, you need not be a saint. Ten visits a day would still be hitting a home run. The total daily time of this intervention may add up to only five minutes.

Finally, keep in mind that this is only the first step. If you were rewiring a house, the first step would be to get to the wire box. This step is the equivalent. The work we do here sets the stage. We can't mess around with the wiring unless we have proper access, and these techniques will open that door. Once you're in, you can set out to virtually rewire the way in which your child chooses to function.

Obviously, while you are laying the groundwork with the initial interventions, many difficult behaviors will continue. For now and for a few more weeks, until the timing is just right to set up consequences that will work, avoid as much as possible giving undue attention to negative behaviors. If a rule is broken, as a temporary measure issue a consequence with as little discussion as possible. Very clear instructions will be recommended later in the book when the stage has been properly set.

Chapter Six
Step 2: Experiential Recognition
Instilling Those Wonderful Values

THE THRUST OF THE THINKING AND INTERVENTION IN THIS NEXT STEP is to further heighten the level of successes and to capitalize on the momentum and opportunities created in the first step.

Here's where parents, teachers and others who work with children can instill some of the cherished values that are dear to their hearts.

When parents are asked about the positive qualities and life skills that they find important, most begin with: using a good attitude, showing responsibility, being respectful, being cooperative, getting along with others and using good manners. A handful of additions typically follow: playing nicely, being helpful, making an effort, expressing feelings in appropriate ways, making good choices, using self-control, showing compassion.

Any quality that fits in your family's value system or that may be valued in the broader scope of the community, or any quality that you would like to see occur more often, is worth cultivating in your child.

One of the existing myths is that these qualities can be largely instilled through lessons or lectures. **However, we find, especially with difficult children who are extremely experiential in nature, that information about life is not internally organized or absorbed unless it has relevance or context in the child's personal retrieval system.**

Upside Down and Inside Out

In many ways, our traditional methods of instilling lessons of this nature are upside down and inside out. We attempt to teach the rules when they are being broken and we attempt to teach important positive qualities of life when they are not happening.

We typically attempt to give a lesson on responsibility or self-control when the child is not using responsibility or self-control. We tend to give lessons on not whining or not hitting when the child is performing the misdeed. The receptivity to the lesson is low at these moments.

The larger problem with bringing up these qualities when they are not being used is this: we ultimately wind up rewarding the very behavior we least wish to reinforce. Given our heritage of parenting ways and means, it is relatively easy to wind up making a big deal when a child is not using a good attitude, self-control, good manners or respect.

Even if we deliver a world-class lecture or reprimand or appeal to our child's sensibilities, we wind up giving a great deal of emotional energy to the problem. **Any way you slice it, five minutes of reprimand or five minutes of lecture translate to five minutes of energetic reward of your time attached to the problem behavior.** No one would dream of giving their child a hundred-dollar bill for being disrespectful; but energetically, we inadvertently do it all the time.

We can certainly continue to give lectures, but we must reserve them for when they will shine light on aspects of the desired qualities, even when they emerge just a little bit. When aspects of the undesired qualities rear their heads, the only real choice we have is giving a consequence, without the payoff of our energy. More on that when the timing is just right.

Imagine a folder in the desktop of a computer. In the folder are two items. One is disrespect and the other is respect. If we habitually point and click on disrespect, the wisdom of the computer will always follow our lead and bring us down the pathway of disrespect. It will have no other way of operating, unless we begin pointing and clicking on respect.

Children operate in a similar fashion. They follow our lead as they learn, assimilate and eventually integrate the values we introduce to them. What we point to and click on and what we give energy to is what is deemed important. Unfortunately, if the only times we go into the "values" folder is when things go awry, then the child will come to think that it is the negative side of the value that we truly love. Children readily equate what we put our energy into with what we love. That's how they decode our behavior.

We may mouth the words that clearly state that disrespect and irresponsibility are unacceptable and undesirable. However, if we put our energy into the negative side of those qualities rather than the positive side, our children will unfortunately come to feel that we "love" the disrespect and the irresponsibility. If we water the weeds, the weeds will grow. And, as any gardener knows, weeds do not need much encouragement.

What we choose to put our energy into is the nutrition that largely determines what grows and what doesn't. It is also the basis for children's deciphering what we truly love and how they can best obtain quality time. Some children come to believe, on the basis of our actions, that they can get the best quality time when they are misbehaving. Some children feel those are the only times when they can get solid one-on-one, heart-to-heart emotional exchange. Regardless of the negative venue, many will seek the closeness and the intensity.

If we give three hours a week of focused, undivided, excited attention to football or anything else, our child will witness that and will often explore his options until he finds a way to compete. Sometimes, the only other ticket in town is obtained through acting out. We now want our child to see that the ticket is on the other side of the same coin. We want him to see that he can get us focused and excited about all the positive aspects of the qualities and skills we value. The burden of proof is on us. And *we must provide these lessons in the context of the child's actual experience.*

Schools and religious organizations are also notable for attempting to teach lessons out of context. Certainly lessons on valued qualities embedded in interesting stories, fables, lively discussions or role plays can touch a child's life. However, literature is still removed from personal experience: It is an artificial version of an experience.

If the only time we connect the qualities we cherish to actual experience is in the middle of a problem, then we have an unfortunate situation, especially for the difficult child who is set up to make frequent and intense challenges to the limits.

If you were a difficult child, what would your relationship with responsibility or respectfulness or cooperation be if the only time you heard those words were when you were having a problem? They would eventually sound like dirty words.

One reliable way we can help children to believe in themselves and to believe that our valued qualities are truly within them is to massage aspects of those qualities *when they are actively happening,* even if those instances are in underdeveloped states of emergence. Every plant was once a seed. Think of it as coaching, mentoring, or cultivating the qualities that you wish to see grow.

All of what's been said points in an encouraging direction. First, we as a society maintain a clear vision of positive qualities that we value and wish to convey to our children; and second, most adults are willing to see themselves in the role of teacher. This is good news. The framework to move forward is present, even if the tools that we have been given to construct the valued qualities are in need of revision.

In other words, if you as a parent or a person who works with children have the desire to teach positive qualities and life skills to your children, we can help you.

Let's focus on positive lessons. Is it possible to add new context when these qualities are being introduced? Is it possible to embed the lesson in an actual experience so that the message has increased impact? You bet. It's actually very easy. It builds smoothly onto the new context of experience that we've already begun. It just requires a little bit more cleverness and creative thinking and the willingness to apply what you're learning here.

Giving the Moment New Meaning

We want to be in a position to reformat any given moment with our child and be able to make it into a successful experience. We want the lessons we wish to convey to have context and real meaning. That is an *empowered* position.

A *disempowered* position is one of waiting for positive experiences to happen and having a limited view of when and where those kinds of successes take place. An empowered position is one of co-creating those experiences in a determined manner.

If you are not sure about the emotional energy you can reflect when your child is going along in an ordinary manner, ask yourself if you're pleased when your child isn't causing problems. If the answer is yes, then you have some emotional excitement to reflect. Or, conversely, ask yourself if you are upset when your child is acting out. If the answer is yes, then you have some emotional excitement that can generate powerful successes. Just tap into your emotion and let it show.

Saying "Thank you" more often to your child might be of some help, and adding some hint of real pleasure in your voice along with it might get more positive events to occur. However, if it's your core desire to help your child reinvest his or her fund of energies and intensity into successes, then a slightly more intense strategy is called for. Bring on the transformation.

Experiential Recognition is a technique that calls for uniquely capturing a moment. **You create for your child's benefit a positive picture of an event that is either presently unfolding or that has been completed in the recent past. And you re-frame that moment in such a way that the child not only can digest it as a nutritious experience of success, but in a way that lets her perceive your excitement in connection with a positively valued behavior.**

You are using your parental creativity to enrich an experience that might otherwise have passed unnoticed or been given no thought, especially by the child.

Here are illustrations:

Brandon is playing a video game. He thinks his mother hates the game. She approaches him, does a Video Moment, and adds some Experiential Recognition:

> "I see that you are very focused and that you are using a lot of concentration. I really like the effort you are making."

She values those qualities and is thus enhancing those qualities. She is creating a specific lesson on effort and concentration in context of an actual experience.

Hannah has tried to use words to get Alex to stop chasing her, but he continues and she walks away frustrated. She thinks she has mishandled the situation. Here are several possible approaches applying Experiential Recognition:

> "Hannah, you made several good choices. Even though Alex didn't stop, which looked frustrating, you used your words very well and then you made another good choice to walk away when he didn't listen. I'm proud of you and the wisdom you used." Or:

> "I really like the self-control you just used. You could have gotten very angry when Alex didn't listen. You stayed cool and handled your feelings very well by walking away. You were thoughtful and used good judgment. I also like that you tried to use your words first. I value that."

Julio, who has alienated many peers by pushing the limits, is playing soccer with a small group on the playground. The game has just started and Julio has not yet shown his normal aggressive attitude. He can honestly be told:

> "Julio, I notice that you are using a respectful attitude and that you are being cooperative. That's considerate and an excellent choice." Or:

> "Julio, I appreciate the positive control you are using. That is very helpful to your teammates and a healthy way to be powerful."

Yes, these comments are truly being pulled out of the sky; out of left field, so to speak. However, that is part of the nature of creativity. A child like Julio might otherwise believe that he is screwing up as usual. He certainly could have the impression that the only way to generate attention and interesting adult and peer reaction is to stir up trouble.

When kids like Julio are not causing trouble, our natural reaction more often than not is to feel relief and to take advantage of the break by doing other things that need to get done.

To form an opinion of himself other than feeling that he's only interesting to us when he's causing trouble, Julio needs us to stay conscious and determined. By so doing we provide new experiential evidence that it's not a question of whether he can or can't embody any of these valued qualities…he is.

He's not likely to form these new opinions on his own. He needs our help in creatively sorting his experiences out loud, providing affirming and acknowledging documentation.

Experiential Recognition: Critical Points

- **Experiential Recognition freeze-frames a picture of success for your child in a meaningful here-and-now instant.** This strategy heightens the level of successes given to your child. This level of recognition tremendously expands your child's perception that he or she is valued and recognized for positive behaviors and creates for him or her a heightened perception that it is not necessary to go to the trouble of acting out to get noticed.

- This strategy provides **clear, specific feedback to your child regarding values, behaviors or attitudes that are considered desirable.** This form of experiential, moment-centered and heart-centered teaching is our choice as the most effective means of shaping positive values for the difficult child.

- **It allows you to transform a relatively neutral experience in your child's mind to one that is positive.** It gives the desired quality context. Focusing on successful behaviors rather than undesirable ones gives you greater influence as well as the most mentoring leverage with your child.

- Experiential Recognition provides parents with an instant tool that takes only seconds and yet has an enduring effect.

- These acknowledgments expand your child's ability to take in positive self-information and thereby build self-esteem. Each acknowledgment gives a direct experience of being held in esteem.

- Experiential Recognition should be done opportunistically, as often as possible (several times per hour, if possible, during time spent together).

- During your Experiential Recognitions, it helps sometimes to underscore the value or skill at play by saying "you're being successful right now in the way you are showing respect" (or substitute any other quality that applies). You can also enhance the quality even further by saying that this respect, thoughtfulness, or wise decision is a quality of *greatness* you admire in her.

- This technique is like a video playback that heightens your child's level of perceived success. It also begins preparations for effective consequences because this step begins the process of defining the true distinctions between desirable and undesirable behaviors.

Experiential Recognition: Prescription

- Try to find several instances of Experiential Recognition per hour that you are with your child, keeping these freeze-frames short, specific and positive.

- Focus on times when your child is acting appropriately alone or while interacting with others.

- Be creative in pointing out both small and big positives. Both count equally in the process of teaching and supporting your child. In fact, in the beginning, the small behaviors may even count more to your child.

- Teach this recognition technique to other adults who are care providers for your child or significant contacts. The more support and positive pictures given by others, the faster the transformation will occur.

Remember:

You are assisting your children in figuring out what to make of experiences in different situations. Don't assume that he knows that he is doing okay. A child who has been living out a predominantly negative pattern of behavior for some time may well be under the impression, at any given moment, that he or she is doing something wrong, or not doing anything particularly positive. Help such a child size up both new and familiar situations in a favorable light.

Adding a dash of emotion to your description, along with some appreciation, will deepen the healing effect and will make the success more powerful.

Keep Shamu and the tollbooth attendant front and center in your consciousness: Where are you going to start the rope? How are you going to choose to view the things you see?

You are producer and director. You get to choose the moments, you get to angle the camera any way you wish, and you get to choose the voiceover to the frame. Everyone sees everything in different ways, anyhow—you might as well take full advantage and choose to see through a positive lens. Once you begin to make this shift, you will find that there are so many moments of success for the taking. And *you never have to depart for an instant from telling the truth of the moment as you choose to see it.* Shakespeare's Hamlet said it well: "There's nothing good nor bad but thinking makes it so."

When you think you couldn't possibly find a positive side to what your child is doing, keep in mind that every desirable quality has many facets. A positive quality like respect or good attitude can be reflected and given recognition from many angles, at many different stages of its emergence. Each angle is an opportunity to teach nuances of that quality as well an opportunity to show your love.

Think of it as polishing yet another facet of an incredibly precious gem. The more attention you pay to each detail, the more it shines.

Chapter Seven
Step 3: Proactive Recognition
A New Spin on Rules

A S PARENTS, ONE OF OUR MOST IMPORTANT ROLES is in helping our
children to interpret and shape their experiences. We cannot assume that
children can automatically and accurately size up a situation, or that they
can consistently discern whether or not an experience or a choice was a success
or a failure. Myriad emotions and reactions can short-circuit a child's objective
assessment of self or of a situation.

Often, a child with a pre-existing pattern of attracting negative responses
will be hypercritical of her own experiences and be supersensitive to picking up
on their negative aspects, placing her at risk to perceive and register them as
failures. For these reasons, your response as a parent becomes crucial to
building and maintaining perspective for your child.

As a parent, you are privileged to have a broader perspective and can draw
on your own greater experience to help your child make vital distinctions.
Parents are essential in directing traffic in regard to their child's inner experience and choices, which are more or less likely to become experiences of
success or failure, depending upon how they are viewed. The experience may
not wind up in the right bin on its own. It needs sorting. That's where your
help is needed.

Parents give closure and meaning to their child's experiences. The way
parents choose to give their attention to those experiences makes all the
difference in the world. **Where you choose to expend your energy, and the
way in which you expend it, gives children important clues as to what is a
success and what is a failure and, ultimately, on how to translate life itself.**
This process is going to occur regardless of whether we become more conscious
of exactly what is going on. We might as well use our awareness creatively and
advantageously.

If a parent pays attention to undesirable aspects of behavior at any given
moment, the child unfortunately gathers a negative impression or a failure
message about herself. If you focus on the smart, thoughtful or rule-related
choices your child makes, she receives a success message from you about who
she is as well as about her positive capabilities. It's almost as if we lend the
experience our energy and wisdom. The loan eventually becomes an inheri-
tance.

Parents who hone their intervention skills can create a wealth of successes that would not otherwise exist. The role of success-building has become incredibly more important for every child. To stand up to the pressures of our times, children have to be stronger on the inside than ever before.

Not long ago, we had the privilege of meeting two wonderful families with adolescent girls who had been doing extremely well at both home and school up through early adolescence. Both girls had been sent to private schools to help insulate them from peer pressures. To their parents' dismay, both children wound up involved in serious situations as a result of peer pressure, illustrating the point that there may no longer be any real insulation from dangerous temptations, other than fortifying children to be much stronger and centered from the inside out.

Because both girls had relatively easy temperaments up to that point in their lives, very little parental imposition of rules had been necessary for either of them. The rules were therefore relatively unclear and had been given little parental attention because both children were basically self-motivated. Their parents certainly appreciated their daughters, but there didn't seem to be a high need for them to demonstrate it.

When they realized that their daughters were having problems, these parents wisely made the rules more clear and began to give more and varied recognition, including recognition when specific rules were not being broken. Both children became dramatically stronger and far less vulnerable to peer pressures.

For the difficult child, the stakes are higher and the role of success-building becomes incredibly more important than in these cases.

Now that you are trying a new approach, it is time to re-examine the rules and to reintroduce them to your child in a way that will help her learn better, in a way that truly makes sense and clicks for her, and in a way that she will ultimately respect and in which she will find comfort and safety.

The Old Rules

If you walk into the typical mainstream classroom, what you will most often find are ordinary rules that unfortunately are too unclear for the difficult child. Rules like "Be respectful," "Use good manners," "Follow directions," "Hands and feet to yourself," among others, are generally marginally effective with the average child. However, they simply do not work with the more challenging child.

And by the way, there are fewer children who fit the description of mild or average temperament than ever before. For every intense child that externalizes or acts out an energized or conflicted inner state, there is another child in the same classroom who is under-functioning in a withdrawn, depressed or under-energized manner.

Somewhere along the line since the time of the Ten Commandments, we've somehow gotten the notion that the rules need to be framed in a positive context. This notion is rampant in mainstream classrooms.

Positively framed rules such as "Be responsible" make it much harder for challenging children to function. These children do not have a clear sense of when they are out of bounds and when they are in. It's like trying to play a basketball game on a court where the lines around the court are staggered or zig-zagged. It would make it harder on the players as well as on the referees. Children I've observed in these classrooms still get the bigger energetic responses when things are going wrong, and still feel relatively invisible when the rules are being followed. Actually, with positive rules they often have to break the rules in even bigger ways to get noticed. Little bits of rule-breaking often go undetected because of the "fuzzier" line, and inconsistent consequences amp up the uncertainty and the energy around rule-breaking. From an energetic point of view, these rules create a scenario that's upside down. This contrasts the reality of sports, where a limit need only be exceeded by a tiny bit to yield a penalty.

Difficult children have an especially hard time with fuzzy rules. Positive rules and unclear consequences invite escalating patterns of testing. It is no accident that intense children systematically fall off the educational conveyor belt.

Inclusion, or working with challenging children within the mainstream classroom setting, can be achieved, but not without clarity. Without clarity, *inclusion* is more like *exclusion.* How can children focus their energies on successful classroom endeavors when so much of their energy is bound up in useless bouts with confusing limits?

The New Rules

If you sit with groups of challenging children, which we have done on many occasions, and you ask them what kinds of rules are needed, they will invariably reel off a host of rules that are much more clear and more structured than the current conventional rules. They will state rules in a negative way: "No bad words," "No aggression," "No breaking things," "No whining," "No name calling," "No arguing."

These rules resonate much better for the difficult child. Remember that they cannot live their lives with clarity unless we lend them clarity.

Think again about the example we gave earlier concerning video games. So many children can throw themselves into playing these games successfully because the rules are so clear. We don't advocate video games; however, challenging children are often drawn to their simple, clear structure. Similar threads run through nearly all of these games: when you're on track—when you're not breaking rules—you score, and when you do break a rule, you get a consequence. The rules are as clear as day. Usually, "No crossing the line" and "No getting hit by the enemy" are the basics.

In addition to the rules being clear and concise, what truly helps children reconcile their experience of rules (i.e., helping regulations truly make sense in their ways of thinking) is the feature that recognition follows *not* breaking the rules.

In video games, that recognition amounts to more energy: higher scores, sounds, visuals, access to higher levels of success. If the higher score and the attraction and excitement of higher levels were not present, the desire to avoid breaking rules would decrease.

Most conventional parenting paradigms have it backwards: the higher payoff goes to occasions when the rules are broken, and the payoff is minimal when the child is just going along in an acceptable yet ordinary fashion.

The Old Switcheroo

When parents switch the menu of payoffs, the remarkable happens. When they verbally provide a larger response when rules are not broken, the child begins to sense a new relationship to the rules. The rules are no longer the bad guys. The rules begin to have their merits. **In fact, the child begins to perceive the notion that more rules are better, because the more rules they do not break, the more recognition flows into their lives.**

If you talk to successful people, you will generally find that they have a fairly positive relationship to rules. Of course, some rules, like those regarding taxes, may truly be annoying. However, most rules are perceived positively because they help organize lives and businesses and help insulate us from haphazard events.

Children with pre-existing patterns of challenging the limits are definitely at risk of exiting childhood and entering adulthood with a negative opinion of rules and with an adversarial relationship with them.

For most challenging children, the only times they hear about the rules are times when the rules are being broken. At the same time, they are inadvertently and unintentionally rewarded with various payoffs when rules are broken. Numerous kinds of negative excitement such as lectures, reprimands, critical expressions and raised voices are really rewards because these are major payoffs of an adult's energy and relationship. They contribute to the difficult young person's emergence from childhood with—at best—a confusing relationship with the rules.

Our experience is that challenging children, upon entering adulthood, do not easily leave their old patterns behind. They either take them along or have to struggle with great effort to change them. Have pattern, will travel. If an adversarial relationship with the rules has been established, then that pattern is likely to be lived out and acted out for a lifetime.

With these techniques, you have the power to alter that confusing pattern for your child.

Success Rules

Now is the perfect time to move into a new gear and proactively tune your child to a still higher key of success. This will involve specifically verbalizing recognition when the child has not broken a rule, as well as raising the level of appreciation when the child is showing glimmers of valued and desirable qualities or other positive behaviors. It is time to polish the facets of the gem from several directions.

Difficult children typically get nailed for their problems, rather than commended for the efforts they have made. *Proactive Recognition* flips this upside-down dynamic right-side-up. It involves **nailing your children with** *appreciation* **for even small degrees of appropriate effort, choice, attitude or behaviors.** This shifts the dynamic in favor of the rules you set up for your child and family.

Giving your children close attention when they are using self-control gives them a new sense of connection to their capacity for steering clear of problems. Tying the control to specific rules that have not been broken strengthens a child's sense of being on track. It strengthens her belief in herself rather than in a belief that the best way to get attention is to break rules. It makes *not* breaking rules the focal point of the excitement and fireworks. And, best of all, the child develops the ability to learn the rules in a receptive manner.

Noticing and acknowledging when rules are *not* being broken shows your child, proof positive, that you value his ability to use his power in healthy ways.

Instead of waiting for your child to break rules, you are now the ruthless opportunist who proactively fixates your attention, deliberately and determinedly, upon *even the smallest steps* in the direction of success. To do this, consciously find moments when nothing seems to be happening, and capture those moments by acknowledging your child for not breaking the rules or pushing the limits in that given instant.

Examples of Proactive Recognition:

"Brandon, I appreciate that you have not used foul language all morning long. Thank you for following the rules."

"Jason, I like that you have not been teasing your sister. Keep up the good work."

"Susie, I notice that you have stayed with your reading and have not gone into my room without permission. Thank you for obeying that rule. I also love that you have not argued or fussed about your homework."

"Marge, I want you to know how much I appreciate that you are not being bossy to your brother or mean to the dog. Keep up the good work."

"Frankie, I like how you are using your power to control your strong feelings. You did not take your frustration out by breaking anything or hitting anybody. Your power is a great quality."

It is about seeing the glass as half-full, rather than half-empty. You are seeing and verbalizing the positive steps your child is making in the right direction, *even if the behavior is rare, infrequent or short-lived.* **This attention and affirmation magnifies what is already present, lending proactive (positive) rather than reactive (negative) energy to the healing/ tuning process.** It says to your child in ever-heightening ways, "You do not have to go to all the trouble of breaking rules to be noticed by me. I have plenty of energy for so many successful aspects of your life."

Once in a while a parent will report that, as soon as proactive recognition has been given, a child will turn around and blatantly act out by breaking a rule. Rather than taking this as a sign that the strategy is not working, our experience indicates that just the opposite is happening. The child likes the attention and hasn't yet formed the backup ability to keep you attuned in positive ways, so reflexively reverts to ways that have worked in the past in an effort to capture your continued contact. It is precisely this kind of attitude and testing that allows you to reaffirm your focus on the positive.

As an illustration, at the extreme end of the continuum, we have even had tremendous success with children who have been dangerously fascinated with fire. Many have been through other kinds of fire-starter programs unsuccessfully. What we have seen in these and other hard-core cases is that, when the parents or caretakers begin to express their valuing of self-control when fires or other aggressive behaviors are not happening, the child no longer has to go to that extreme to get the fireworks. He is getting it in a rule-related way. The fear that reminding a child about fire-starting will prompt him to go out and burn something down turns out, in our experience, to be completely unfounded.

Be a Ruthless Opportunist

If you sense that negative behavior appears to be on the horizon, we suggest you maintain a neutral attitude and creatively utilize the situation as an opportunity for proactive recognition. Proactive recognition is the cement that holds together the rules that you are now using to frame your child's behavior. Its use creates a different magnetic pull and a new message about your belief in your child. For example:

> "I see that you have strong feelings right now and that you are trying very hard to control them. I appreciate your effort."

> "It looks like you were thinking about lashing out just now, but you are managing to control yourself. I appreciate that you did not hit your brother." Or:

> "I notice how frustrated you are with your little sister and I really appreciate your success in not calling her names back or being mean to her. I like how you're following the rules."

Compare these statements to more common (and non-therapeutic) reactions to a child's impending escalation:

> "I can tell you're ready to bother your sister! You'd better leave her alone!"

> "You had better control your anger. If you argue you won't be watching TV for a week."

Unfortunately most of us have used these common and almost reflexive approaches with an acting-out child. Much to our own and the child's disadvantage, this type of intervention sends the child a message inferring his or her inability to exercise self-control. It is more likely to provoke further loss of inhibition or a loss of control.

It is, in effect, an inverted message: "I affirm your out-of-control nature and behaviors of the past, and I dare you to continue to use that behavior right now." This is certainly not a message of trust.

Teach Our Children Well

Most parents are already trying to teach their children the rules. However, with an intense child they often wind up on a merry-go-round, caught in the downward spiral of trying to teach the rules on the fly during or just after the breaking of the rule. These are not exactly excellent teaching moments. Receptivity is sure to be poor at these times.

Although to do so defies conventional thinking, it is amazingly effective to teach rules when they aren't being broken. You and your child may both find it odd at first, but this is, in fact, exactly the right time to demonstrate to a child that she is within the expected bounds. That's the absolute truth of the moment. She is not breaking rules. The child, under the new circumstances of success, is becoming more psychologically and emotionally receptive.

Parents are only uncomfortable with this approach until they try it. Once they get used to it, this method becomes more natural than the old ways.

If I praise a child for not yelling and not arguing, I not only create a few successes; I also make a shift toward his believing that the rules are not completely bad and that he is capable of success in this important aspect of life. **Most difficult children think rules stink because the only time that they hear about the rules is when they are breaking them.** So they wind up getting a high dose of negative reaction and payoff in the context of a problem behavior, and they wind up at least partially habituated to pushing the very limits that they hate. No wonder the life of a difficult child is so confusing.

It's not as if they want to break the rules. Nor do their parents want inadvertently to reinforce the negative behaviors by responding to them. As you can imagine, the situation can become very convoluted, very fast. The way out is to adopt a proactive stance.

One way to understand the meaning of proactive is this: If you find out that you have a heart problem for which a gene runs in your family, do you really want to wait for your first bypass surgery to do something about it? Or do you want to look at changing some of your attitudes and stresses and habits of rest, exercise and eating *before* the problem develops? You get the point.

A Temporary Measure

Even though we are a few short steps away from being in a position strategically to recommend limits and consequences that really work, you might find yourself in a situation where consequences are called for. Challenging children require limits and consequences to help them feel safe and protected from their own feared loss of control. Until we get to the point where we can recommend consequences that work with this approach, use a consequence that is somewhat familiar to your child, but not excessive. **As a temporary measure, until we take a more formal approach, time-outs or lost privileges can be appropriate consequences, but should be given in a decidedly matter-of-fact (neutral) and straightforward manner.** *Do not give negative behaviors your energy.* No lectures, reprimands, pleading, strong voice or threats of a consequence. Unplug the gift of you and your relatedness.

Simply give the consequence as a result of a rule being broken. Get it over with and get back to successes as soon as possible. Much more on this when the timing is perfect. The new consequence will support you being unplugged.

The nonverbal message to your child is this: "Yes, I see you need a consequence now, but I'm not going to let you pull me back into negative reactions when you act out. I will respond to your behavior in a way that maintains control. When the consequence is over, my primary focus will continue to be pointing out your successes and the great steps you are making, rather than your failures or inadequacies."

Being neutral when your child is out-of-control or is escalating is difficult, to say the least. However, *this is a much more powerful stance in the long run.* You maintain control, and your child is unable to control the situation by pulling you back into a frustrated or reactive stance. Stay aware: some children will test their parents' commitment to staying neutral. This is often done as a way of verifying that the success messages are permanent or as a way of sizing up the new results of pushing your various buttons. The child needs to see that you won't be derailed by the challenges. Give the child a chance to learn what the buttons are doing now that they weren't doing before. As long as you stay consistent, the child will get the hang of it just as fast as she gets the hang of a new video game.

More often than not, however, the proactive, early interventions serve to de-escalate the child's behavior. The child feels reassured or fortified by acknowledgments of successful behaviors and is reassured when reminded that he is on track and valued for not breaking rules. A parent's modeling control—by demonstrating control—also becomes a support to the intense child's precarious internal structure. When a parent verbalizes specific recognition and appreciation for unbroken rules, the child's belief in her own ability to have self-control and make successful choices increases.

Almost anyone can show integrity when things are going well. If a parent loses control when faced with a child's difficult behaviors, the child, in effect, learns that it is okay to lose control under difficult circumstances. Integrity is a quality best taught when the going gets rough.

On the other hand, if a parent is able to demonstrate an effective yet neutral response to challenging behaviors, the child not only learns a crucial lesson about self-control, but also learns that negative behaviors no longer yield a payoff.

Proactive Recognition: Critical Points

- **Proactive Recognition supports your parenting efforts by giving recognition and appreciation specifically to the rules of your household.** It reshapes the rules by giving them more definition. It is the basic beginning of a new focus for your child's behavior. It is a critically important way to teach the rules to children who are habituated to the payoffs of response that come with breaking the rules.

- Proactive Recognition gives your child vital information on how to act. It also helps him gain confidence in his capacity to use desirable and rule-related behaviors.

- Proactive Recognition accelerates and deepens STAND I by pulling your child into a new realm of successes and by counteracting her past adversarial relationship with the rules.

- Proactive Recognition is specific to your family and your child's needs. It is derived from your list of rules via your custom-tailored take on what your family needs and what your child needs as filtered through your family values.

- Proactive Recognition requires parents to be restrained in their reaction to negative behaviors and give much more animation and magnetism to the child when she is not breaking rules.

- **Proactive Recognition teaches and reminds the child of rules and good behavior from a non-adversarial stance, which is of particular importance for defiant children who need to know exactly where the line is drawn.** As you praise your child for not breaking rules, the unspoken message is that the rules exist and are in force. It's hard to enforce a limit with clarity unless it exists with clarity.

- The negative rules that provide the foundation of Proactive Recognition give more opportunities to acknowledge successful behaviors than traditional positive rules. Unless you are artfully creative, a rule like "be respectful" requires waiting for an act of respect to occur before you can offer rule-related recognition, whereas a rule like "no disrespect" provides a wide range of honest opportunities to create appreciation; you need not wait until special behaviors happen to provide the warm regard of success.

Proactive Recognition: Prescription

- Use this type of recognition and appreciation throughout the day, especially first thing in the morning and after school. **Focus on the times when your child is in control, not out of control.**

- Begin shaping lists of rules and positive behaviors to support more consistent interventions and as a way of teaching *all* the rules, not just the ones that are particular problems. You can keep the lists as a private reference point until you are ready to formalize them and present them to your child.

- View your child's capacity at this point as "half-full" rather than "half-empty." Regard small steps your child makes in the right direction as the precious seeds of the harvest to come. Point out whatever you notice in this positive, growing direction. Express your appreciation and excitement. Be creative and water every seed that you can.

- **Recognize and appreciate 10 or more rule-based successes daily.** Be *ruthlessly opportunistic* in finding the positive choices your child is making, no matter how microscopic. Keep in mind that it always takes effort to refrain from breaking rules. It doesn't just happen. Appreciate the effort, power and control being used. Just as you, as the parent of a difficult child, are working harder than the average parent, your child is making more effort than the average child to control her extra dose of intensity. (We have worked at psychiatric settings where children and adults were truly, acutely out of control. It is not a pretty sight or a heartwarming experience. This is why, in part, we are so appreciative when self-control is being used and why we credit children for the effort.) When we give children this kind of heartfelt payoff for their good choices, problem behaviors become negligible.

- **Use Proactive Recognition in conjunction with the previous steps: Visit your child, do a Video Moment or two, and then add on recognition for a few rules that have not been broken.** You can also weave into the exchange some appreciation for the positive qualities that you want to see grow.

- Even if you were to do this 20 times a day, which would be above and beyond our recommendations, and even if you were to elaborate upon these interventions so as to take 30 seconds for each of them, this would not total more than 10 minutes a day to exert a tremendously powerful therapeutic influence in your child's life and a wonderful new pull toward successful behaviors.

- Use Proactive Recognition with a *calm, neutral attitude* during red flag times associated with your child's escalation to misbehavior. Even as Samantha seems to be on the verge of climbing the ladder she's been told to stay away from, calmly say: "Samantha, I see that you're tempted to climb Daddy's ladder, and that you're choosing to follow our rule not to do that. You're showing great restraint and consideration for your own safety."

- Try to "beat your child to the punch." Notice the early signs of problem behavior and praise and appreciate the self-control being used, *before* the rule is actually being broken.

- Once a rule is broken, your choices are limited. Until the timing is just right and until we fully develop the consequence strategy, you can give whatever consequence you normally give, as cleanly and as neutrally as possible. In Step Five, you will learn how to give an effective consequence without ignoring the problem or inadvertently giving a payoff to the negative behavior with warnings or lectures. Do the best you can for now.

- **If the opportunity to build the new pattern of success is diminished temporarily, focus on resuming it at the next opportunity.** *Stay intent.* Keep in mind that the true purpose of this intervention is in shifting your child from a pre-existing habit of failures and attachment to negative response to a new habit of excitement and investment in successes.

- If your child crosses the line and breaks a rule, calmly and neutrally impart a consequence that you can readily control and monitor.

- **Now and then, after giving recognition, mention that you might be willing to give "credits" for this kind of effort and self-control.** Just say that you've been giving it some thought and you'll let him know what you decide. You might add that it could be a good way of earning extra privileges.

Chapter Eight
Step 4: Creative Recognition
Creating Successes That
Would Not Otherwise Exist

CLARITY IS AN INCREDIBLE GIFT to give one's self or to give one's child. Without clarity, it is virtually impossible to successfully parent, and it is virtually impossible for a child to be fully successful. Remember, difficult children lead unclear lives, almost by nature. Unless a parent has intervened to create the necessary level of structure and clarity, the challenging child is at least to some extent floating in a world of confusion.

The child knows all too well that breaking rules and other acting out has pushed the envelope beyond the acceptable and senses the stress that will surely result. Nevertheless, he is compelled by the desire for the payoff of energy and relationship that problems draw. **Even when desperately wanting to do the right thing and desperately not wanting to disappoint the adults in their lives, many children are, for all intents and purposes, addicted to pushing the limits.** The bigger reactions that negative behaviors typically draw inadvertently reinforce their belief that acting out pays off.

It's a classic double message. Traditional methods of parenting have us scolding or admonishing a challenging child for some transgression, telling him never to do it again—while at the same time, we psychologically slip him the equivalent of a hundred dollar bill, via the energy of our reaction. It's a confusing mixed message and a confusing way to live. Difficult children are, unfortunately, under the impression that they get more reliably exciting quality time when things go wrong. No wonder so many challenging children have depressive symptoms. Confusion is inherently depressing.

Removing the Clouds

Every spring in San Francisco, the famous "Bay to Breakers" 10K race is run along a beautiful course from San Francisco Bay through Golden Gate Park and to the breakers at the ocean's edge.

The distance of seven-plus miles might well be achievable for a child's cardiovascular system, but most children would need a good deal of coaching and training, as well as shorter races, to build up the endurance and the mental focus required for such an endeavor.

In a sea of thousands of runners, packed shoulder to shoulder, one false move could be disaster. Even if your child were in great shape, would you let her run the race alone? Probably not without some solid assurance first: some proof of her capacity to stay on course and be safe during the run. Even then, you might feel the urge to run along and be supportive step by step, at least during the first part of the run.

Every day is like a Bay to Breakers race for the energy-challenged child. Being able to channel energy wisely, stay on track, not get distracted, not be run over or run someone else over—all take training and successful experience in evolving toward attainment and mastery.

This next strategy builds on and creates new successes begun by the first intervention, Active Recognition. It is about training your child by using shorter "runs," which build stamina, focus and, most of all, a sense of success and a welcoming of the challenge to take on bigger events.

Creative Recognition is about **pulling your child further into progressing in a successful direction through the use of clear and simple commands and through feeding back bigger-than-ordinary reactions to gradations of compliance.** It's another way to allow a child to experience the new circuitry you are installing and to feel a new flow of energy.

If a child is out of shape or inexperienced, would you require him to run a 10K race right off the bat? Many parents inadvertently do the equivalent by the way they communicate both expectations and requests. Believing that, because a child is high energy and able-bodied, he automatically has other skills needed to succeed at life's challenges can sometimes lead to setting him up for failure, despite the best of intentions.

Willingness and interest in complying, as well as the necessary skills, must be cultivated through training, and by a coach who is willing to cheer the first steps around the track, rather than asking the child to accomplish the entire seven-mile stretch before any applause occurs.

Initially, acknowledging your child's efforts and ability to run an eighth of a mile would more surely both ensure a successful outcome and encourage your child's motivation to try longer and more difficult runs. **It is the small and doable steps that pave the way to building success and training for bigger accomplishments.** Baby steps lead to quantum leaps.

Focusing on and appreciating the positive steps your child has already taken, rather than focusing on what the child has not yet done, changes the nature of the interaction and the message to the child.

This type of focused recognition will bolster your creative parenting as it produces an increasingly positive environment—by virtue of setting the child up to succeed with clear, achievable requests and by attending to the child's efforts made in the desired direction.

Creative Recognition is a technique, but also a *benevolent attitude.* It creates a flow of successes that would not otherwise exist.

Creative Recognition is about learning to shift the traditional ways we make requests to new ways that foster more success. It is also about strategically acknowledging children's efforts at progressive compliance. It is a way to stack the deck differently for your child—with more success and competency, rather than failures. Pure Shamu! Pure tollbooth attendant!

This is not about training a child to be a prize-winning athlete. **It is really about teaching him how to reinvest his energies successfully, constructively, productively, creatively and enjoyably.**

Most of us have raced with a child to a tree or wall. It is absolutely magical to see a child's face light up when she wins. Children usually love to win, and don't want to race unless they have some reasonable assurance of success. **Without some winning or at least some trace of success, some children may stop racing altogether.** This technique is about creating more assurance of success so children will want to try harder and further increase their efforts… as well as about dissolving the pull toward being non-compliant just to obtain your reaction and gain stimulation from your response.

Remember, most difficult children are unquestionably under the impression that more parental energy and emotion are available when they are not doing what they are asked or required to do. This is one of the core issues we are setting out to address.

With Creative Recognition, it is essential to cultivate a *microscopic view* of the child's successful behaviors, slanting your awareness toward small steps, choices and behaviors that are appropriate, desirable and laudable. A common mistake is to assume that the little things we notice don't make a difference to a child. **To the contrary, it is precisely the microscopic focus that helps a sensitive or highly reactive child resist becoming overwhelmed by the larger tasks to which these small behaviors lead and of which they are comprised.** When beginning with small, relatively easy requests with which the child will likely comply, the child is set up to succeed—moving ultimately in the direction of overall cooperation in responding to larger requests and assuming more responsibilities.

Children who begin to feel more successful on the inside want to show what they can do. They are naturally more responsible and helpful and less inclined toward instances of being resistant or defiant for the sake of "fishing" for reactions from others.

Removing the Confusion

Creating a home or school environment that is far clearer than the one that previously existed will help a difficult child enormously. We meet all the time with parents who are extremely well-intentioned and honestly believe that their children have had things spelled out to them in the clearest possible terms.

Time and time again, however, when these same parents are given an approach that makes their child's life even less ambiguous, these children begin to live their lives with more zeal, intelligence, competence and comprehensibility.

Beginning with simple, clear requests with which the child is easily capable of complying increases the chances of acquiescence and therefore of experiencing success. Children need requests to be simple and clear. They need to receive the true content of the request and they need to know when compliance is required and not optional.

In an effort to be tender, polite and diplomatic, many parents inadvertently dilute their requests or send the child a conflicting message that compliance is unimportant or optional. This, of course, is far from what is intended. Conventional parenting plays right into the problem of feeding the lack of clarity.

Request-like phrases such as…

"Would you—?"

"Could you—?"

"Please—?"

… heighten an intense and obstinate child's confusion about the expectation being communicated, who is really in charge and whether the child really has to do what the parent is asking.

Phrases like: "I need you to put the truck away," or "I need you to put your shoes in your room," send clearer messages than the polite requests.

Phrases like: "Could you please put your truck away?" or "Your bed is still not made," or "Would you take the garbage out, okay?" contain mixed messages regarding whether or not compliance is important. To the difficult child, they unfortunately imply an option.

Despite the obviously pleasant aspects of compassion and good manners that polite and well-intended requests imply, and despite the fact that softer requests work for the average child, these conventional requests create a host of problems for a child who perceives that negativity nets them greater payoff.

Such a child will see, in an unclear or confusing request, an implication that she has a choice—and, therefore, an opportunity to get a larger payoff for noncompliance than for following directions.

A child who believes he gets more mileage out of negativity senses, in advance, when the payoff for doing what has been asked will be low-key: "Thank you," "Attaboy" or "Good job" at most. The child also knows that if he does not comply, the reaction may well be a progression of more animated reactions: warnings with increasing pitch and emotion, displays of frustration, anger and perhaps even yelling. Despite its being negative attention, most difficult children predictably will be drawn to the bigger reaction… the fireworks.

The turnabout begins to take shape when the child senses that bigger reactions and emotions, animation and fireworks will occur *when compliance occurs*—and this often requires a creative form of jump-starting.

A second crucial aspect of Creative Recognition is reinforcing and energizing the child's efforts and response to your requests. This form of recognition is best comprised of equal parts of Video Moments and heartfelt appreciation.

An example of a Creative Recognition to a simple request might be: "I notice that you picked up nearly all the dirty clothes off the floor and put them in the hamper. I really appreciate how well you listened and how you are doing what I asked. Now I need you to get the last two shirts over on the chair."

Much of mainstream parenting would charge right into pointing out what wasn't done and completely ignore what had been accomplished. In the above example, the parent is skillfully making a "big deal" over aspects of success that might normally be underplayed or overlooked.

A more complex example might be this: Jeremy has just been asked by his mother to pick up his toys. He begins to stomp over to the first toy and then slowly drags his feet. A typical frustration response from a parent might be:

"Stop stomping. Stop dragging your feet. Please hurry up!"

A Creative Recognition might go like this:

"I see you slowly walking over to your truck. I appreciate that you got up and are starting to do what I asked."

Another might be:

"I guess you heard me, Jeremy. You are beginning to follow my directions. You are walking to your toys. Thank you for moving when I asked you to, even though you seemed to be angry."

As a parent, you are literally changing the focus of your relationship, your relatedness and your verbalizations to a heightened positive slant. This sends a message of success and recognition to the child for even small steps in the desired direction. It resists a negative interpretation of the manner or quality of the child's walking, but more importantly, *it acknowledges that he is moving in the right direction* (toward the toys, as requested). This shifts the energy to a positive spin and conveys a message that every movement in the right direction is valued.

After all, on a microscopic level, every movement in the right direction really is a success, even if we only give recognition to a few at a time. Imagine having spent years of your life constructing and engineering a robot. When it was finally operational you'd most likely be excitedly cheering every correctly directed step of its journey.

Sometimes parents have to heighten their level of creativity to match a child's level of intensity. When necessary, we have advised parents to be as clever as they need to be to get a handful of successes in a day and thereby gain the working edge: obtaining therapeutic opportunities to reinforce any success by showing their appreciation and delight.

David

One of our favorite stories involves an extremely defiant six-year-old whose wonderful parents were entirely frustrated in their attempts to gain compliance. The father's response to our technique was a roll of his eyeballs and these words: "There is no way that David is going to do anything we ask him to do. It won't work."

The father was simply told: "For now, be as clever and as simplistic in your requests as possible to get the successes going. That's the secret."

David's dad then had to leave to pick him up at school. When he returned he had a broad smile on his face. It appeared that he had accomplished his mission, and we asked how he managed to do it.

With great pride he reported that David had gotten in the car and was in the act of closing the door when his father requested: "I need you to close the door."

It was, of course, already a done deal and all that was left was to congratulate David for following directions, which was done in excellent fashion. Several other exceedingly doable requests yielded the same kind of outcome. The family was on its way. To make a long story short, within a relatively short time, David was predominantly compliant with both simple and more complex commands and his parents were quite pleased with the change. They could now even ask him to go clean his room or do his homework and he would just stop what he was doing, and with the best of attitudes, take care of whatever was needed.

What David's parents did brilliantly was to back up and begin by *making their requests as simple as they needed to be to get compliance to start trickling in.* They were willing to suspend the polite requests that they valued and to make their requests simpler and clearer. And, they were willing to be appreciative of small successes, even though they were angry about his years of defiance.

They brilliantly created successes where they would otherwise not have existed through their attitude and their creativity in setting tasks at which it was virtually impossible for David to fail.

The power of this technique is also based in its ability to be "in the moment" with the child. Rather than pushing for finished products and the ultimate behaviors you want to see, you help shape your child's behavior in a beneficial direction by operating on the principle of partial credit and applause for smaller steps. Your child will be much more likely to achieve the larger end goals by beginning with this more narrow focus.

More examples of simple requests that tend to elicit straightforward compliance are:

"I need for you to hand me that pair of scissors."

"I want you to hold this book for a second."

"Hold the other side of this blanket and let's give it a few shakes."

Ironically, as this step gets solidly underway, bigger and more complex requests become surprisingly easy to achieve. The proper psychological pathways evolve through this intervention, as does the child's internal desire to do what needs to be done. Verbal reinforcements and acknowledgments are at their best when they are descriptive and specific… just as in Active Recognition. This engages the receptivity of the child and gives her concrete evidence of the esteem in which she is held. Examples are:

"I notice that you paid attention to what I said and handed me the scissors right away when I asked. I appreciate that very much."

"I love that you held the book just like I told you to. I noticed that you did it with a very helpful attitude."

"I appreciate that you followed my directions and helped me by shaking the sand out of the blanket."

Details further help you maintain your parenting conviction not to be pulled back into the negative soup with your child. The detail in your response both is felt by the child as a success and deepens the new flow of energy that makes future compliance that much more accessible and probable.

Here are some examples of Creative Recognition as it might occur in an everyday sequence or application:

"I need you to pick up your toys right now." (clear command)

"I see you picking up toys off the floor." (video moment/ recognition)

"I like it when you do what I ask." (defining the specific compliance)

"Thanks for clearing the floor on time!" (specific appreciation)

"I need you to wipe off the counter." (clear, simple command)

"Thanks for using a clean cloth." (detailed appreciation)

"I can really see the effort you are making." (video moment)

"I appreciate your help in the kitchen." (specific appreciation)

The simplicity and brevity of application of this strategy provide its

effectiveness. It cuts to the heart of information that is needed to motivate a challenging child. When requests are vague or long-winded, your child may not get the right message.

If the acknowledgments and recognition are not detailed and specific or are too general, the child's defensive radar comes into play. It absolutely has to be made clear what specific actions were valued.

Remember:

Appreciative comments like "Thank you" or "Good job" are simply not specific enough for this level of intervention. The child's trust and perception of success are engendered by detail and by really feeling *seen*. It is far more powerful and nurturing to describe exactly *why* you are saying "good job" and exactly *why* you are thankful.

Creative Recognition: Critical Points

- This strategy **pulls your child toward further success and cooperation by adding appreciation for any positive efforts.**

- Requests of challenging children are most effective when simple and in a clear form that doesn't imply an option.

- **Recognition and appreciation are most powerful when they are specific, detailed and based on observable behavior.** Avoid general and global praise.

- Creative Recognition should be offered frequently throughout the day to continue a flow of success for the child.

Use these opportunities to also point your child to aspects of his greatness. "The way you listened and did what was needed is a great quality you have." "The ability you are showing now to be collaborative is a wonderful quality of your greatness."

Creative Recognition: Prescription

- Use simple and clear requests to create five to 10 "successes" per day. Make this a daily goal. In the beginning, as many as 20 creative "requests" may be required to make five successes happen.

- **Encourage your child with requests that are very doable and that your child might predictably perform without a struggle.** Then, as time passes, gradually make bigger requests. Eventually there will be accountability for requests not followed once consequences have been properly set up; you will learn how to do this in a subsequent chapter.

- Use your parenting creativity through requests that invite compliance and applause, rather than conventional requests that are less clear such as "Please do your chores." Requests such as "Be responsible" might be redefined more specifically as: "Be home by 5 p.m.," or "Put your dirty clothes in the hamper every morning," or "I need you to check in with Dad before going outside after school."

- As a parent, **consciously practice and use command-type requests versus question-type requests** (i.e., "I need you to…" versus "Would you please…?"). Sweet questions like "When you get a chance," or "Could you please…?" water down your parenting authority and make compliance seem optional instead of necessary.

- **Recognize and appreciate small efforts your child makes.** Be specific with examples of behavior you observe. Advance your level of awareness and appreciation also to include the following:

  - Efforts your child makes that are in the "right direction;"

  - Evidence that your child is showing a good attitude; and

  - Instances when your child makes a smart choice (even a little one)!

This step is called Creative Recognition because you are using your parental creativity to create successes that would not otherwise surface. You are *making the successes happen.*

Be prepared for your child to feel some discomfort with all the unaccustomed recognition. Some children are so used to receiving negative attention that they still do not quite know what to do with positive attention. Expect your child to test whether the positive attention will continue. It is fairly common for children to try to either brush it off or to act out to see if they can pull you back into the territory of negatives merely because they are not yet comfortable with the shift to positives. Ignore the little stuff whenever possible and if consequences are needed give them calmly. Eventually, you will be able to provide accountability for all noncompliance. And most of all, don't back off the positives. If anything, turn up the dial.

Remain firm and remember your Parent Stands: "Absolutely No – I'm not going to let my child pull me into a pattern of failure and payoffs for negativity. I am doing what it takes to pull my child in the direction of success!" This mantra is the focus of Creative Recognition in a nutshell. Write it down and tape it to a place where you will see it several times a day. Say it aloud when you see it. This affirmation represents your resolve to change your child's situation. It is a very powerful stance and will anchor you for future strategies involving rules, boundaries and consequences.

Again: Keep in mind Shamu and the expectations that creatively helped him to flourish. And remember the tollbooth attendant whose attitude made all the difference in the world.

And one more thing: Make sure to give *yourself* recognition for all you are now doing to create this major change in the life of your child. You could have given up or said, "This is too silly!" but you haven't, even if you felt either of these things strongly. Your perseverance and determination are qualities of your greatness. Your creativity and clarity of purpose are also great qualities that you are demonstrating. We are here applauding you. Keep up the great work.

Chapter Nine
Step 5: The Credit System
Bless the Child Who Has His Own

Consistent positive recognition promotes a family atmosphere that is upbeat and reduces the risks of children having to draw attention to themselves for other than positive reasons. In our busy, stressful lives, this sort of "drip irrigation system" provides a steady flow of positive, affectionate, emotionally nutritious parental relationship.

Every child's home becomes a classroom of life. Qualities she does not initially know she possesses are first brought to light, then consistently reaffirmed. Your recognition polishes your child's many facets *in action:* the ability to show respect, for example, is recognized when the child is actually talking nicely or using good manners, and when the child is not being disrespectful, such as when not arguing, swearing or name-calling. With these techniques, you build your child's sense of connection and comfort with the experience of success, as well as a sense of mastery and accomplishment. To further enhance your enactment of the techniques already described in these pages, you can add a credit system.

The Credit System solidifies the flow of successes started by Active Recognition (Video Moments), Experiential, Creative and Proactive Recognitions. It offers the parent more leverage to reinforce rules and other increments of a child's efforts in a positive direction.

Credit systems are not necessary for the Nurtured Heart Approach to work. We did not realize this when first writing this book; but years later, we've seen clearly that the majority of children do just fine without it. If you decide that the credit system is not something you want to enact right now, you can just skip the rest of this chapter.

How does a parent know whether the credit system could be an important piece in his or her application of the Nurtured Heart Approach? Let's consider which circumstances beg more strongly for at least a consideration of a credit system:

- **If you wish to effect change in your child's behaviors at school, but there is little hope that the school will consider new approaches.** With a credit system, your impact stretches into the school setting, whether or not the child's teacher is willing to help in ways that align with the Nurtured Heart Approach.

- **If you want a way of getting a resistant child to take a consequence.**
  Some children resist consequences, and this can become a major obstacle
  for some families. A credit system can help a great deal with this problem. **Fortunately, our new form of consequence is much easier to
  enact, and resistance is minimal. This will be explained in the next
  chapter.**

- **If you want a potent way of fanning the flames of success that you've
  ignited through the techniques discussed up to this point.** A credit
  system can serve as insurance that opportunities for positive feedback
  and praise are rarely missed. And a credit system can serve as a great
  reminder to be appreciative even in the midst of a stressful period of
  time.

If you're even considering implementing a credit system, we invite you to
read this chapter. If you wish to skip forward, you can always come back to this
if you determine that it would be helpful to you. The material in these pages
will help to reinforce the other aspects of the Nurtured Heart Approach, even
if you ultimately choose not to use a credit system.

We Are All On Credit Systems

It could be said that we are all on credit systems. For better or worse,
whether we like it or not. Whether on welfare or earning large sums of money,
virtually every adult alive is faced with the dilemma of managing his or her
resources. To illustrate this point, let's take a fresh look at several important
features of our lives.

Essentially, we all acquire money, which is a symbol to which we ascribe
value and meaning, and we then exchange this symbol for objects and services.
Money itself cannot be eaten, used for clothing or provide shelter or transportation, but it can be used to acquire any of these, and is required to obtain a
wide array of other necessities and extras.

If we have our necessities budgeted, we then are faced with choosing what
to do with whatever is left over. This discretionary money can be saved for
anything from retirement to vacations to more frivolous or adventurous
spending. Even a homeless person who acquires a dollar by begging is faced
with deciding how that money will be spent. Whereas rent and car payments
may be our necessities, cigarettes and sweets might be his. Even those who take
vows of poverty are faced with money-related challenges. Currencies of many
kinds comprise the systems that are used worldwide. There seems to be no
escaping economics, like it or not. And this adventure does not end when we
retire.

A child does not roll out of bed on her 18th birthday with a profound knowledge of how to manage her own economy. Without a few years of apprenticeship where she has a chance to deal with the realities of necessities and discretionary spending dilemmas, the child is likely to be missing a few very important pieces of the puzzle when she emerges into the adult world.

Although most children spend substantial time indirectly experiencing their parents' credit systems, most remain unequipped psychologically to venture out competently and confidently when the baton is passed. Instead of having had their very own experiences of being in charge of an economy and its complexities, they have only picked up on the highlights of the economies that they have vicariously experienced, and quite often they harbor grave misunderstandings of how things really work. For example, they may not comprehend all the hidden expenses of owning and operating a television, let alone a car or a house.

Having the secondhand experience of living in the parents' economy is like trying to get exercise by watching people exercise on television. Until the experience is firsthand, much is left to be discovered.

The problems are multiplied for a difficult child en route to leaving the safety net of childhood and experiencing adult life.

The life of a difficult child is typically much more incongruent than that of the average child. She probably has only a minimal understanding of economics, having failed to pay close attention to learning opportunities. She also may be under the impression that the things she wants are acquired through the labors of manipulation, begging and duress. Her appreciation of the concept of sought-after possessions and acquisitions being the fruits of hard work is not likely to be well-established.

She also is unlikely to feel connected to the little things involved in running a household. She might think toilet paper magically appears within arm's length or that the toilet paper fairy sees to it that the roll never ends.

The point is that *difficult children frequently have only a vague sense of what their jobs are in the household or at school, or of how things work in the systems of which they are a part.* Their ability to acquire things depends on the whims and moods of their parents and, in their minds, their windfalls may not be at all connected to whether the child had a good day, a great day or a bad day.

Many parents of difficult children are understandably so resentful about their child having adversely affected their lives that, when the child is no longer annoying them, they continue a moratorium on recognition, privileges and rewards. A child's acquiring anything from such a parent can be a walk down a depressing, dimly lit street.

Other intense children may acquire all their hearts' desires easily, despite poor behaviors, as a result of last-ditch attempts by parents to attain closeness or gratitude. Concessions such as gifts and favors may be given in poorly designed efforts to gain compliance and leverage. These efforts typically backfire and deepen the gravity of the situation.

Attracting negative attention, unfortunately, is a well-advertised enterprise. Many bright children end up applying a good portion of their superior intelligence to the convoluted endeavor of figuring out how to acquire relationship and coveted things through various forms of manipulation, begging, guilt trips and bullying tactics. That will not help them in the adult world unless they are planning on a life of crime or misery.

A credit system is a powerful device for parents both to acquire a healthy quotient of needed leverage and to provide a child with a much-needed apprenticeship that combines powerful life lessons with a strong blend of mastery and accomplishment.

Apprenticeships are no longer readily available to children. Schools can somewhat suffice as a substitute when school-based apprenticeships are engineered on the basis of successes. Unfortunately, success-oriented apprenticeships at most schools are far more readily available to children who are *not* challenging.

Difficult children, however, frequently fall into *negative* apprenticeships on the basis of their failures. The child quickly figures out the reality of any given classroom and concludes that getting recognition and being of interest for doing poorly is a much stronger economy than that for doing well. The child perceives that sought-after relationship and privileges are obtained through poor choices, and this becomes the style of acquisition.

This is particularly unfortunate because positive apprenticeships for difficult children are very easy to set up in any kind of classroom, given the proper knowledge, skills and tools. Credit systems afford parents and teachers a systematic way of making each child an apprentice, and of acknowledging and encouraging every child in their care.

Many people who work with difficult children are under the false impression that telling a child, "If you try harder, you can do it!" is encouraging. In reality, this is a very discouraging statement to a child who is *already* trying harder. It takes so much more effort for a difficult child consistently to modulate his intense impulses and energies, and it is deflating to be trying very hard and be told to try harder. Besides, the meta-message the child gets when you tell him to try harder is "You're not trying hard enough right now."

Just like the brakes of a 10-ton cement truck have to work much harder to stop at 20 m.p.h. than a small car at the same speed, intense, energy-challenged, hyper-needy children have to apply much more effort to gain self-control successfully. Like the cement truck, their control mechanisms ultimately have to evolve at much more powerful levels. We need to purposefully build the additional control by applauding what's already there rather than accidentally delivering deflating messages.

The Marlboro Sign

From a distance, one passes a billboard sign and takes in the basics of the overall presentation—usually a picture paired with a caption. Someone who moves in much closer and adjusts the focus sees that a multitude of dots comprises the picture. Each dot contributes to a variety of colors in different arrangements. These are the elements that make the big picture happen. They are like the bricks of the house. During a cold or rainy spell, it becomes easier to appreciate every last one. If weather conditions start removing dots or bricks, the big picture gets compromised.

Children are going to do much better if they are creatively recognized and given credit for the micro-efforts they are already putting out.

"I see that you have the first part of your assignment done. That took a lot of effort. Now I need you to focus on part two."

"David, you have six of the eight levels completed. You are using a lot of focus and concentration."

"Gabby, I notice you trying very hard to not ask for treats. It looks like a real struggle for you, but you are doing it."

How are our children going to learn that what they are capable of accomplishing if we fail to validate the things they do when they actually do them? If we fall into the trap of only validating their actions when they *can't* do something, how in the world can we expect them to turn things around? Does success arise out of frustration or motivation? How motivated are you to improve on your job performance when a supervisor notices only your shortcomings?

Just as the energized, intense child has to work harder to control his energies and intensities, parents of hyper-energized, hyper-needy children concurrently have to parent at more intense levels. Your job requires more determination, more resolve and more reserves. You deserve more credit, not less.

The Credit System is a means of putting determination and resolve into action in a powerful, efficient way.

This system allows for easier discernment of positive facets of your child's day and easier distribution of successes, on a daily and ongoing basis. The Credit System is the final phase of the first stand: doing what it takes to pull your child in the direction of attainment while refusing to revert to old, unproductive attempts to manage misbehaviors. It is the Credit System that also dramatically increases the level of healthy leverage you, as parent, can exert in a powerful and neutral way.

The Credit System is also the first phase of the final stand: "Here are the rules and here's what happens when you break a rule." The Credit System begins formalizing the rules in a very clear way. Now your child will know exactly what happens when a rule is not broken. This is an essential strategic phase in preparation for being in a strong and clear position to enforce the rules effectively, which you will be positioned to do in the very next step.

The Credit System as a Way To Create "Time-In"

We can use the credit system as a systematic, predictable tool to further create and deepen a growing sense of what we call *time-in*.

You are, most likely, familiar with the concept of time-out as a consequence for rule-breaking. Many parents have found that time-out doesn't work for them, but in our experience, *this is because of the lack of time-in*. Without time-in, time-out doesn't mean much.

The better and richer the time-in, the better the impact of time-out. The higher the interest and excitement of being in the game, the more being out of the game creates a powerful sense of missing out. This is what makes the time-out as a consequence effective—that desire for the child to be *in the game*.

The time-in is the final piece you'll need to understand how to give effective consequences in the form of a brief, un-energized time-out.

Time-in is the time when the child feels like he is in the game, being recognized and appreciated for success and steps toward success. During time-in, the child receives psychologically and emotionally nutritious comments that he comes to interpret as evidence that he is valued, meaningful and held in esteem. He is where he wants to be, accruing inner wealth, confidence, and faith in his own abilities and strengths.

Keep in mind however, that you do not have to use a credit system to accomplish a rich, rewarding, inner wealth-creating time-in that becomes, to the child, infinitely more rewarding than the un-energized time-out we recommend as a consequence. You can create a wonderful time-in by using the techniques described in previous chapters to recognize positive qualities and choices with strong, focused energy and relationship.

The hinge of the limit setting to come, psychologically, becomes: "I can't stop you from breaking a rule, but I can give you recognition and credit when you make a smart and helpful choice not to break a rule…and a consequence every time you decide to break one." You will learn much more on this subject in the next chapter.

Getting Started With a Credit System

In this case, the first phase relates to giving your child credit to the extent that each rule is followed every day. Through this process, once a child knows exactly what happens when a rule is not broken, you will be in a far more advantageous position to say what happens when a rule is broken and to have consequences have meaning and take hold. It makes the defining line much clearer.

The previous four steps of the Nurtured Heart Approach have been geared toward your providing a new, positive form of nutrition for your child regarding his or her behavioral pathways. You are affirming and appreciating your child's presence in general (Active Recognition/Video Moments). You are creatively pointing out the great choices made, despite the presence of the existing problem behaviors (Creative Recognition). You are proactively showing gratitude to your child for everyday successes and for being responsible and controlled in relation to the rules (Proactive Recognition).

Now it is recommended that you increase the level of clarity and the level of impact to a point that is truly meaningful to children whose lives are often confusing, frustrating and disempowered. You will be creating a daily system that will allow your child to experience the benefits of choosing to follow your rules as far more alluring than choosing to break the rules.

The more unclear the life of the child, the more appealing the adventure called clarity. Some of our children's lives have the texture of the fuzziest video games imaginable. Especially for our challenging children, the methods we have had at our disposal have set this up. Again, it is not the parent or the teacher, but the available conventional methods of parenting and teaching that manufacture this lack of clarity.

For however long an unclear, difficult, acting-out child may be put in a clear environment, that child will try it on, like any new environment —like a personal video game, if you will. Watch what happens. The child will size the situation up, down and sideways to test it and assess whether it's for real. Do I really score points in these ways? Do I really get consequences in this way? What happens if I choose this doorway? The more clearly the environment is set up in terms of positive structure, the quicker the learning. Acknowledgments and limits must align interactively.

The more frequent the exceptions, the slower the learning and the greater the frustration and the testing. Testing is a child's way of telling you, "Come on, come through with the clarity... the structure... I need it!" If the clarity makers (parents and teachers) come through with structure at the right level, the testing typically stops and the successes roll in. If the clarity the child requires is not provided, the testing typically heightens.

This step is about how to set up and award credits for all the recognition that you have initiated thus far. Seeing rules that are *not* broken as successes and communicating your appreciation through words and credits, as well as crediting productive, successful behavior, make this strategic level different from conventional point systems, which typically fall into the trap of deducting points for misbehaviors or rule breaking. Such systems do not emphasize partial successes, but rather inadvertently emphasize partial failures.

This difference is deceptively powerful in setting the stage for limits and consequences that really work. Re-emphasizing partial successes is an essential step toward establishing limits that are clear and building your child's self-esteem and sense of competency. This is achieved by pointing out nuances of movement in the desired direction. This step also paves the way for allowing a difficult child to withdraw her energy from negative behavior and reinvest it into being positive with equal intensity.

The Allowance Lesson

Remember that we are all on a credit system of sorts. We work so many hours for so much pay. If we miss a day we may not receive our full check. We are also on a "token" economy—where it is necessary to pay for privileges. We pay a parking meter a certain amount to use the space for a specified period of time. Different brands of shampoos have different prices. If we take in a movie, it costs us so much extra for a popcorn and soda. The extras are not givens. These are obvious examples of life's credit system and privilege price tags.

One of the most common tools to teach children aspects of responsibility is from the system of allowance payments, which also helps the child learn from autonomy. Not every child is old enough for this lesson, however, or sufficiently motivated by money. Neither does every family have the luxury of extra funds on a regular basis to make an allowance system workable. Most allowance systems only tie earning potential to chores rather than to clear links with behavioral expectations.

Many parents of difficult children who have tried this traditional approach prior to applying our credit system report that the money/allowance system typically works in only a limited fashion. One situation in which it fails is when a parent needs something to be done and the child refuses, often digressing in a manner that accidentally rewards defiance. A parent of a difficult child needs both more leverage than exists in an allowance system and a system that will hold up over time. Parents need healthy leverage for a child of eight as well for an 18-year-old.

Of course, most parents of difficult children are already using pieces of several credit systems in attempts to get leverage, often without realizing it. For the most part these negotiations are done on an informal and unorganized basis. "If you eat all your dinner, you can have dessert." "If you have a good week at school, you can stay over at your friend's on Friday night." "If you get good grades, we will let you have driving lessons." "If you do the following chores, we will give you this amount of money every other week when we get paid."

These are time-tested methods. They often work like a charm with children with less intense temperaments and children who have no pre-existing patterns of negativity and failure. Any parent who has ever tried them with more intense children realizes that something more powerful, more organized and more inclusive is needed to accomplish their goals and to have their child thrive more consistently in a climate of ongoing motivation and success.

Inside a Video Game

In effect, when you set up a credit system, you are creating a custom-made, heart-centered video game, tailor-made to your child's needs and abilities. In this game, you decide the rules, you award the points or tokens. Your child will not only want to play, he will want to play at increasingly more challenging and successful levels.

Even though you will give your child a choice as to whether or not to commit to the Credit System, you will be armed with powerful leverage to convince her that this really is the only game in town—so it's well worth trying. Even the most hesitant, defiant, anxious child finds it is much better to play than not play (more on this later). As the child commits—whether reluctantly, cooperatively, angrily, excitedly, sadly or pensively—once she begins to experience the success this new system engenders, you will see her react with surprise, pleasure and a new fervor to cooperate.

Designing a Credit System, Part I: Ways To Earn

To design your credit system, you'll first decide how the child can earn credits by taking three steps: establishing a list of written rules; formalizing a list of desired qualities of behavior and action; and devising an appropriate list of chores and responsibilities for your child. Once you complete these steps, you will have comprised your child's **Ways To Earn** category.

1. Establish rules.

At this point, rules must be in a written form that you can post. This is as much for your awareness and commitment as it is for your child's. We urge you to make the rules as clear as possible and to have not only the essential rules, but to include some "gimme" rules—a few that are easily achieved on a consistent basis.

For example, instead of a rule like "Be respectful," incorporate component aspects of respect such as "No back talk," "No bad words," "No yelling," "No name calling," and "No arguing."

Be inclusive. Even though you may know in advance that your child has, for example, a history of arguing or name calling, he may virtually never yell or use bad words. Include "No yelling" and "No cursing" in your rules anyway. This system needs to be set up for success as well as leverage. It is also vital to have rules that are within your ability as parent to monitor or evaluate, directly or indirectly.

2. Formalize a list of desirable, sought-after behaviors and qualities.

This also should be written out, because under this system the items on it will be tracked and credited. Think of any behaviors that merit recognition: aspects of living for which you would be willing to give credit or bonuses, behaviors that you would like to see more often or desired behaviors that you value and wish to cultivate.

Examples of these are behaviors like good attitude, extra effort, being respectful, using good manners, showing responsibility, making a good choice, taking no for an answer, following directions, sharing well and playing cooperatively.

3. Devise a list of chores and responsibilities that are appropriate for your child's age and range of abilities.

Chores can be anything from raking leaves to folding towels to taking out the garbage. Any household or neighborly tasks that contribute to life on the home front and the family's efforts along those lines are appropriate.

Responsibilities, on the other hand, are those daily incidental aspects of life that are essential to the well-being of the child and the family. They range from doing one's homework and keeping one's room neat to brushing one's teeth, getting ready for school on time, being ready for bed on time and putting one's dirty clothes in the hamper.

These first three lists are then combined to comprise Ways to Earn, the first of two essential categories of the Credit System. The combination of credits and bonuses earned for rules not broken and for positive behaviors and efforts applied to chores and responsibilities become earned credits. These credits will be used to purchase privileges that are detailed on the final list.

Designing a Credit System, Part II: Ways To Spend

Then, establish **Ways to Spend**—a list of privileges you find acceptable for your child to work for or earn through constructive behavior.

If this book were produced for the average child, we could spin off a few simple extra privileges that would suffice. However, since the book is designed primarily for children who exhibit challenging behaviors, we must design a privilege list that provides the necessary leverage and attains the necessary level of structure. **Our general rule of thumb for challenging children is that the**

more intense the child, the more intense the intervention.

For most moderately to high-level difficult children, this translates to a privilege list that incorporates *most privileges other than food, shelter and clothing.* This may sound drastic, but think for a second about what privileges are denied when your child is on some kind of restriction. When your child is grounded, do you allow visits with friends, phone calls, TV time and the like? In the real-world economy, we pay for almost everything. This credit system emulates a real-world economy by being somewhat as encompassing.

Ironically, **by taking a stand that includes almost everything as a privilege on the Ways to Spend list, you actually get a much better chance to be the good guy.** You get to demonstrate to your child that, with the credit system in place, he will never again be grounded or arbitrarily restricted from privileges. The only ways to miss out on future privileges is not accumulating the necessary credits or while a consequence has yet to be fulfilled. Your child will quickly figure out on his own that if he indeed misses out on a desired privilege, no one but he is actually responsible for the "grounding." He will not have to be told this. He will arrive at this conclusion as he sizes up and figures out his new reality. Unless a privilege is otherwise unavailable because of resources or timing, or if the privilege cannot be purchased at the moment because of a consequence owed, the child soon should come to realize that you basically favor his having privileges, given the proper exchange of credits, and that you are all for helping him figure out ways to earn more.

In a nutshell, the credit system operates like this: If your child follows a rule (from list one in the Ways to Earn category) or shows an example of good behavior (from list two in the Ways to Earn category) or performs a chore or responsibility (from list three in the Ways to Earn category), he will be entitled to earn the corresponding credits, which in turn he can spend on any of the designated privileges (the Ways to Spend list).

Under this system, you are clearly defining, in writing, what the expected rules, behaviors, chores and responsibilities are; and you are assigning a value, or a certain number of credits, to each one. Don't forget to include some "gimmes" in each category to ensure your child at least a handful of successes. No child wants to run a race he can't win. Then, as your child earns credits with each success, he can begin earning privileges.

Generosity

Generosity typically means a noble attitude of abundant giving and sharing. It means establishing this position of generosity and success-building that sets this system apart from others we have come across.

Cost response—where the impact on a difficult child's behavior is greater when desired or earned credits are taken away—is a predominant trend in the behavior management field today. Current research generally supports strategies based on this conclusion. What we see, over and over again, is that such conclusions only are true from a limited perspective. If one greatly enhances the early stages of treatment—all the phases of recognition—and glues them together with a credit system based on generosity, positive impacts on behaviors can be achieved in enormously different, exciting and simple ways.

Let's discuss a few fine points on the application of generosity to the credit system.

Properly define the rules so the child can be generously awarded credits.

Be specific and clear. When the rules are clear, awarding credits flows easily. A generous approach to crediting gives you the empowered option of responding by rewarding success and bestowing recognition rather than assuming a negative and punitive stance. Rather than simply declaring "Be nice to your sister," quantify the rule more clearly: "No hitting" makes it possible to recognize and give credit when that rule is not being broken.

Commands tend to be infinitely easier for both you and your child to reach agreement on. If the rule is "Be nice to your sister," you then essentially have to wait around until some form of nice behavior occurs. This could limit your opportunities as a success finder. However, if you use the clearer rule "No being mean," you can generously find as many opportunities to recognize and encourage as you have time to harvest. You will also have far more opportunities to offer "partial credit," as in the following examples:

> "Alex, I am going to give you half points today [instead of the full 10, for example] for following the no-hitting rule because I'm proud of the way you controlled your hitting most of the day."

> "I'm giving you the entire 10 credits for the no-disrespect rule. As far as I can tell, you were respectful all day."

> "Also, I'm giving you five credits for the no-interrupting rule. Even though you had a hard time when I was on the phone, you did your consequence well [this is covered in the next step] and I could see you were trying hard the rest of the time."

You most definitely want to underline, emphasize and credit the portion of the day when the rules aren't being broken.

Remember the story of Shamu and the great achievements accomplished by knowing how best to initiate the learning process. This is an essential and decisive aspect of intervention that will not only increase the amount of healthy self-control your child uses, but will help convince the child who is heavily invested in negative behaviors that there is more than enough attention available for positive efforts and healthy aspects of self. A child can come to realize that she does not have to be perfect to be valued in your eyes. This sets the stage for her making the decision to reinvest her energies in successes.

A focus on generosity in crediting the rules enables your child to experience how not breaking rules contributes to his economy in a predictable fashion. You will find him standing on the threshold of a somewhat unbelievable conclusion: "The more rules the better." This translates internally for the child to: "The more rules that I don't break, the more credits I earn." It is not unusual for a child to suggest new rules once it dawns on him that the rules are no longer the bad guys.

This budding attitude helps to defuse opposition. It decreases the defiant tendencies of the many difficult children who feel claustrophobic around rules and tend to push the limits simply because the limit exists. In addition, as the child sizes up the new scheme of things and sees how much positive attention is available for not breaking rules, the tendency to go to the trouble of breaking rules to get a payoff diminishes.

To apply generosity to crediting the child for daily chores, break tasks into manageable, specific chunks.

Rather than "Clean your room," a more generous intervention might be broken into several specifics, such as: "Things picked up off the floor, clothes in the hamper, toys put away and the bed made neatly." This gives you many more chances to credit each action individually and breaks the work down into less intimidating tasks for your child. Again, specificity represents clarity for your child and easier crediting of any positives.

For example, each of these four aspects of room cleaning might be valued at up to 10 points, with a total of 40 points available for all four done well. Even if your child blows it on one task, she still has an incentive to try on the others. (Remember, moving in the right direction is valuable, even if a child doesn't hit the finish line every time.) Recognizing incremental job performance provides a safeguard for the child who is distractible or who may be easily overwhelmed or frustrated.

Tasks that absolutely have to be done will be addressed in the next section on consequences. For now, remember Shamu and the importance of creating successes that wouldn't otherwise exist.

What criteria constitute work well done? Defining and listing specific qualities and expectations regarding job completion can often be essential… particularly with manipulative, distractible or defiant children.

For example: "Take out garbage" may be broken down more specifically as: 1) Get all trash to the outside bin by 6 p.m., 2) Wipe off all trash containers, 3) Return all containers to their proper place. Generosity. The tolltaker would be proud.

Breaking down activities into smaller components is particularly helpful with younger children or with children who are easily frustrated. Not only does it provide better information about specific expectations, it provides you more chances to reward successes. It becomes a powerful tool for teaching about what constitutes excellence and also how to work toward it systematically in smaller, less intimidating increments... a great life lesson.

Some children look at a dirty room and are so overwhelmed by the idea of having to clean it in its entirety that they never start. If the task is broken down into smaller parts, most will accomplish some "success" (even if that "success" is only putting dirty clothes in the hamper that day).

It pays to redefine "success" this way to give your children the message that they not only can be successful—that they are, indeed, being successful. Then, over time, expectations can be increased and factored into the Credit System. Success becomes habitual and small successes grow into larger successes.

Another way to incorporate generosity is through the number of credits offered for following each rule, for positive behaviors, for chores completed and responsibilities performed. Assigning larger point values that reflect generosity and that accommodate wider margins for partial credit is a wise strategy as long as prices for privileges are equally inflated. (Another great lesson about the economy the child is likely to encounter as an adult!)

You can assign higher credit values to rules and expectations that are most important to you. Sometimes, offering higher credits for successes in relation to particularly challenging behavior serves to stack the deck in favor of quicker change in these areas.

Reserve the executive authority to refine the values as time goes by so you can keep upgrading the system, like a merchant trying to make her enterprise work better.

For example, Jeremy's arguing is a behavior that provokes an angry response from his father. In this case, "No arguing or no talking back" might be the rule, with the potential of earning more credits than would be earned for obeying other rules. Jeremy may be able to earn up to 30 credits per day for not arguing or talking back, compared with 10-15 credits for observing most other rules. This serves to increase his incentive and the likelihood that higher motivation will affect his effort and focus.

Also, the option exists to creatively credit other positive facets of "No arguing." You can choose to give bonus points for nuances such as "Listening without interrupting" or "Discussing things calmly," to mention just a few. Recognitions such as these have the effect of further pulling Jeremy in the desired direction by highlighting more of his successful efforts.

It should be noted that some parents absolutely have to have a condensed version of the credit system, either because of time constraints or because they know in advance their own need to keep things simple if they are to maintain their efforts. Some seem able to streamline the system effectively by making all values the same. If they do this, most choose to value each rule, chore and positive behavior at something like 10 credits each so they can still give partial credit, or at 15 credits so they can easily give a few different levels of partial credit. They may also choose to pare down the number of items on their list. In any case, we highly recommend maintaining a stance of generosity by including a number of items that almost always lead to successes ("gimmes").

Don't remove rules, chores, or responsibilities from your list just because your child seems to have mastered them.

As adults, we certainly would dislike having employers change the basic expectations of our jobs by removing the aspects that we have become good at while keeping only those that were hard for us. Imagine working at a large retail outlet store where employees get bonus credits toward a Caribbean cruise for not being rude to the customers, not using foul language and observing a few other basic rules. Those of us for whom these criteria are easy to maintain would not want our employers substituting new rules that are hard for us without at least retaining the opportunity to earn the easy credits as well.

Offer Bonus Credits.

Your ability to convey an attitude of generosity can also benefit from the use of bonus credits. What are the special behaviors, chores or responsibilities you are willing to credit? Keep in mind that every time you are giving recognition, you are massaging your child's spirit and massaging your child's true self with a song of success.

Examples of bonus behaviors might be anything from showing compassion for one's self or towards others, to taking criticism well, to apologizing when appropriate. Consider as bonus behaviors other qualities of greatness like being collaborative, thinking things through, or doing some especially helpful or thoughtful task like changing the sheets, folding the laundry, sweeping the walk or dusting the blinds.

The basic message to your child is: "There are lots of ways for you to be successful, and I'm going to be creative in finding them and letting you know about it." You can assign however many credits you want for a bonus behavior or act, but be sure to add them to your child's credit accumulation.

Again, the underlying message to the child is: "You don't have to go to the trouble of acting out to be noticed. You are going to be acknowledged and appreciated for a host of everyday events, not just the big deal stuff."

Introducing the Credit System to Your Child and Overcoming Resistance

Having implemented the first four steps of The Nurtured Heart Approach, you should, by now, be seeing some response from your child to the many kinds of recognition you are providing throughout the day and evening. The cumulative effects of acknowledgment and recognition typically provide a strong flow of emotional nutrition, a restoration of perceived psychological support, and an increased interest in family life. This is a signal that it is time to present the Credit System and to involve your child in this powerful means of magnifying " time-ins" for your child's good behaviors.

Although we have not yet detailed the How To Spend part of the Credit System equation, we would like to broach the topic that many parents find most intimidating: presenting the Credit System to the child. **Parents may fear that the child will reject the system, negating all their conscientious efforts up to this point and leaving them feeling more disempowered than ever.** They may be afraid that the child will proclaim that paying for privileges once enjoyed for free is preposterous. (If this latter point comes up, remember that eventually, your child will have to pay for those privileges; he or she may as well get used to the idea now, with the safety net of your supervision.)

In the end, the child has to enroll in the system for it to work; it can't be forced. So, it's important for the parent to broach the subject with the child in a way that makes the whole thing sound appealing. As you'll see, this isn't hard to do at all, as it is empowering for the child.

You have worked hard to cultivate a consciousness of determination. You did not come this far only to back down now. You are well into the process of taking an effective stand. Although it may not feel that way, you hold all the cards. Here are some strategies for presenting the Credit System to your child—and ways you can respond if your child initially rejects your suggested version of it.

Scenario 1

"Jeremy, I have really seen you use more effort lately in following the rules and using positive behaviors. I also have heard you say you would like to be able to have more privileges. I think you deserve to earn credit every day for the efforts you've been making. I've come up with a way you can 'buy' privileges with the credits you can earn every day for all your great efforts to follow rules and make good choices. Here is what I have in mind...."

Scenario 2

"Jeremy, the past few weeks have been so much better and because of that I want to start helping you to get the privileges I wasn't willing to give when things weren't going well. In addition to all the appreciation I've been giving I am now going to give you credits you can spend to get these things. It's up to you whether you want to start using this Credit System, so let me explain to you how it would work...I will keep track of the credits you are earning for following the rules, doing chores, homework and making great choices. I've decided this is what I need to help me to help you. The good news is that you can probably wind up with more privileges than ever and you will never get grounded again as you have in the past. If you have credits, you can get privileges. If you decide to be on the Credit System, let me know. Then, you'll be able to begin to spend your points on privileges."

Persuasive Ideas for the Reluctant Child

"You have worked very hard the last few weeks on not hitting, talking nicely, and other positive behaviors. On the Credit System you would have earned points every day for each of those efforts, so I know it's possible for you to earn lots of points for following the rules. It's up to you, but if you decide to start the system today, I'm offering a one-time-only startup bonus of 500 points. This is in addition to the points you earn today for doing things on your list of Ways to Earn."

"Unfortunately, the only way you can have anything on the privilege list from now on is by using the credits you are earning. I will continue to give you credits that you deserve, even if it takes you a long time to decide to buy into the system. Just let me know if and when you decide. I will do everything I can to help make this work. Here's what I have in mind and I'd really like your input."

Intermission

At this point in the chapter, we think it is advisable to offer you, the parent, a dose of encouragement. You may be finding the Credit System a bit complex, but we urge you to read on. It will all become more clear, and we also interject ways for you to simplify it if needed. We will also provide specific samples of actual lists of Ways to Earn and Ways to Spend. The effort you expend in understanding this approach and diligently applying it with your difficult child will have an amazing payoff. Think of a credit system as a device for furthering the cause of inspiring and appreciating your child—a cause you have already begun to undertake!

Privileges

Now let's take a look at privileges. A privilege is anything that is nonessential to your child's survival and basic health and well-being, but that is doable, realistic and appropriate for the child's age and capabilities. Ultimately, it is up to you.

Many of the privileges you come up with may have already been considered by your child to be things to which they are entitled. TV time, bike riding time and phone time are examples. For these suddenly to be considered privileges requires their being counterbalanced by the availability of some other privileges your child really wants, but may only have access to on rare occasions. Be sure to place a full spectrum of privileges on the list, with a wide range of prices. If possible, include bigger, high-priced items for which your child must save. This will help him learn the value of pursuing a goal strategically over time.

Let's look at how generosity might apply to your child's privilege menu and privilege prices. Keep in mind that we have helped many families who didn't have two nickels to rub together develop perfectly workable privilege lists. Forming effective credit systems does not have to involve money, nor does creating an attitude of generosity require the use of dollars and cents.

Before you present the Credit System to your child, devise a rough draft list of privileges and the costs associated with them. This list will probably give your child strong incentive for investing in the Credit System, so be sure to include privileges you know are desirable to him or to her. Going beyond basic privileges makes the system far more enticing, even to the resistant child. Ultimately, you as the parent must approve every privilege on the list and then decide how much of a privilege will be available (example: 30 minutes of computer time) and how often (example: three days per week). However, involving your child in creating the final version of the list and giving strong consideration to your child's suggestions are essential.

Examples of Common Privileges and Appropriate Prices

Most of these can be easily customized to your family. Change or eliminate those that aren't a good fit. Add privileges that work for you and your child.

Even if the privilege has been earned, it is not available when the store is "closed"—after bedtime, while you are working, or when your service or participation is unavailable.

Watching TV. To have the privilege of watching television, the child could be charged 20 credits for a half-hour show, with a maximum of 2 hours per day. Parents will alter the charges and maximum privilege times depending on their own family values. Some parents ban some shows altogether and some allow a questionable show but will charge a far higher price. For instance, approved educational TV could be very inexpensive and shows with aggressive themes very expensive. Most children will alter their viewing habits on their own in response to managing their own economy. Some children will create successes much more frequently by making greater effort to earn in order to gain the extra level of privilege. Of course, this gives you all the more to applaud.

Desserts or treats. Dessert, sodas or extra treats can be a privilege item with specified limits as to exactly how much per day is allowed. This privilege can be set at high credit values. Of course, some families prohibit sugar items altogether, and some find alternative healthy treat choices. In any case, we recommend that they be deemed a privilege, perhaps allowing the first one to be free.

Extra bedtime story or delayed bedtime. An extra bedtime story or an extra 15 minutes of stay-up time could be listed as a privilege. Longer staying-up-late privileges might be made available on weekends or holidays.

Computer or video game time. Computer time or video game time can be charged on the basis of 15-minute or 30-minute intervals, with sensible daily maximums. Most families choose to charge higher rates for computer time than for TV, except for educational games they wish to encourage.

Phone and stereo/personal music player time. Phone time and radio time are sought-after privileges for older children. Charge accordingly.

Special clothing items. Some families will stipulate that they are willing to buy normal items of clothing when needed, while selection of special name brands at higher prices must be earned. One way to clarify this issue is to make your child responsible for the cost above and beyond the cost of a regularly priced item. Pricing at 100 credits per dollar usually works. Of course, this should only be made available if you can afford it.

Fun outings. Items like roller-rink time, bowling time, swim time or bike riding time are viewed by most parents as privileges. Again, value these according to factors of cost and your desire to encourage or discourage the activity.

Social time with friends. Most parents view time with friends or social visits or events as privileges. Certainly, if you have ever grounded your child, these activities would have most likely been placed on hold. This is often the most reliable measure of whether something is really a privilege.

Special concessions. Any special concession, such as a sleep-over, a movie with popcorn, a driving lesson, or the use of a family possession like the car, is most definitely a privilege.

Classes, lessons, or participation in a team can even be regarded as privileges. Charge according to your cost and effects on family life. One 14 year-old, who had become progressively defiant through many years of outrageous behaviors, several hospitalizations and various other therapies, began to act responsibly when his parents charged credits for both football games and practices. He missed one practice and tried to blame his parents and the "stupid credit system." His teammates told him to get it together and make sure he had enough credits the next time. He did. To get the credits, he had to be all the more conscious of his actions and deeds.

An argument or negotiation with a parent. Several families have made it possible for their child to buy an argument or a negotiation as a privilege. Of course, arguing without prior request and permission should result in a consequence. The first mother who was creative enough to design this privilege described the results with her son with great excitement in group training. She said it was great. She made the cost of an argument high for each five-minute interval. She found that, instead of getting drawn into the fray, she was simply able to stay aloof and say, "Your five minutes are up, would you like to buy another argument?" The child said, "No, that's okay," and walked away calmly. This mother was able to compliment her son for handling the situation and his strong feelings well, as well as for numerous thoughtful statements he made in arguing his case.

Other ideas and inspirations: Another child worked diligently and responsibly to save credits for extras on the family's planned trip to Disneyland. Another worked extremely hard for the privilege of seeing at home a previously restricted movie to which he had free access at a friend's house. A third did spring cleaning for the family virtually by himself because he was strongly motivated to have the privilege of attending a special sporting event. A ticket to the game had been offered by a friend with a few days' notice. His parents gave permission, but placed a high credit value on this privilege. Both the child and the parents got to see him apply his intensity productively and at a high level of functioning. In this instance, creating special opportunities to earn extra points gave one family a chance to generate an enormously successful experience. More opportunities lend themselves to more recognition, which feeds the new pattern of success.

Many families consider wearing makeup or certain items of clothing a privilege and charge accordingly. The element of fun can be easily introduced as a theme with a little bit of creativity. Adventures like art projects, a mystery trip (picking a direction and a mileage number out of a hat and driving to the location for a picnic), an indoor or outdoor treasure hunt of some kind, a family board game, or a privilege allowing the child to be boss for a limited period of time can be lots of fun. Other possible privileges are letting the child choose a family game, have time alone with a parent away from siblings, or choose a family outing or video.

Examples of Services You Might Offer as Privileges

Some families we have worked with have been tremendously creative in preparing their list of privileges. Some even began charging for "services" that the child had taken for granted—even maid service and chauffeur service! This is another way in which generosity can be brought into the Credit System: by offering as broad as possible a menu of privileges—as rich an array of choices as possible.

Maid Service. We all do a certain amount of picking up after our children. Services of this type could either be a way for the child to earn credits or they could be added to the Ways to Spend list as a provided service you charge for. The latter approach would be most appropriate in the event your child tends not to perform (or earn credits for) her chores and responsibilities. This privilege might be made available either upon your child's request or applied when you want a child's room straightened up by a certain time.

One strategy is to inform your child that it's okay to do as little or as much as he wants, but that the maid (you) will finish up whatever remains to be done and the maid's time is expensive. Instead of issuing an order with a negative or punitive tone, it should be proposed neutrally and simply charged as an expensive privilege. Most kids will initially find this strategy novel and amusing, but will quickly begin to covet their precious credits and choose to do the room themselves. This choice will not only save on maid service, but will give the child extra credits for cleaning the room and making a good choice. We will also discuss how this same situation can be handled with a consequence in the next chapter if you decide maid service is not an option.

Food Preparation Assistance. This would be a privilege made available when a child requests something different from what the family is eating. Of course, these services are expensive (your time is valuable) and should be available only by prearrangement and on a limited basis at your convenience (perhaps once or twice a week at most).

Chauffeur Service. This could be bought with credits on an occasion when your child needs delivery to any privileged activity, a trip to the store to spend money he has earned, to a friend's house, or to a sport or play activity. If you choose to charge for this privilege, it would be listed on the Ways to Spend list along with its cost to the child and it would, of course, only be obtainable when you, the car and the gasoline are available.

Other occasional, fun services you can offer in exchange for points accrued might be an extra bedtime story, a foot massage, special one-on-one time, special homework or project assistance, or breakfast in bed.

Privileges and the Credit System

Again, a privilege is any activity that involves the parent's time and family resources and is not a necessity for survival. The dictionary defines it as any right, favor or immunity granted. Defiant children often undervalue privileges. Rather than viewing them as something special, to be earned, privileges are often seen as things to which the child feels entitled.

Privileges can also be catalysts for material manipulation of the parent. Many children attempt to influence a parent in this manner: "I'll be good if you buy me something at the store." Likewise, parents often give away their own power to the child by offering incentives beforehand for behavior that would generally be expected of the child. This child-powered form of manipulation can be eliminated.

The Credit System virtually removes this false, problematic notion of entitlement by defining most everything that is not food, shelter or otherwise essential as a privilege. It shifts the balance of negotiation power back to the parent through a clear daily system. You are now the manager of the store.

It should be stated that this system does not stop you from occasionally making something a freebie. If you want to take the family to a movie or go out for a treat, you certainly can play that out in any way with which you feel comfortable. It's also okay to have "red apple days" where some privileges are half-price. However, it will be advantageous to your purpose of orienting your child to success to generally stay on course, using the system with consistency.

Beginning to manage their own economies well gives children an internal model of how to manage their personal economies of energy and emotions as well. Also, when these activities are earned, they gain more value in your child's frame of reference.

Allowance and the Credit System

If money or an allowance is to be part of your Credit System, we encourage you to have the allowance be one of the possible ways your child can choose to spend credits, rather than a separate system unto itself. You will have much more teaching control over behavioral issues if the allowance is a privilege on the list rather than money earned separately.

In other words: **if you decide to offer money on your list of Ways to Spend, we recommend giving credits first and allowing your child to "cash them in" for money.** Most parents tie in a child's potential to earn an allowance to the child's age and the parent's pay schedule. Money would only be available to be earned every other week or even every month if that is when the family's income flows.

Obviously, families should not exceed their comfort zone by exceeding the limits of their economy. An allowance is not a part of the credit system in every family. Younger children do not need a big allowance to be inspired. However, if you want money to be a part of the crediting, limit the amount that can be earned to what you would normally give your child, based on age and a reasonable level of responsibility on her part.

Some parents go slightly beyond the old maximums by offering a potential number of bonus dollars, available at higher credit prices. For example, a child who can normally exchange 100 credits per dollar for up to five dollars every two weeks (corresponding with his parents' normal pay period) might be offered the possibility of a sixth or seventh dollar in exchange for a higher than normal rate, such as 200 to 300 credits per dollar. If this child is typically motivated by money and his parents can afford a few extra dollars, this extra incentive can ultimately result in more to cheer about.

Combining diverse privileges made available on the basis of productive behavior and constructive responsibility results in a system that gives both you and your child what you want. You want to see your child using his intensity well and want to see responsible behavior and completion of chores and homework; and your child wants access to privileges and the possibility of special privileges beyond the necessities.

Younger Children and the Credit System

Younger children may benefit from pictorial representations of behavior on their charts. They may also benefit from morning and evening reviews, and use of stars or stickers as a means of reinforcement in addition to the tokens or markers, perhaps given on the spot instead of being given all at once at the end of the day. However, remember to offer verbal acknowledgment during an actual event or experience whenever possible. Receiving and spending tokens can help the younger child understand the exchange system for privileges.

Teens and the Credit System

For parents of teens, the Credit System allows vast creativity—especially when it comes to money, privileges and negotiating a system that your teen feels is fair and doable. It permits the option of earning the bigger privileges teens usually want (i.e., having a friend over, spending a night at a friend's, movies, negotiated curfew time, being driven to the mall to shop, driving privileges, makeup privileges). It also can turn potential conflict areas into negotiated privileges with clear stipulations in terms of how to acquire the privilege, along with limits to safeguard their misuse.

When teens realize they have the ability to choose how they will spend their credits, they not only become interested in the challenge of earning, they feel more autonomy because of the options offered through clear and specific menus of Ways to Earn and Ways to Spend. An example comes from a teenage girl and her mother who constantly had arguments about her excessive phone use. Because she had her own phone line, she felt entitled to use the phone as often and long as she liked. On the Credit/Privilege system, she spent credits earned to talk daily, with a 30-minute maximum; but could occasionally obtain extra time at a higher cost. She also spent credits monthly to "pay" for her separate phone line.

Paying credits for phone privileges resulted in the teen's valuing this more as a privilege, and because she chose how she would spend her daily credits, she regulated her own phone line use, eliminating the arguments with her mother. She monitored incoming calls and became more selective about those with whom she chose to converse. This parent's creativity demonstrates a way of linking the Credit System to accepting the real-world responsibilities associated with acquiring and maintaining a privilege.

Expectations and Partial Credit

Keep in mind that, even for older children, the system is still founded on the basic flow of acknowledgment and recognition. The Credit System, should you choose to use it, does not stand apart from the flow of creative acknowledgement described in earlier chapters.

It is our experience that children will work harder and more successfully when the consequence of this hard work becomes acknowledgment, appreciation and recognition along with concrete opportunities, such as privileges. This focus serves to rewire the child's energies to pursue positives, rather than merely behaving to avoid punishments or negative experiences.

The power of this system is in its broad, encompassing scope. You as parent can ease off of larger expectations and judgments and focus on the fulfilling aspects of parenting that come from observing your child's successes. Acknowledging these successes and providing a concrete privilege exchange system, based solely on your child's constructive day-to-day choices to do well, lets the larger picture of success fall into place in a natural progression.

Consider the case of Tamara and her mother. At age 12, Tamara has started to show interest in boys and they are starting to show interest in her. Her mother is concerned, and feels she has to be super-vigilant: how is Tamara being affected by this shift? Will she still be that "good child" her mother has so wanted her to be?

Her wariness about Tamara no longer modeling good behavior brings her to aggressively seek evidence that this is happening. When her daughter gets angry or falls short on a school assignment, Tamara's mother is likely to view this as a spin-off of her interest in boys. The accusations progress rapidly, and suddenly their relationship has become very negative.

The larger general expectation of being good has become a weight around everyone's neck. The way out is for Tamara's mother to give credit for all her child's efforts and successes. The relationship will then be permitted to heal as Tamara's mom gets to see evidence that her daughter is still an excellent child, despite her inevitable social interests. Staying rooted in noticing the specific details of the small successes, rather than concentrating on the shortcomings in relation to the grand scheme, offers a powerful alternative route that is grounded in the present moment.

While you are implementing a Credit System, continue to resist giving payoff to negative behaviors. If your child breaks a rule this week that cannot be overlooked, give a consequence calmly and immediately, with as little "hoopla" as possible. Remember: you are refusing to give relationship, emotion, connection and energy (payoff) to problem behaviors.

The Credit System allows a neutral focus on negative behaviors. In reviews of credits earned at the end of the day, simply give only partial credit if your child displayed a negative behavior, without undo attention to the problem that occurred earlier. Your child will understand the implication of partial credit. No need to re-emphasize the problem. In fact, it would work against you. Examples of this style are:

> "Here are your credits for not teasing. Most of the day you used excellent control. I'm going to give you nine of the 10 possible credits. Good work."

> "Here are your credits for the 'No Hitting' rule. You did your time-out and recovered very well and most of all I'm happy that you used your power to be non-aggressive the rest of the day. I'm also giving you two bonus credits for not hitting the dog when he growled at you. That was a good choice to walk away. You might not have done that in the past. You're really learning to use your control well."

Do not take away points that your child has already earned for any reason other than spending on privileges. For example, during a credit review for a child who has hit another child that day, offer partial credit for the "No Hitting" rule rather than rehashing the problem. **We strongly recommend that you do not refer in any way to "taking credits away" or "losing points."** This is an important distinction, especially to your child. The former feels fair under the Credit System. The latter feels depriving, critical and punitive.

A child's perception that she will receive no further credit that day in a category will often lead to a sense of license to continue to break that rule because she has nothing left to lose. Many school-based credit systems that give one star or one point every 15 to 30 minutes fall into this same trap. Emphasis on partial credit gives you the distinct advantage of having many more vantage points from which to foster, create and reflect successes. In truth, the problem behavior took only a small fraction of the day. Partial credit is a symbol of appreciation for the larger part of the day when the same problems did not occur.

No matter how you feel about your child's behavior on any one day, do not refuse to do a credit review and do not deduct from other points earned or saved. Very serious infractions might call for an added consequence of community service, which will be explained in the next chapter, and result in a "Spending Freeze" only until the community service has been performed. However, it is extremely important that the child continue to be given credits due for all categories of desirable behaviors.

Being deprived of the ability to spend any points earned helps a child realize that she is grounding herself. Your continuing to notice positive actions and attitudes heightens the therapeutic tension and reinforces the vital flow of successes. This keeps you in the good-guy role and not only reduces the power struggle, but serves to communicate to the child that you are ready and willing to lift the spending freeze as soon as the community service is done.

The predictable flow of credits allows the child some sense of competency or esteem, even on a hard day. On particularly hard days, it allows you a neutral and more objective system of feedback to your child, when you might be otherwise inclined to send failure messages by not communicating or refusing to do the daily credit review. No matter how you feel about the behavior that day, always do a Credit Review at the end of the day. Even if you make a serious mistake at work, that mistake does not comprise the entirety of the day's efforts. You still expect to be paid. If you don't pay your child this same respect, she will associate the Credit System with deprivation, punishment and failure rather than viewing it as a calm, enduring window of success that's there even on a stormy day.

The key focus of the Credit System is on creating an expanded menu of opportunities that enable you and your child to delight in growing mastery and a sense of accomplishment. It remains equally important that you sustain your level of encouragement by consistently acknowledging desirable attitudes and actions, day in and day out.

The more we can delight in our children, the more our children can learn to delight in themselves and in others. This is important for the difficult child in particular, who is at risk of having poor regard for himself and others.

More Strategies for Giving and Spending Credits

Create a system that you can live with. As mentioned before, many parents decide to award all behaviors equally to make accounting or daily reviews easier. Offering a potential 10 points per rule not broken, per desirable behavior and per chore or responsibility allows you to easily remember how much to award for each item. It serves to streamline the system while retaining an empowered position from which to award partial credit.

For the most benefit under this alternative, additional credits and other verbal appreciation should supplement the recognition techniques previously described. During the credit review, specify the particulars of why the credits are being given. Take five minutes or so to go through the details.

However, if you have the time or inclination, we encourage you to evaluate the cost of each privilege separately. This provides a better view of the real world for your child, where everything in the store does not have the same value or cost to the shopper.

To figure privilege prices, estimate how many credits your child may typically earn and how much time your child normally spends doing privileges each day. The total cost of your child's average, daily privileges (i.e., the number of credits charged for time playing outside, watching TV, playing a video game every day, and so on) should add up to approximately 50% to 75% of the total daily credits the child can potentially earn. This allows your child to continue usual activities by exerting a reasonable amount of effort and provides incentive to work and save for bigger, less frequent privileges, like going to a movie or something else that's special.

For a more intense child, values can be recalculated so as to produce more leverage by making privileges increasingly expensive. However, we recommend starting out with the general accounting described.

The heart of the system is to create and to cultivate a healing level of successes over an extended period of time, not to put the child through a wringer.

The Daily Credit Review

Create a specific time to do the review and credit assignment with your child daily. Most parents find evenings, after dinner, to be the best time. It is generally a settled time and allows the child to spend some earned points that evening, which reinforces the child's basic need for trust by creating a flow of positives in a consistent, predictable fashion. It is also a powerful daily ritual, giving you a consistent window of opportunity to let your child know how strongly you value his efforts.

Basically, the accounting involves daily credits earned, minus daily credits spent or planned to be spent by your child later that night. Although many children love to do the accounting themselves, it is up to you to award the credits. The parents should always remain in charge of the Credit System. Down the road, you can expand your system to respond to degrees of accurate self-evaluation and self-recognition.

Credits not spent that day become credits saved and can be applied to larger privileges or longer-term privileges, most of which must be scheduled in advance. This means, for example, that your child might have to wait until the weekend to spend credits on staying over at a friend's house because of a "weekend only" scheduling requirement or an "as available" stipulation.

Some privileges are only available to purchase within the parameters of convenience for the family. For example, for many parents, payday comes every two to four weeks. Your child may have earned the limit of possible dollars per period and set aside those credits to cash in later, but must wait for the proper time to do so. Likewise, she may have credits to exchange for staying up late, but must accept that this privilege is typically available only in limited quantities and on non-school nights only.

In the long run, this strategy also gives you more power in the form of authority, convenience and neutrality. Just as you can only spend your credits at a local store during store hours and in accordance with their policies, your child's choices within the Credit System are based on its rules and stipulations. **Within the mutually understood structure of this system, you are now free to be a supportive consultant, relaying positives and credits earned and credits spent.** You no longer are judge and jury responsible for deciding your child's fate; this system and your child's efforts decide that. Your child will ultimately feel that you and the world are more fair, consistent and predictable. These are welcome anchors to a child who has previously been confused about how he fits into the big picture.

Markers of Success

It is generally easier and more convenient to use some customized form of currency as physical markers of credit, even with older children. Using some sort of marker lets the accounting take care of itself.

Many families choose to use poker chips, play money or homemade tokens or tickets. One creative family makes reduced-sized copies of real money in different denominations, then cuts the children's school pictures in circles to fit over the presidents. Each child has his or her own separate currency!

This kind of creativity around designing markers or tokens for the Credit System works especially well in families using the system with more than one child. Each child having his or her own color or special currency avoids concerns about credits being lost or stolen. After all, the real-world credit system uses markers: the various currencies used in differing denominations in hundreds of countries worldwide. Children love having their very own currency.

You need not concern yourself with how many credits your child has on hand. You need only concern yourself with giving credits and collecting credits spent. In families that use this system for several children, using different colored markers can also help keep the credits separate, avoiding confusion. Most families find it convenient to have some markers valued at 10, 20, 50, 100 or even 500 credits.

Many children rapidly improve their basic mathematical abilities through the process of managing their real-life economy.

Children often take great pride in their stash of credits. Like having money in the bank or a fat wallet, having a canister, a sack or a wallet with their earnings is a concrete representation of the successful efforts they have made. A child who is beginning to feel rich in credits will begin to feel rich on the inside. His credits are a tangible representation of appreciation and success.

Grounding Oneself is a Learning Experience

Few children can resist the intense gratification of experiencing recognition and appreciation. If your child persists in rejecting the Credit System, continue to give generous verbal recognition for all levels of success throughout the day. Review credits earned for positive efforts with your child and give recognition and tabulate credits as part of your daily review. Do not allow yourself to be derailed at this juncture. Hold your ground by keeping the flow of recognition high.

Let your child know *she will not be able to obtain privileges except by purchasing them through the use of credits.* That is what the system is for, to help her get her privileges. Even children who defiantly hold out typically decide to accept the system, perhaps grudgingly at first, when they realize they have, in effect, grounded themselves by not agreeing to it. Most children who take their challenge to this level will angrily announce within a day or two that they'll do the "stupid credit system." At this point you have your foot squarely in the door and can utilize your position beneficially.

Of course, it is up to you and other adults supporting the Credit System startup not to allow any privilege for your child unless it is acquired through the new system. Waiting out resistance in your most neutral manner, while graciously inviting your child to partake of the privileges available only through credits, is crucial to successful intervention for the most defiant children. **Continuing to give recognition and credit despite resistance is the key.** The idea is to "pull your child in a positive direction" despite his attempts to keep things the same.

Certainly, if you discover that a privilege has been enjoyed without permission, you must charge for it accordingly. Some families hasten the process by telling their child in advance that the cost of privileges taken without permission will be doubled.

Some children are suspicious of any credit earning system because they think it may deprive them of privileges and focus on a critical rather than a positive review of their behavior. This is only fear. You can prove it not to be the case. Hold your ground.

For the ambivalent or mistrusting child, you can encourage full participation by offering additional privileges and additional ways to earn credits. The preceding weeks of recognition and appreciation should have served to promote a healthy interest in what you are suggesting. Encourage the child by assuring her that, after a trial period, future changes to the Credit System can be negotiated.

If the child asks to go off the system sometime down the road and you feel staying with it will continue to benefit him, continue to assert that this is simply the only alternative through which privileges can be acquired. Calmly and neutrally state the impossibility of earning privileges other than through the system.

Most children are convinced of the system's benefits within one or two weeks. Hearing, "These are the credits you earned for your efforts with…" is very fulfilling for most children. The daily process helps them feel more confident in their ability to purchase a fair amount of privileges while accepting that they will, in essence, be paying their own way from this point forward . For most children, the system soon becomes a mix of fun, mastery and pride in accomplishment.

For the child who has enjoyed negative control, a shift toward appreciating the greater benefits of positive control begins. The most successful position to take with such a child is: "It's up to you to decide what you will put your effort into and how you will spend the credits you've earned. I will make sure you get credit for the efforts you make." You are now out of the critical role and into a more powerful one of support. Expect your child to test the strength of this new role and system. In our experience, children who challenge the system gain a great deal of benefit from the process.

The predictability and consistency of both recognition and limits provided by a credit system support a healthy level of accountability. Accountability is not simply taking responsibility when something goes wrong. It is just as much, or more so, about opportunistically appreciating the small things that are going well… that are *not* going wrong. This is "really being there" for someone.

Siblings Too

It is our experience that families do best when all the children in the family over five years of age are also on a Credit System. This prevents jealousy and any sense of preferential treatment among siblings who otherwise might resent not having a daily review and begin to act-out to try to obtain one.

This system can easily be tailor-made for each child's needs and with age-appropriate expectations. It has been used successfully with children younger than four and as old as 21. Keep in mind, though, that many families choose to use one inclusive system when that is possible. It might entail having a few extra rules or chores to compensate for individual or age differences, but it helps keep things simple.

We have seen this system produce wonderful results with siblings who have not had problems but do relatively well. With extra recognition, successes and incentive, they have begun to thrive beyond where they had been before. This approach will help *all* children to be much stronger on the inside, and to make good choices in our high-pressure, complex world.

The Credit System, along with the clearer limits and clearer consequences to come, will build a sense of predictability and consistency that will help every aspect of any child's life, be it school, family or even adventurous endeavors. The more adventurous, the more predictability and consistency have to come from within. Risk takers in business or science, for example, have to have copious amounts of resiliency, reliance and discipline to be prepared for unpredictable conditions.

For siblings who are not having behavioral problems, an extra layer of success-building can be fostered by focusing on how they handle situations when a brother or sister acts out to get a reaction. "Leaving the room when Billy teases or fusses" or "Taking care of self" or "Handling difficult situations well" could be appropriate bonus categories for a child who may be overlooked when a difficult sibling is stealing negative attention.

Sometimes, it's appropriate to make expectations and privilege prices higher for older siblings. Siblings' treatment of each other around credit and privilege earning can be a relevant issue. If necessary, you can add a rule related to sibling teasing or competition to offset jealousy-based provocation related to the Credit System. Give credits when the rule isn't broken and when instances of cooperation can be discerned.

It is frustrating when more than one child is vying for notice. However, we have found that sibling competition can be shifted to a positive rather than a negative in direction. When children begin to trust that recognition is readily available, they not only relax more but can find healthy combinations of cooperation, collaboration and competition. The broader message of the Credit System is that there is more than enough recognition to go around.

Teamwork

Before you present the Credit System to your child, it is advisable that all adults intervening or monitoring your child in your home be in clear agreement with the proposed system. This strengthens the approach and makes it less likely your child will be able to negatively manipulate things to his or her advantage. If there is not agreement between parents or other in-home care providers, request that you alone handle the Credit System and any consequences with the child, for the time being, until agreement between adults can be reached.

If there is another adult in the home who is interacting with your child in a way that is counter to your purposes and plan, try to do your best under the circumstances despite his or her influence. You may be pleasantly surprised once all the steps are in place and you have demonstrated your positive influence. As you increase your clarity with your child, the effect you have will influence all your interactions and everyone around you. It will come through in your voice and your actions.

The Drip Irrigation System

For all intents and purposes, most children come to accept the Credit System as a reality. From their point of view, it is the credits that they find ultimately important. They need the credits to make things happen. They need their credits to acquire the privileges they want and to maintain their lifestyle.

The Credit System, from this angle, is a device that is extremely helpful on a day-to-day basis for consistent delivery of emotional nutrition to the child's very roots. For the parent, this is akin to putting a drip irrigation system where the old "drip aggravation" system used to be. Your child will be primarily interested in the bottom line—the credits and how the credits translate into privileges, just as a plant's primary interest is in turning sunlight and water into food so that it can grow. You as a parent or caregiver constantly distribute beneficial emotional nutrition, just as a well-tuned drip irrigation system constantly nourishes a garden, by verbalizing your delight and having your children feel that their efforts and their successes have indeed been seen. On this level, it is the consistent emotional nutrition that is the real bottom line.

This system, at its heart, is a device that aids parents in remembering to distribute and attribute successes on an ongoing basis. Keep in mind that without such a system, it is easy to back off from a high level of recognition, especially after things improve for a while. It's natural. Before you know it, you're no longer remembering to offer recognition, and you may end up back at square one.

With a system such as this, you have a built-in alarm mechanism. If you happen to skip a day or two or if life circumstances dictate that a day is missed, your children will likely sound the alarm by asking for their credits, just as you would object if some compensation due to you were to be delayed. You've earned it and need it to keep your economy going.

Credit System: Critical Points

- This Credit System accentuates the positive. It gives credits for clearly defined rule-related behavior, positive actions and deeds, and chores and responsibilities on a daily basis. It accentuates *greatness.*

- The Credit System solidifies the flow of successes started by Active Recognition (Video Moments), Experiential, Creative and Proactive Recognitions. The system gives the parent more leverage to reinforce rules and other increments of a child's efforts in a positive direction.

- The Credit System allows your child to "purchase" clearly defined privileges (potentially anything that is not food, shelter or otherwise essential) for specified amounts of credits or tokens earned.

- The Credit System mirrors responsibility and accountability needed to be successful in the real world. It serves as a modern-day apprenticeship.

- The Credit System allows parents to be neutral, supportive and less susceptible to manipulations regarding privileges.

- The Credit System provides a crystal clear view of expectations, rules, values and motivational incentives required by difficult children.

The Credit System also brings your child therapeutically to the next step of this treatment intervention: "Now you know what happens when you don't break rules. You get appreciation and credits. You can spend the credits. Now let's come up with a simple solution for when you do break a rule." (That solution is presented in the next chapter.)

Credit System: Prescription

Prepare the following before presenting the Credit System to your child:

- Ways to Earn (rules, desirable behaviors, chores and responsibilities). Include several behaviors your child already does well. To this list, add a separate list of positive/bonus behaviors. Include credit values for each item. Expectations should be very clear. See the example list at the end of the chapter.

- Ways to Spend (specified privileges with costs, terms and limits clearly stated). See the example list at the end of the chapter.

- Potential to earn between 200 and 500 points per day for most children over six and a more basic accounting system for younger children (20-50 stars, tokens, or other markers, depending upon age and counting ability).

- Calculate what you want to charge for the privileges on the list. Charge according to what you would like to encourage or discourage. Keep in mind that you can revise your prices as needed or as you discover that you may have initially over-charged or under-charged.

As you introduce and use the Credit System:

- Set clear parameters as to when privileges are available and exactly how much of each privilege is available. Keep your own resources of time and money in mind.

- Maximize your opportunity to appreciate aspects of your child's success. You can keep refining and enriching the system. If your child begins to feel rich in accumulated credits, she will also begin to feel wealthy in terms of self-worth and self-esteem. This is true inner wealth.

- Have daily, weekly and occasional privileges (which require saving and scheduling on your child's part). As much as is appropriate and possible, include your child's wishes and reasonable requests in the Ways to Spend list.

- Plan a meeting time with your child to discuss your proposal of the Credit System. Recognize your child's specific efforts from previous weeks, introduce a plan to give credit for your child's efforts and discuss how it will now be possible to obtain more privileges based on effort.

- Offer your child the option to go on the Credit System with a start-up bonus of a few hundred credits for accepting the system now and/or a larger bonus in relation to successes of the past week.

- **If your child refuses the system, accept his skepticism. Show compassion, but let him know that you are going to adopt it anyway.** Let him know you will continue to keep track of credits being earned. Let him know that privileges are available *only* through the Credit System. Then continue all the various forms of verbal recognition, but withhold any privileges until your child decides to be on the system. Be matter-of-fact if the child refuses the system and complains about having no privileges. Persist with your recognition despite the resistance.

- Give your child the space and time necessary to come around. She eventually will realize that you are not grounding her but that she is in effect grounding herself. Younger children hardly ever refuse the system. They are generally excited and challenged.

- **Review the Ways to Earn list daily with your child** (5-10 minutes maximum time needed). Be specific about the positives you see, be generous with credits and give bonus points if your child participates appropriately during the daily review.

- Remember to **give partial credits whenever possible.** At the end of the day, do not give any review or energy to any problems that occurred, but rather give as much energy and recognition to the parts of the day that went well. For example: "Sammy, I appreciate that most of the day you followed directions well and most of the day you didn't bother your brother. Here are the credits I'd like to give you." Maintain your generosity. Give partial credit whenever possible, emphasizing the efforts made. If a rule was broken, put it in perspective of part of the effort made all day to not break that rule. Reinforce the control used during the positive part of the day and give partial credit.

- Above all else, **do not remove points already earned!** The only way to lose credits is to spend them. Do not take them away as a penalty. Doing so will backfire.

- Each day, tally the credits earned and subtract privileges purchased by your child. Your child gets to accumulate the credits that are left over.

- **Be neutral and objective in your review**—particularly about behaviors for which your child did not get full credit. Do not lecture, but rather be matter-of-fact and complete your review in a supportive and encouraging fashion.

- **Maintain your important role as giver of positive credit and not critic of the shortcomings of your child.** The daily review and privilege system provide the child with all the information needed about problems where more effort is required and where more credits might be earned. Let your child figure it out unless she inquires. Hold off on the lectures, no matter how you are tempted. Ignore complaints and excuses. Award bonus points if your child listens, controls outbursts or participates in a polite way during the review. Recognize any effort toward improved behavior or attitude.

- **Focus only on the credits your child did get and why.** That is where a big deal can be made. Positive 'lectures' have great impact. Focus on the areas where effort was shown and commend them. Focus on the growing edges where control was used. In addition to the review, continue giving lots of recognition during the day. This sets the stage for the next strategy and continues to teach your child the rules at times of increased receptivity… when he isn't breaking them.

- Simplify your Credit System, if necessary, using 10 credits per behavior.

- Support your child's efforts by awarding "bonus" points when there has been exceptional behavior or circumstances during the day. **Be generous!**

- **Keep your daily list or chart in a visible place, and don't give reminders to your child regarding chores... other than to "check your list today."** Do not give any undue energy or payoff to noncompliance. Many parents advertise and give bonuses for chores done extra well and for chores done without reminders or with an especially good attitude. If a chore was done with a grumpy attitude, the child should still obtain the base rate. **A bonus for good attitude is the fastest way to make it happen more often.** Not giving credits for chores completed with a grumpy attitude is the fastest way to incite your child to go on strike.

- Surprise your child with "Bonus" stickers, credits, stars or written recognition/appreciation when a job has been exceptionally well done. A little goes a long way.

- Don't give in and allow privileges unless they have already been earned and formally "purchased" by your child with confirmed credits. **This is vital and lets your child know you will not be manipulated on this system!** If your child is home alone and you discover privileges were taken without prior approval, you can develop a policy that in the future there will be a surcharge or that unauthorized privileges will cost twice the regular price. It is fine to stipulate that privileges for the "home alone" child are available or only after homework and chores are completed.

- It is fine to offer occasional freebie privileges or have red-tag specials in terms of price reductions.

- Privileges that require scheduling or have limitations should be clearly noted by parents on the Ways to Spend list. **Privileges that require scheduling should have top priority in terms of making sure you see them through once the privilege has been earned and paid for with credits.**

- **Keep notes** throughout the day if they are needed so you can remember acknowledgments to recount during the credit review that night. Attempt to take note of effort and credit it whenever possible.

- Always verbalize your recognition and appreciation for each item as you award credits. Remember to be generous as well as specific in this regard. Your force field of positive attention (magnetism) must be considerably stronger than the force field created by the attention you may inadvertently reward to negative behaviors.

- **The Credit System is worth the setup and worth the energy involved in maintaining it.** Once you fine-tune it to fit your daily routine, it becomes a system that promotes the ongoing structure and support that a challenging child needs. It ultimately contributes heavily toward shifting your child from nonconstructive to constructive behavior.

- Many parents feel this daily credit-review time is a vital ritual to provide needed structure for their child and to maintain a positive orientation. It will also be extremely useful in relation to changing school behaviors.

- **Consider the added benefits of using the system with siblings.** It is highly recommended to maintain an even playing field by abundantly recognizing their successes as well.

- **Formally including teachers in this program comes later**—generally, after the home game plan has been established. Letting your child's teacher know you are beginning a credit system at home can prepare her for the possibility of noting baseline behaviors or improvements at school. Schedule a meeting with the child's teacher to take place two weeks after starting the Credit System, so that you can fully explain the home program and request a consistent approach to dealing with both successful and difficult behaviors.

- Lastly, **keep in mind the attitude of the tollbooth attendant and Shamu's secret to success: It's all in the way you choose to look at things and all in the way you work with the rope.** Rope your child into success. The way you choose to see things is an art form and the way in which you choose to create successes is an art form as well. The Credit System is a great tool to make it happen.

Watch how this makes you feel and how it makes your child and the other people in your house feel. Studies have revealed that the "feel-good" neurotransmitter serotonin not only occurs in higher levels for the person receiving appreciation and compliments, but the same is true for both the person giving the recognition and for others witnessing the recognition.

Ways to Earn Points

Sample List

RULES			
Points		**Points**	
10	No lying	10	No arguing
10	No stealing	10	No being disrespectful
10	No aggression	10	No teasing
10	No yelling	10	No whining
10	No name calling	10	No bullying
10	No bad language	10	No disobeying

BONUSES FOR POSITIVE BEHAVIORS			
Points		**Points**	
10	Being polite – respectful	10	Taking "no" for an answer
10	Doing things when asked	10	Cooperative or compassionate behavior
10	Taking criticism well	10	Being helpful
10	Handling strong feelings well	10	Good manners
10	Expressing feelings w/o hurting others	10	Responsible behavior
10	Good attitude	10	Good self-control

CHORES/RESPONSIBILITIES			
Points		**Points**	
20	Making bed	10	Putting dirty dishes in sink
100	Good day at school	30	Washing the dishes
50	Good behavior at sitter or after school program	30	Good daily hygiene (brushing teeth, combing hair, etc.)
20	Keep room clean	50	Doing homework and turning it in
20	Taking the trash out	I	Good grades *(Bonus)*
10	Feeding the dog	I	Extra helpful efforts *(Bonus)*
10	Clearing the table	I	Good bus stop and bus behavior *(Bonus)*

Ways to Spend Points

Sample List

Cost	Privilege
60	$1/2$ hour of acceptable TV programs *(2 hour max)*
10	$1/2$ hour of educational programing *(2 hour max)*
50	Extra treat
50	Soda *(3 per week max)*
150	Rent acceptable video game or movie *(2 hour max)*
500	Go to movie theater
300	Rollerskating at rink *(2 hour max)*
30	$1/2$ hour skateboarding time *(2 hour max)*
30	$1/2$ hour bike riding time *(2 hour max)*
40	$1/2$ hour staying up late *(weekends only / one hour max)*
100	Allowance per dollar *($5 max every two weeks)*
300	Allowance per dollar *(purchase up to $2 bonus per week)*
150	Maid services *(per 15 minutes / only when available)*
100	1 hour chauffeur service *(prorated / only when available)*
100	1 hour trip to store to spend earned money *(prorated)*
50	1 hour friend time *(per hour / only when available)*
50	1 hour computer or computer game time *(2 hour max)*
500	Sleep-over *(four times per year max)*
200	Meal at fast food restaurant *(limit of two per month)*
500	Trip to fun-type amusement park *(limit of once per month)*
100	Ice cream *(only when available)*
200	Meal different than family is having *(once a week max)*
???	Mystery adventure *(when available)*
100	1 hour special one-on-one time *(when available)*

Chapter Ten
Step 6: Consequences
Perfect Timing

T HE TIMING IS NOW PERFECT to take a stand through limit setting. It would be wishful thinking to believe that recognition or appreciation for positive behaviors alone are enough to fully restructure and re-energize the challenging child. **The preceding strategies begin to shift your child into new modes of productive energy use: in essence, they create a time-in, where energy and recognition come to the child in response to positive choices and for a lack of poor choices These recognitions bolster the flow of psychological and emotional nutrition in a fundamental way. They also begin to construct a container that structures and supports your child's efforts toward success.** The strategies are also designed to set up a perception in your child's mind that it is not necessary to go to the trouble of pursuing negative energy and relationship: that he or she is literally surrounded by readily available positive connection.

If the child has been at a high level of intensity in the past, or has had a long-lived pattern of undesirable behavior, you may find at this juncture that you are only partway to your goal. Those negative habits may still seem to have a life of their own.

Now that your child is perfectly clear about what happens when rules are *not* broken, he or she may be even more fixated on just what results when the rules *are* broken. The stage is now set for you to simply present the situation to your child:

> "You know, you've been doing a much better job using self-control and not breaking rules. Because things are so much better, let's just come up with a consequence that is simple and easy so that we know in advance what happens when you do break a rule. Here's what I have in mind."

What *do* we have in mind, anyway? Before we can effectively explain the mechanics to you, let's rekindle some thoughts already discussed and introduce some new ideas that make this intervention understandable.

Remember the story of the two-sided back brace? This brace would cinch up in the particular spots that are problematic. The more it is cinched, the more the structure compensates for whatever instability is occurring in your back. When the right amount of torque is acquired through trial and error, you can get on with your life while healing takes place.

Obviously, if you were to wear just one side of the brace, no real support could be achieved. No balance; no torque; no therapeutic tension. Both sides together produce the required structure. **In this model, those two sides that brace the child's course into positive choices are: 1.) the positive recognitions you learned to give in earlier chapters, perhaps reinforced by the Credit System; and 2.) consequences for rules broken.**

The Credit System and the underlying purposeful and intense use of recognition provide your child with a strong sense of the positive side of the bracing. When the positives are sufficiently in place, the child has reached a critical juncture at which he is prepared and ready for the essential and balancing other side of your intervention. One side of the brace is in place. Now, it's time to apply the other side and cinch the whole contraption into its most comfortable, supportive adjustment.

Consequences serve as the all-important limits side of this intervention. Consequences meet your child's need to be assured that the structure of her life is predictable and protective and can withstand being tested. They are vital to energizing the integrity of the structure you have built so far, and to achieving the therapeutic tension that makes everything fall into place. **Together, the positives and the limits form a safe and enhancing environment for a child.**

A child needs to experience that the adults in his or her life can handle both positive and challenging behaviors in an easy, sure-handed manner. This experience paves the way toward a sense of wholeness and being okay with his or her own intensity.

You can be world-class either at being positive or at limit setting, but one aspect of the structure without the other results in little or no therapeutic tension, leaving the structure flawed and only half-built. This may be adequate for the average child, but it certainly will not suffice for the intense child.

Keep in mind that the goal is transforming the difficult child. The goal is to help the child shift his investment of energy from primarily negative behaviors that arise from being convinced that acting-out is the best way to get the payoffs to positive and successful behaviors. When this happens the child can finally relax, convinced that doing the right thing will lead to all his needs being met. It naturally follows that positive attention is infinitely more nourishing and leads to further horizons of success. Successful choices can be as exponentially driven by the child's intensity as the old, poor choices were.

To achieve this, you now have to get out of the way and allow your child to have a clearer version of consequences than ever before. Fortunately, this is fairly simple to achieve, now that the stage is set.

Time-In and Time-Out/Resets

As we move into a discussion of consequences, hold in your mind and heart the idea that limit setting does not have to be severe to be effective once you have established your time-in. This need for a powerful time-in is the reason why we have not talked about consequences in detail up to this point. We wanted you to really grasp the time-in before considering the time-out/reset.

Is It a Time-Out? A Reset? What's the Difference?

As the approach has evolved over the years, we have recognized that **"time-out" and "reset" can be used interchangeably.** For some children, particularly very young children, "reset" may be a better choice, because it doesn't sound like a consequence; it sounds like a new opportunity for success—and that's exactly what it is. It leads the child right into the next moment, where a whole cornucopia of positive choices is possible. In this context, the time-out has this same function, but because the time-out is traditionally seen as a punishment, "reset" may be easier to introduce without anyone having preconceived notions about this new sort of time-out. Parents and teachers have come up with lots of other versions: "Pause" or "red light" for time-out and "play" or "green light" for time-in, for example. They're all versions of time-out, and eventually you'll find your own way of using them.

Think of a basketball court. If the in-bounds area were undefined and didn't have the allure of excitement, fun and scoring, the out-of-bounds area wouldn't hold magic as a deterrent and a consequence. The clearer the line of demarcation, the easier it is calmly to blow the whistle. The more interesting, exciting and present the activity within the game, the more a turnover serves to make a player determined and focused to stay on track. That's the essence of time-in.

We are going to recommend the time-out/reset as the mainstay of consequences. If you have tried various permutations of the time-out without success, don't worry: our version is really, truly different. It works beautifully not because it's more threatening, drastic or punitive than other versions really, the opposite is true but because it's balanced by an energized, rewarding, congruent and connected time-in.

Conceptually, we are more or less stuck with time-outs as a consequence. Almost all consequences essentially distill down to the same thing energetically, from the point of view of a child's inner experience. *It's all time-out,* whether the child has a restriction on TV time, computer time, or friend time, or whether the child has additional chores or assignments, such as cleaning up, making reparations, extra research, or writing. Whether they are out of the flow of what they really want to do for an hour, a day or a week, the child's inner experience is the same as a time-out. To whatever extent they have that consequence, the child's inner experience is that of being out of the loop, missing out or having temporarily lost access to life's privileges and payoffs—in essence, a time-out.

So: if that's the case, and if we are indeed "married" to time-out, with no divorce in sight, then we might as well invent a version that has a purpose, direction and impact different from traditional versions.

The underlying essence of our version of time-out is this: **it is a reset from the current problem to upcoming next moments of success**. It moves the child from the present moment, where things are going poorly, to the next "now" of positivity and greatness.

With very challenging children, parents easily get sidetracked in providing increasingly drastic and punitive results, believing that if they can find the right words, they can provide the "awakening" that will turn things around. The real power of a consequence gets lost in this unpleasant shuffle. Having come this far in learning about this approach, you now know that escalating consequences will inadvertently energize the very problem you wish to extinguish. More gas on the fire.

We contend that the true awakening happens through the child coming to see who he really is through continued exposure to successes. From this point of view, all that's needed is for the child to perceive a result each and every time for poor choices, but that inevitably, on the other side of that consequence is a welcoming again to his new and growing relationship to his greatness.

The Speed Limit Story

Imagine that I live near a main thoroughfare and that I frequently drive on that street. I'm used to going just about any old speed that I want to go. If I'm in a hurry, I go as fast as I need to. If I'm not in a particular hurry, I still go pretty darn fast, even though the few times I slow down feel nice in an unfamiliar way. My mindset is that I'm simply keeping pace with the other cars and that I am entitled to this way of proceeding.

It is perfectly clear that I don't pay much attention to my speed. In fact, I don't recall the last time I actually checked the speedometer. I simply go as fast as I please. I certainly don't have a clear idea of just how fast I am going. I do know, however, that it feels excruciatingly slow when I'm stuck behind someone who is actually obeying the law.

Then one day, I read in the newspaper that the speed limits on that particular main thoroughfare are going to be vigorously enforced. In my mind, I say: "Yeah, right, they're always saying that. Don't they have anything better to do?"

The forewarned day comes and the admonishment has completely skipped my mind.

Sure enough, two minutes after I turn onto the road, I get pulled over. The officer greets me with a pleasant "Good morning," and hands me a ticket. "Have a nice day," he says, and walks away silently, without any song or dance, discussion, interrogation or even explanation. I glare down at the ticket, and it's not the dreaded $200 fine or even a $50 fine. It's a ticket demanding that I remit two dollars. My mind, in its infinite wisdom, registers an automatic "No big deal." I take the ticket, place it on the empty passenger seat, and take off again at my accustomed speed.

A minute later, I'm pulled over again. I put on my grumpy face but silently take my medicine. Another two-dollar ticket. The days roll by and, as they do, the pile of fines accumulated on my passenger seat grows higher and higher. Every time I get a ticket, the officer remains perfectly neutral and pleasant.

Finally, out of frustration, I go into Plan B. For most people Plan B would be taking another route or choosing to drive within the speed limit; however, having a history of being challenging, I am stuck to this dilemma like Velcro. I must try my entire repertoire of anything and everything that has ever worked to throw another person off balance. I try my customary ploys and manipulations to see if I can get this madness to stop. I try to deter the officer from writing the next ticket. I try guilt. I try threats. I try wheedling and cajoling. The officers remain perfectly neutral. I try joking. I try pleading. I try being a bully. They are immovable. Every excuse fails. Nothing I say, at least as I see it, has the slightest effect on limiting their purpose… which seems to be to enforce the speed limit scrupulously.

They are unflappable. If I'm angry or in a rage they reflect at most, "I see you're very upset. I'll have your ticket ready in a second." In most cases, they just hand over the ticket without any fanfare, only speaking to repeat the new mantra, "Have a nice day," as they leave me fuming there on the shoulder.

The officers are very pleasant in their demeanor. However, they refuse to spare me the experience of being ticketed whenever I go even a hair over the speed limit. They are certainly not giving me anything that resembles a warning. It's almost as if their unspoken attitude is: "Have a field day: speed all you want. I can't stop you from speeding, but I can give you a ticket every time I see you go over the limit."

The tickets continue to stack up. Not only has it become perfectly clear that the outcome of going over the speed limit is completely predictable, but it is also clear that I can't get to first base with excuses. And while I'm detained awaiting each ticket, I'm missing out on my life. Not only is this all getting old, but the tickets have piled so high that I realize I could have had at least a small vacation or a new wardrobe with the fines that have accumulated into a substantial sum of money. I'm increasingly frustrated, and this frustration leads me to the next crucial juncture. "I don't want to do this anymore. This is boring and disempowering."

The moment of truth comes when I arrive, through my own perceptions of my own experiences, to the point of deciding to go 38 miles an hour in the 40-mile-an-hour zone. Now, no one is telling me to do it. It's my conclusion and my decision.

That's where the light dawns. I start noticing my speedometer. I hadn't ever paid much attention to it, but now I begin to marvel at the relationship between my right foot on the accelerator and the movement of its needle. WOW! I can make it go up and down. I can ease up on the accelerator and I can gently touch the brake pedal. The miraculous. I can control my foot. I can keep it pretty steady below forty. My first personal biofeedback machine.

"I'll show them. I can keep it at 38. Hey, this isn't so bad. Hey, I haven't had a ticket in a month. You know what? I haven't been late for an appointment for a month. I even allow a little extra time between appointments. I even notice that I'm no longer driving through the rear view mirror to see where the flashing lights are. No paranoia. I'm relaxed. I'm a new person."

I was angry at the whole deal at first, but now I'm used to it. I even kind of like it now. I used to be deeply offended when I was stuck behind somebody who was actually going the speed limit. It felt like slow motion. Now it feels just right. I have come to recognize the relationship between the brakes, the accelerator and the speedometer.

For the intense child, the internal relationship among the brakes, the accelerator and the speedometer is simply underdeveloped.

An intense child cannot be assumed to have developed the skills involved in using self-control and being adequately aware of limits. Using self-control and learning to assess how well he or she is doing in relation to the rules at any given time are a function of resolve, confidence, belief in oneself, and the way in which brain pathways have been nurtured, strengthened and organized.

Pieces of the puzzle are not missing. They simply have not yet come together consistently enough for the child's self-control to be adequate for his or her level of intensity. A predominant reason for this is that, until now, the limits have been far too confusing.

Far Too Confusing?

So many parents come to our office or our classes with the perception that they have tried virtually every limit setting technique available in the strongest possible ways. They are under the impression that they have put their foot down in no uncertain terms.

Unfortunately, however, the ways traditional models of parenting deal with an intense child involve a great many uncertain terms.

Most limit setting and consequences used in conventional parenting fail not only because they are confusing, but generally speaking, they turn out to be more like rewards than punishments—contrary to what the parents are desperately trying to create.

As we stated earlier, a great deal of what is conventionally employed as a consequence is one form or another of time-out. Any consequence that sets out to remove a child temporarily from aspects of his life or her freedom is, in essence, a time-out. Even writing "I will not bother my brother" a zillion times distills down to a time-out. Time-outs, in one form or another, are probably the single most common category of limit setting.

The parents of difficult children are not coming to see us because they want to chat about the weather. They are frustrated. They have often tried ignoring misbehaviors, giving gentle warnings and then stronger and more systematic warnings, and have often escalated into harsher, more punitive measures: threats, yelling and even spankings. They have tried the week-long groundings, the restrictions on privileges, the deprivation of precious "screen time," and even the old standard time-out of one minute per year of age. They've tried all of these consequences and more, and are convinced they do not work. **They have, typically, arrived at the conclusion that nothing works with their child.**

Quite a few parents have taken parenting classes where they have been taught either to use natural and logical consequences or to sit down with the child when misbehavior has taken place. They are commonly instructed to think of an ingeniously related consequence or to let their child know just how upset or angry or sad that it makes the parent feel when a particular behavior takes place.

Other parents quietly discuss the problem or go to great lengths to explain how it affects other people or how other people will view it. Still others lead the child though more elaborate processes designed to help the child arrive at his own solutions and a more internal sense of discovery.

Many parents of intense and difficult children find themselves giving little sermons, lectures, brow-beatings, admonishments and the like. Even if they give the world's best talk or deliver the perfect words of wisdom, they often end up feeling they have wasted their breath.

Even natural and logical consequences, the Rolls-Royces of techniques that work very nicely with the average child, seem to consistently backfire with the intense child. All too often, these kinds of consequences serve to maintain the child's addiction to pushing the limits.

Children who act-out with frequency and velocity may see their parents squirming on the ropes as they try to remain sufficiently clever and inventive without knowing what to do next. In this situation, the child often winds up further confused and further engaged by the resulting sequence. He muses, "Let's see: If I do this, they do this… and if I do this, then they do this…I wonder what will happen if I do *this?*"

If it were a video game, this would represent the child's getting sidetracked by exploring what happens when every different kind of rule is broken instead of focusing on a successful outcome.

None of these techniques are awful. On the contrary, most would work well with easier children. They would have a strong probability of working with an average child who has a milder temperament and only occasional, normal bouts of challenging behaviors.

Let's examine more closely why traditional ways of setting limits—including physical consequences like spanking, which will be discussed separately in a later section—typically make matters worse with the difficult child.

Why Traditional Consequences Backfire

Most conventional approaches to limit setting that have been mentioned not only lack the inherent intensity of structure to serve an intense child most effectively, but also have one common fatal flaw. Understanding this fatal flaw will generate the necessary resolve and mindframe for embracing the simple innovation we are about to suggest.

While we are in the process of giving what we think of as a consequence, far too often, and to far too great an extent, we are simultaneously giving our most precious gift, our energy. This is the part that is upside down and is tremendously confusing to a child.

The primary reason traditional consequences backfire is energy. Your energy, or the ways in which you choose to assign your life force through your words, thoughts and actions, is the single greatest gift you have to give anyone, especially your children.

Your children are not out to get you. They are out to get your energy. How you choose to give your energies in relation to limit setting and providing consequences is pivotal.

To return to the video game analogy: these games do not give any energy to a broken game rule. No points are scored. There is no payoff. **The game's response to any such violation is totally predictable.** *Oops—broke a rule.* **The consequence: temporarily missing out on the action.**

Our Energy Is the Reward

What therefore fails every time in conventional approaches is that we are accidentally rewarding the very problem we want to extinguish.

When your child fails to obey a rule and you sit down and have a heart-to-heart, explaining how important it is to listen carefully and to be responsible, you probably have the best of compassionate intentions. But even if the heart-to-heart has the most wonderfully chosen words, if it lasts seven minutes, you have just showered your child with seven minutes of your heartfelt energy. Seven minutes of browbeating and yelling would have showered the child with seven minutes of your angry energy. In either case, you would have given a portion of your most precious gift to a behavior that you wish to curtail. On a purely energetic level, your child weighs this as having gotten seven minutes of your time and energy. Seven minutes of you being present and connected. Is this how you want to offer quality time to your child?

Meanwhile, the child is aware that he has broken a rule, which makes this situation confusing to him on other levels. Although the parent's emotional reactions to negative behaviors are usually intended to have impact as a consequence or at least as a deterrent to further infractions, this kind of input is perceived by the child as a payoff. The child, expecting a real consequence, does not feel a price has not been paid for his wrongdoing. He has received seven minutes of your time in relation to a problem behavior. If he doesn't also receive relationship and connection in response to good choices and following the rules, it doesn't take long for him to figure out that he can get more by breaking a rule than for positive behaviors. He knows you do not want him to break rules and that it upsets you, but he can see from experience that following the rules nets little to no relationship and energy compared to the strong connection for breaking rules.

This is an upside-down world for the child, who feels energetically paid to keep breaking the rules in a way that contradicts the verbal pleas of the adults in his life.

How often do we go on and on emotionally and intently for seven minutes about some level of positive behavior? If told to take out the trash, a child might get a far-from-rousing "Thank you" (a low energy payoff with low emotion or excitement). However, defying you by not doing as she is told may obtain multiple warnings (mid-level payoff with heightening excitement and emotion) on the way to a true display of fireworks (high-level payoff with lots of emotion and excitement). From the vantage point of energy, the warnings are rewards, the heart-to-heart is a much bigger reward and the yelling is a greater reward still.

Of course, no one consciously wants to reward children for misbehaviors, but we wind up doing it all the time. The traditional array of available techniques lends itself to this inverted situation. And difficult children wind up being rewarded in this way more often than we care to think.

No wonder so many difficult children are depressed. Their world is so confusing. All they want is for it to be clear and to make sense so that they can get on with their lives. If you view the acting out as a way of signaling a need for more structure, for things to be clearer than for other children, you come to realize that the behaviors are not malicious; they reflect a plea for help.

When that plea is answered by clearer limits and truer consequences, the acting-out stops, as does the depression and the confusion. If this request for clearer limits is answered by accidental rewards and payoffs, the acting-out expands into more and more dramatic attempts to find out where the true limits are.

Of equal importance to understand is that *even the heart-to-heart is internalized as criticism and failure*, no matter how carefully it is worded. Besides which, the child, knowing that this dialogue is occurring as a result of her wrongdoing, is far from receptive to any inspirational message. She still internalizes the interaction spiritually, on the most primary level, as "failure, failure, failure." And worse, the next time she needs your attention or energy and senses that you are otherwise unavailable, the pre-existing tendency will be to do more of the same acting-out.

The perception will be that she will be more likely to get her parents' undivided relationship and concern by doing the things that have proven to concern her parents most, as measured by their actions, emotions and levels of excitement.

Unfortunately, these things are typically problem behaviors.

We have all inherited images of problems as things to be chased after and solved. This is exactly the essence of TV parenting. Think back to some of the classic TV family shows. The dramatic arc of problem, attempts to solve the problem, and then the triumphant solution just before the credits rolled was exactly what made these shows interesting. The more interesting the problems, the higher the ratings of the show, the more seasons it ran and the more it lives on in our collective memory and culture.

Even in celebratory episodes of any of these family sitcoms, the problems were often inseparable from the humor. If someone was getting married or graduating or being honored, the humor invariably focused on what went wrong. And, tragically for our images of our own roles as parents, every problem was solved in 30 minutes, with every parent came out smelling like a rose.

The tradition lives on in current programming. So much energy is given to problem behaviors because that's what sells. All news media perpetuate this same phenomenon. In comparison, they give only lip service to positive behaviors. A show like Bill Cosby's may well do an excellent job of highlighting important aspects of family life, and may well be a thoroughly enjoyable respite from the day, but invariably the underlying theme—what we attend to—is the inevitable "problem of the day." Children equate what we attend to with what we love.

Some parents say that they know their children hate getting negative attention and wonder why they seem purposely to seek it. Why would they perpetuate having problems?

We assure you, they are not doing this on purpose. They simply become addicted to the level of reaction and energy they get from the adult. It's the higher intensity closeness that comes through problems that is nearest and most readily available flavor of intimacy that they feel they can acquire. We all want intimacy and if we can't get it in positive ways, and inadvertently discover we can get it in negative ways, then negative ways it is. Of course, they hate the lectures and the yelling and the shame, regardless of whether they show remorse or not. Most alcoholics and substance abusers hate their addictions too, but they compulsively continue to abuse until they approach their lives from a different angle. Children can rarely break the chains of addiction by themselves, even with the best blend of conventional coaching. We as parents or influential others hold the keys.

The energy must be expended when rules aren't being broken. Passionate parenting must surface for every positive aspect of the qualities you feel are desirable.Polishing our treasures, our children, with recognition and appreciation is the first step. **The limit has been set when recognition has been given that the rules were not broken. Your child now knows that you know the rules, and you now know for sure that your child knows the rules. In this way, the line has been drawn. The warning has been issued.** And now the stage is set for an approach in which the child receives a true consequence from which he can learn, rather than confusing rewards for misbehaviors that he finds repugnant but addicting.

Just a few more things before we're completely ready to break the addiction.

The Stage is Set

It's time to take the all-important stand: "Here's what happens when you break a rule." The timing is perfect because the time-in is now working. Time-outs/resets can now work in a way that they have never worked before.

You may be saying to yourself "Please don't tell me after all this buildup they are going to recommend using time-outs. We tried them and they don't work."Just about every family we have helped feels this way to some extent. You must realize, however, that at this particular moment in time, if you have started implementing the previous steps, what didn't work in the past can now work like a charm, with a slightly different version of time-out and a radically different attitude.

Time-outs *can* be a worthless intervention unless time-ins also are in place. Time-ins consist of the excitement a child feels in partaking of life and its adventures, along with the emotional nutrition and recognition that come with being "in-bounds." The child is in the game, so to speak, and the fans are cheering.

You have gone to a great deal of trouble to change the nature of time-ins. If you are underway with our prescriptions, you deserve a lot of credit for your efforts and your willingness to change your techniques and your attitudes. This is a wonderful step forward.

Time-outs, on the other hand, become temporary "absences" from life, where the child misses out on the excitement, emotional nutrition and the freedoms that come with family life. Time-outs take on an even more heightened effect when time-in is upgraded and predictably available. When the game is exciting and rewarding, the child can't wait to get back in there and play.

Excitement and adventure do not refer to a Disneyland version of life. Think of the wonder children have over even the little things in life. That wonder is amplified and made exciting through children's adventurous natures when they are being recognized for even small accomplishments. As they are acknowledged for their efforts, they begin to trust that the most important adults in their life really care enough to see them for who they are. Life becomes sweeter and safer.

Getting Out Of The Way

If ever you were to put a new roof on your house, you would want it to rain. You would want to see if there were any leaks and where. You probably would want to know how well the job was done, just in case the roofer was getting ready to leave town.

Similarly, most anyone who has had to parent an intense child feels a certain amount of dread of possible "leaks" in the form of bouts of defiance, outbursts of anger or aggression, calls from the school, or even the sundry little annoyances that may comprise the typical day.

Given even a little of this type of apprehension, it is relatively easy for parents to fall into subtle modes of reacting or responding that get in the way of an effective consequence. Here are some examples:

- Ignoring the latest incident, either because of being worn down or temporarily giving up because it seems that no response will make a difference.

- Out of compassion, letting an incident go because "it was really no big deal," or you felt the child couldn't control herself, or you're either not sure the rule was actually broken or that the child actually knew she was breaking a rule.

- Letting an incident go because the child has already been though a lot and had a hard life, or because it was someone else's fault, or because he already feels so bad.

- Out of stress, letting incidents go because you're running late, have a zillion other things on your mind, or are already so frustrated. The feeling might be: "What's the point? Let's just walk away."

- Out of compassion, giving what you think is a consequence in the form of a lecture, heart-to-heart, admonishment or reprimand, but in actuality is a reward of attention and energy.

- Out of compassion, making subtle or direct warnings in order to give your child another chance, not realizing that even a warning is a "reward" of our energy.

One of the reasons children learn video games so rapidly and pour their energies into succeeding at them is because video games do not get in the way of learning. They never look the other way when a rule is broken, even fractionally. The game does nothing to try to keep the player from breaking a rule. The same is true of sports. They are predictable, clear and consistent. Without any interference in the learning process, unlike what conventional parenting introduces on so many levels, the child can progress rapidly. The game scrupulously avoids accidentally rewarding negative behavior.

The fantasy is that holding a difficult child accountable for every last rule that is broken will land the child in time-out all day long. The reality is that, with clear rules and clear, predictable consequences, along with solid time-ins and a prevailing tone of recognition when problems are not occurring, the opposite is true. The more clearly the rules are defined, the more easily children can play out their lives like a great video game, putting their intensity into avoiding problems and focusing on ways to score.

As in the speed limit story, clarification of limit setting can be achieved in several simple ways:

Be neutral. Children become aware that they are not able to extract a reaction from you in relation to their poor behavior. It is predictable that the child will attempt to push many of the buttons that have worked to extract energies in the past. This will be one of your child's main barometers for determining whether things have really changed or if he can still pull you in.

Once your child determines that there is little to be gained in terms of payoffs for problem behaviors and that she will be held accountable in a non-reactive, neutral manner—with you remaining unflappable—she will withdraw her investment in negative behaviors and reinvest in positive and constructive endeavors.

Pretending to remain neutral may be a significant challenge sometimes. At times, every button you have will be pushed simultaneously. However, the task is to handle those feelings privately and to not let your child know in any way, shape or form that he has gotten your goat. Even subtle facial expressions are rewards for children with pre-existing patterns of negativity. Exceptions are not the end of the world, but they slow down the child's learning curve and extend the treatment process.

We've asked quite a few moms and dads who felt they could not keep from overreacting to pretend they were a famous actress or actor in the role of a parent whose child pushed a personal button and the script called for not showing it. It may help to pretend that you're being paid a million dollars to play the role successfully. Like the officer in the speed limit story, you must stay pleasant and neutral in delivering a consequence.

No warnings. Yelling and other emotional explosions, which as you now know are major rewards of energy, are almost invariably a function of warnings. It stands to reason that yelling would be the end product of heightening frustration. Most people do not yell from the get-go. Most parents yell after giving numerous warnings that do not lead to the desired actions.

So many parents who identify themselves as "parents who yell a lot" find that the yelling mysteriously stops when they substitute an effective consequence intervention for a warning. Many parents feel that it is kinder to give warnings, and this may be true for easier, basically compliant children; however, for challenging children who are habitually invested in negative behaviors, warnings are a reward of your energy.

A warning is tantamount to telling a child, "Don't do that!" and handing her a 100-dollar bill at the same time. Here are two additional reasons why warnings can confound your best efforts to create time-in and effectively use time-out/reset:

1. They imply that breaking rules will not consistently yield a consequence. Up until about 1993, we used to recommend that parents give warnings for minor violations, but the warning was deemed a privilege that had to be paid for through the Credit System. The system worked very well for many families. For some reason, however, the downside of warnings started to become more evident and we started recommending no warnings at all. The initial presentation of the rule is the warning, and giving credit and recognition when rules aren't broken is certainly ongoing confirmation of their existence.

What we noticed then was astounding. The process of turnaround to successful behaviors became much shorter, time after time. Children more quickly reached the conclusion that there were fewer payoffs for problems and greater payoff for positive behaviors. It turned out that warnings were a far greater obstacle than we ever imagined.

It was interesting, however, that we nonetheless found ourselves hesitant to suggest elimination of warnings to the families we worked with—primarily because of the way we wanted people to think of us. We, like most others, wanted to be perceived as the good guys, not as intolerant totalitarians. Many families face the same dilemma.

However, it's worth getting past the fears. Within a short period, it became evident that this stronger intervention was so much more beneficial to the children that the fear disappeared. And our findings about our new attitude on warnings has excited parents as well; they seem to see instantly the possibilities of how this will help the entire family.

2. Warnings themselves tend to be inconsistent; as a result, they cause confusion for the child. If you're having a good day, you can easily wind up giving more warnings and letting more go than you would on a tense or stressful day when you may find yourself giving minimal warnings. The inconsistency keeps the child off balance.

Fearlessness

Parents are often fearful that their child is going to break rules. Being afraid of this is a misappropriation of parental energy. The truth is that even if we wanted to, **we can't stop a child from breaking a rule if she wants to do so.** We cannot stop a child from yelling or from saying a bad word or from being aggressive. We do not have that power. We can't push the bad word back down. Nor can we stop it from coming up in the first place if the child was dead set on saying it. But we sure do expend a lot of energy trying—and on being afraid of the result if we don't manage to stop that rule-breaking train.

Children know this truth and it is time we realize it also. The traditional admonishment of "Don't you ever do that again" is not only a waste of time with the challenging child because we can't control the child's choices, but it also gives energy and fear to the problem.

How do we deal with this? By going to whatever lengths necessary to convince the child that we have no investment in whether or not they break the rules.

We can let a child know that we will no longer try to prevent him from breaking rules. If he chooses to break a rule, what we *can* do is give a conse-quence each and every time he makes that decision, just as the traffic cops did in the Speed Limit Story earlier in this chapter. Of course, if a child's actions involve danger—playing with matches, aggression, destruction or running in the street—safety is fundamental. The action must be stopped immediately, but with the same neutral and fearless manner that we have been describing.

These attitudes, along with the techniques that follow, go a long way toward convincing a child of your fearlessness. You may privately dread another rule being broken, but it is what your child experiences in terms of your new attitude that will quickly lead her to conclude that no longer is anything to be gained from acting out. More recognition and excitement will be found in the positive aspects of life.

Domestic Violence

We should say here that children who have experienced any degree of exposure to domestic violence, whether emotional or physical, sometimes need a longer period of time over which to experience fearlessness. It simply takes more time and trust before they are convinced that they can no longer derail their parents into reactions and fireworks. They need more time to trust that they can reliably obtain relationship in positive ways.

In our conversation with Dr. Dennis Embry, the amazing man who co-founded the successful school-based prevention model called PeaceBuilders and founded the Paxus Institute, he responded so perfectly to these concepts when he said, "I see what you are saying. A reprimand that might work so readily with an easy child is like heroin to a difficult child."

Children who have witnessed domestic violence typically see that they and others in their environment can get tremendous surges of reaction to opposition and defiance, whether these are subtly or blatantly aggressive. Any reaction from the parent—fear, tears, self-pity, emotional explosions, pleas for respite—becomes the "heroin." And their whole being stays invested in where their next "fix" is coming from, resulting in a vicious cycle and a horrible waste of energy and intelligence. As with heroin addiction, even though the user hates the cycle, she cannot quit on her own. She needs our help.

When the child finally becomes convinced that all that ever results from a negative action is a consequence, administered in a neutral and fearless manner; when she is convinced that she can no longer extract your energies through negativity; and when he is persuaded that plenty of attention is readily available for positive efforts and involvement—then the switch to investing his intensity and energies successfully is well underway.

You will want to read the next section a few times before letting your child know exactly what will happen from now on when rules are broken.

Let It Rain

It is at this juncture that *you actually want your child to break rules*. Get out your umbrella and wait for the rain.

To learn what happens when he or she breaks a rule, a child needs you to resolutely get out of the way and allow the experience to occur. The child needs you to have a new level of compassion that prevents your inadvertently rewarding her by giving undue attention to a problem behavior. **At this point, she needs you to no longer ignore broken rules, but rather to compassionately trust that she can arrive at the decision to control herself without your telling her to do so.** Warnings tell a child that she is not trusted in this regard. Warnings keep a child confused and incapacitated.

It is time to get out of the way and let your child see how fearless you are. Even though you care deeply about her, you are not attached to whether or not she chooses to break a rule, and you intend to provide a consequence if the choice to break a rule is made. **At the same time, you deeply appreciate the effort and self-control your child uses when she decides not to break a rule and pulls back from doing something offensive as she might have done in the past. You deeply appreciate her ignoring provocation or temptation or containing or expressing strong feelings appropriately.**

Remember, it is only an illusion that a child can be prevented from doing a problem behavior. We get old trying to by saying meaningless and powerless things like "Don't you ever do that again," "Promise that you won't do that again," "This is the last time I'm going to tell you," or "If you ever do that again you'll be in trouble." We are fooling ourselves, and our efforts backfire by those very warnings giving the problems more fuel.

By now your child should be able to learn to have the necessary amount of self-control to handle his intensity, a skill that will be useful for a lifetime.

It is time to show your child that little or no attention is available for acting-out, only a consequence. This cannot be done by describing your intention to your child. It is done by putting your new attitude into action.

That is why you now want your children to test you. It is through testing that your child will reach the conclusion that a change has really taken place. This is the basis upon which he will decide to reinvest his energies in positive ways.

Here's The Deal – Resets to Success

Even though we are recommending that you completely avoid warnings, you *will* use a warning of sorts when first explaining and introducing this intervention to your child. It functions best if it occurs at the beginning of the first day of the week that you begin using consequences. It can go something like this:

"You've been following the rules a lot more and now you know for sure what happens when you're not breaking rules. You're also showing a lot more respect and responsibility and a much better attitude. We're proud of you for your efforts and for using a lot of healthy power and self-control. We will continue noticing and we will continue giving you as much credit as we can every day.

"Because things are going so much better we are thinking that we can now handle when rules are broken in a much simpler way. We've been thinking about it and we've decided on something very easy. From now on, if you decide to break a rule… even just a little bit… we will just say 'That's a reset,' which is just a simpler version of a time-out. We will no longer ground you or yell at you or punish you. You'll just get a reset every time you decide to break a rule. We won't try to stop you anymore. We really can't stop you from breaking rules anyway. You know that and we know that. It's always your choice.

"You've been getting a lot of appreciation and credits for rules you

Reminder: Avoid Reminders

At this stage in therapeutic parenting, your child should not need reminders about what is and is not acceptable behavior. Reminders are, in essence, warnings; they delay your child's experiencing and integrating on a deeper level why misbehaviors simply don't work out as well as competent behaviors. Although reminders might make you feel more benevolent in the short run, they routinely result in parent exasperation, anger and/or lack of control. Reminders are also a disservice to your child, because they dilute the intensity and immediacy of experiencing a consequence right away. Reminders are a common source of parent-child power struggles that confuse who is really responsible to know the rule— the parent or the child. How many times have your heard a child say: "But you never told me that was going to happen!" The more challenging the child, the more these tenets hold true.

Be aware of the disguised reminders or offers of chances in reprimands like: "No! Don't! Stop it! Quit it!" These are often ingrained, habitual parenting responses. When an already unstable child hears this advice frequently during the day, the underlying message that the child downloads is "failure, failure, failure." If the admonishment has a non-neutral tone, the negative attention factor is increased. Unfortunately, it is virtually impossible to utter those redirections without at least a tinge of criticism. And again, they are not a consequence. In reality, they are always a warning and an underlying reward.

haven't been breaking and, since you are really great now at knowing what the rules are, there will be no more warnings, no more reminders and no more second chances, just like in sports.

"If you are given a reset then we'll just turn away a short while and will not be available until the problem stops. At that point, we will congratulate you for getting it done and over with so well. Being appreciative is our new agenda and we will get back to that as soon as possible."

If you decide you need your child to have a more formal time-out where she goes to sit in a chair, you can explain it this way:

"I will simply tell you to go to the reset chair, and if you go right away without complaining or misbehaving, and if you sit quietly in the chair for a few minutes, not only will your reset be over quickly, but I will give you credits for doing it well (only if you are doing that part of the approach). Reset will start when you are quiet. I won't be talking with you at all or answering questions. We won't be using a timer, so as soon as you're quiet your short time-out will start and I will tell you when it's over.

"If you decide to make a fuss, that's okay, but the short reset will not start until you settle down. Either way, I won't be talking to you or answering questions. I'll just let you know when it's over. If we are away from home, you will either take your reset there or as soon as we get home, before you can do anything else. If you wind up not taking your reset when we're away, then it will longer when we get home. It's up to you. In other words, from now on you can break all the rules you like, but this is what will happen when you do."

The New Time-Out

Since the first edition of this book, our outlook on what comprises a powerful experience of time-out has changed dramatically. In the past, we felt that for the impact to be truly legitimate, the time-out had to take place in a formal manner: in a chair, away from where the problem behavior occurred. We now know this is not necessary for a time-out to work beautifully.

Think again about how great most children get at playing variations of video games. All they want to do is go from level to level to level of attainment and mastery. They have their eyes on the prize; getting a consequence only inspires them to get better and better at not breaking the rules, and improves their focus on further levels of success.

These games give children complete freedom to break rules. When they do, even to the slightest degree, they are immediately held accountable. These games never look the other way, but rather simply deliver the consequence of the violation.

We adults look at these consequences and think they are drastic– heads rolling, bombs bursting, blood spurting—but the child's experience is that she's back in the game in a second or two, even if the previous game is over. The child is not only back in the game but back into it's spell or default setting to propelling successfulness.

In the case of the video games, the awakening is not brought about by the harshness of the consequence, but comes from the awakening of the child to his power in jumping back into the game successfully.

The consequence in a video game is fundamentally an illusion. The child has not even left his chair, but somehow, by way of the perceived closure of the consequence, signaled by the ensuing next moments of success, the child comes to believe that the consequence has been served and is fully over. The move to the success that follows is like a built-in kiss of forgiveness.

And therein lies the secret. **The power of a time-out that actually has more impact than ever before is not in how punitive or drastic it is, but rather in how "clean" it is. A clean time-out**

- **is de-energized, with no energy to negativity at this crucial moment of rule-breaking;**

- **comes across to the child exactly the way a "turn-over" might feel for a rule violation in basketball—un-energized with a rapid return to time-in; and,**

- **leads directly to the next round of his new life of successfulness, where he comes to trust that it the consequence is really over, having given way to the next new moments.**

In The Blink Of an Eye

Believe it or not, highly effective time-outs can take place in a blink of the eye. Just as is the case with Nintendo, it is just a matter of your child perceiving it occurred.

So, from this point of view, it's a matter of announcing the violation, however you reference it (we are liking the word RESET—"that's a reset" or "that's a time-out," with no further words of discussion or explanation), turning your energy away for a few moments (being detached), and then turning back as soon as the shift from the problem behavior permits. At that point, you announce in an appreciative and present way that not only is the time-out over, but the next success *is already happening:* "Billy, thanks for doing your reset so well. I really appreciate the way you are now being considerate of your sister by not teasing her. That is a great choice."

This having been said, we still know that some parents and teachers will want the "formal" version of the time-out—sitting in a time-out chair or going to another room for a period of time—for it to really feel like a consequence has transpired. If you are in that category, allow us to offer a few additional pieces of the puzzle.

Typically, administering consequences that last only for the blink of an eye or a few moments longer gets things back to normal very quickly. Even better, you don't have to struggle with a child to convince him to do his consequence—which, in older approaches, might have meant a wrestling match or having to hold him in a chair.

Even better news: this approach to time-outs has a built-in way of feeding right back into positivity, which is what everyone wanted in the first place. No more pleading, begging, reprimands, lectures or discussions about bad behaviors. These energized responses only serve to feed the old patterns; the new time-out gives you a built-in default setting to feeding the new pattern, showing your child who she really is in light of her greatness. As a result, this new pattern is propelled in even greater ways.

If you decide you absolutely need to have the time-outs take place in a chair then when you explain this new way of doing things you should have a credit system in place and then add the following alternative intervention which has worked beautifully and consistently:

> "If you don't go to do your reset when you are told, that's your choice, but this is what will happen until you decide to do that: I will continue to give you credits for all your good behaviors in the meantime. However, your credits will be frozen until the reset is completed. In other words, you will continue to get credits, but you won't be able to spend any because your - credits are not available. Whenever you get around to completing your time-out is when you can begin spending again."

This removes the power struggle. You can remain the good guy. If your child asks for a privilege, you can good-naturedly say that you'd be more than happy to oblige as soon as she chooses to complete the time-out. The child obviously will need to challenge you to see if you will follow through and to see if you will maintain your neutral attitude. She may storm off grumpily and say that she'll never ever do the time-out. However, our experience overwhelmingly shows that, as soon as the child realizes that you are not grounding her, but that she is indeed grounding herself, she will complete the time-out.

She may come back and say "Okay, I'll do the dumb time-out," but from this point forward she will have changed in relation to your authority. Not that you won't be tested again, but the process of the child taking greater care to avoid breaking rules, using more self-control, and knowing that there is a result of her actions is underway. Remember to acknowledge self-control and the good decisions when you see even small aspects of them beginning to emerge.

As you can see, the parental introduction of the time-out process must be extremely matter-of-fact and neutral, but clear and firm. There is no begging or pleading with the child to calm down. Nor is there comforting of the child during the time-out. These are prime areas where a difficult child can regain advantage or where an unsure parent may lose necessary authority. It is also a juncture at which the child can accidentally get secondary payoffs and regain the impression that dramatic amounts of your energy are available for not complying with time-outs.

Neutrality in using the reset process allows you, as parent, to get out of the way of the child's experience and her need to test your resolve during this phase of therapeutic parenting. It transfers to the child the responsibility of controlling herself—an essential and success-building life skill. Clear consequences allow the intense child to practice and develop this skill.

This new time-out often arouses parental fears—for some, a fear of being seen as totalitarian; for others, uncertainty about whether they can be consistent enough when the child is very angry or resistant. So many people experiment with time-outs and declare them as unworkable. They *are* unworkable if done in an unclear way that accidentally rewards negativity; and they *are* unworkable if time-ins are not significant enough.

Fasten Your Seat Belts

Some children, especially those with previous experience in throwing their parents off track and in regaining control by pulling their parents back into negative attention, will pull out all the stops.

By anticipating and welcoming this, parents can not only avoid the pitfalls of responding in any unproductive way; they can discover, like many parents have before, the turnaround that comes with staying the course. Typically, after an initial challenge—or two, or three—children realize that their parents are not about to fall into the trap. They realize that they are only extending their own agony and loss of freedom. They realize that payoffs are no longer available for ploys and acting-out, only consequences devoid of payoff. As soon as this is recognized, the deeper levels of reinvesting energy in successes begin really to blossom. Remain confident that you now have the tools you need to achieve this, and keep reminding yourself that their steady, calm application is key.

For some children, the transformation comes only when they have taken you on a wild ride through every avenue they've ever taken to throw you off track. They will come around as they see only a clean consequence at the end of all of these avenues, rather than the old payoffs of energy and relationship to which they have grown accustomed.

If you decide to dabble half-heartedly with this aspect of the approach, it won't have its full effect. **It is the intensity and consistency of this stand that gives this intervention its true power. Playing hardball with this approach will yield the best results for everyone.** In this context, playing hardball is about intensity, consistency, and holding onto your Stands no matter what.

The power does not come from long time-outs, but rather from the close connection between an event and its consequences, as well as from your consistently neutral, abiding attitude. Children discover on their own that there's a new game in town, and that winning it is about following the rules and letting their greatness shine through positive choices.

The underlying power comes from the magnitude of the time-in—the powerful level of psychological and emotional nutrition the child receives when things are going right and not going wrong. Resets/time-outs that are not done under optimal conditions cannot work in the same way.

Playing hardball is a matter of getting these factors on the right trajectory for your child. Some children need an enormously strong message of success—more such messages, with more detail and of a more powerful tenor. Some children need to see that even very subtle hints of energy and relationship for negativity are gone without a trace. And some children need the rules to be utterly explicit and absolutely clearly enforced. For them, even a tiny bit of an argument or inconsistency is enough evidence that they can still get that energetic payoff in return for breaking the rules.

Our new time-out, which so many now refer to as a reset, allows for all of this to be handled simply. **Even in the beginning stages of introducing the new time-out to your child, when it's most likely that he or she will be most resistant or explosive, if you see your child cross the line and thereby break a rule, neutrally state, without discussion or explanation, "That's a reset."**

And then, no matter how resentful or angered the child, you detach your connection, turn away, and remove yourself energetically...*for only as long as it takes for some sufficient increment of positive change.* Then, consciously and purposely turn back and declare the reset over by offering an appreciation for the truth of this improved present moment.

The child who resists a reset is in control at that moment, or experiences a semblance of control by way of the resistance. The point is to remove the person being controlled—you—and then regain healthy control by way of announcing, at the first available moment, that the reset is over.

You are the prize. The prize is unavailable during the reset and immediately back when it is over. **You are playing hardball with the gift of your availability, as measured by your child's perception of the energy you are**

radiating. By experiencing the way you relate to her, the child alters her relationship with herself. Over time, she integrates the new texture of a changed relationship that allows her increasingly to be able to acknowledge positive aspects of her own life, to be energetically present for herself, and to use self-control in conforming to real-life limits. In addition, she is no longer terrified of her own intensity, which may have led to problems and uncertainty in the past.

From Structure Comes Freedom

You, like your child, require a certain level of organization and structure to be free and creative in your life. Think of this approach as a way of organizing a consistent, safe background in which your child will thrive and grow into his greatness. It's an escape hatch out of disorganization and inconsistency, which leave us all stuck in debilitating, restricting patterns. This is real freedom—the kind that comes from secure, dependable structure.

A Review of the Mechanics

We all experience times in which wonderful people seem unable to give themselves attention for anything positive. Intense children are set up for this discouragement, and it completely changes their lives to begin the new adventure of living on the positive side of life. A positive inner dialogue—and the inner wealth that springs from this—eventually become as natural as breathing.

By taking such an unwavering stand with them, we can help children arrive at their new destination sooner. The more we make things clear to exceptional children, the more clarity with which they can live their lives.

Let's review the mechanics of the new time-out and the ways in which the rest of this approach works in concert:

- If you are using a Credit System, explain to your children that they are showing improvements in their behavior, and that you will continue to give them credits and chances to earn more privileges for following the rules. Many children require frequent reassurance that they can continue the good work, despite being held accountable for misbehaviors.

- Acknowledge your child's growing ability to follow rules, but tell him that from now on, if a rule is broken, there will be a time-out. Be clear and neutral regarding this, despite your child's reaction to this announcement.

145

- Describe the time-out process to your child. Make especially clear: "Now, every time you break a rule, there will be a short consequence which will be referred to as a reset, a pause, or a time-out and those terms might be used interchangeably." (Use any term that fits best for you.)

- Make sure the child knows that you understand that he gets to choose whether or not to follow the rules:

  "I can't really stop you from breaking rules, can I? I can't stop you from name-calling or yelling. I can't really stop you from arguing or refusing to do something. I can, though, give you a consequence every time you decide to break a rule. It's kind of like basketball—if you step out-of-bounds just a little bit, there's a consequence. There are no warnings. The second chance now only happens after the time-out is complete.

  "The great news is that now that things are going so much better, it's not a big deal. It won't be a long time-out, but it will be a time-out every time. Although it sounds a little weird, you can break rules as much as you wish. It's always your choice."

- Emphasize the no-warning rule:

  "There will be no warnings, reminders or chances when you break a rule now. I'll just say 'That's a reset,' or 'That's a time-out,' and you will be expected to take it right away. I'll just turn away, and you can remain where you are, unless I ask you to go sit in a chair away from where we are."

- Doing the reset right where the child is at the moment of rule-breaking makes life so much easier. It's simpler and faster and keeps you more vividly in the empowered position to declare it over and complete. **The child can even be hiding under a table or walking away and you can still, moments later, claim that it was done well.** "Bobby, I really appreciate that you did your reset and now it's over. Great decision to choose to be not arguing right now." Even if he didn't know he did it, by way of your declaration of completion he comes to see that he is capable of the good choice of getting it over and done.

- Explain to your child how the timekeeping of time-out works: "Your reset will begin as soon as you quiet down for a few moments. I will not talk with you or answer questions. I'm also not going to make you promise never to do it again or discuss the problem with you after the time-out is over. I won't even explain what rule you broke because you are smart and I will assume you know. If you don't, I trust that you will figure it out at some point. Later, if you want some help thinking through solutions or other ways to handle situations, let me know."

- Talking about duration of the time-out usually does not help the child. Use your inner sense of how long it should be, but purposely keep it short. Time begins as soon as the child settles down to a sufficient degree. We recommend that you avoid the trap of going for soldier-style perfection. However, having a rule of no fiddling or playing with anything while resetting might be helpful.

- No talking during time-outs also gives the child a "purer" experience of the consequence of breaking a specific rule. Minimal explanation may seem harsh. However, our experience is that the difficult child makes the necessary connections and inferences sooner and in more stable ways if we keep explanations non-existent or to an absolute minimum.

- **Do not fall into discussions of whether or not a rule was really broken.** Remember that you are in the process of literally breaking an addiction. Rely on your vantage point and your inner sense of whether a rule was broken. In the long run, when habitual behavior is significantly changed, it will not have been a disaster if your judgment was wrong on occasion. It will be far more confusing for your child if you begin an interrogation to find out exactly what happened and realize in the course of the questioning that you actually rewarded the child with an enormous payoff of your energy and quality time by focusing on the problem behavior. Avoid interrogations and discussions like the plague. They will keep undermining your efforts.

- The use of timers and responding to demands of "when is time-out over?" can easily become a cat-and-mouse situation. **Overall, it is of primary importance to avoid accidentally giving your child payoff in relation to the broken rule.** Stick with a consequence devoid of verbal or nonverbal reaction, leaving out any hint of how the situation has affected you emotionally. Refrain from pleas like, "If only you will quiet down, time-out would begin." Avoid getting drawn into the drama for any reason. It will only perpetuate the show.

- Be sure to give verbal acknowledgment when a reset has been done well or when the child has regained control. This will help to make future time-outs go more smoothly, and will encourage coping and compliance with consequences—a skill all of us need in daily living, and that intense children especially need.

- As an even greater incentive, if you are using the Credit System, give credit for days or portions of days where the child has needed no resets.

- If you insist on the formality of having your child go to a designated time-out chair, and your child resists going when given a reset, remember to use the leverage of remaining neutral. This is where a Credit System can be quite helpful, as you can then let it be known that credits will remain frozen until the reset is completed. Continue acknowledgment and credit for all other reasons and possibilities, even if the child holds out on completing the time-out for a substantial length of time. He simply cannot spend his credits. Don't worry about how long it takes for your child to decide to do the time-out, because any urgency on your part will again give relationship and energy to the problem of the child's lack of cooperation. At some point your child will realize that she is grounding herself rather than you grounding her—and this is infinitely more influential.

- Remember that safety always comes first. If some aggressive or destructive action is already in progress, step in to prohibit that action as needed as you say "Reset." Make it your mission to do this with as little emotion, discussion, and perceived relationship as possible. Any such stepping-in should be conducted in as safe a way as possible. If necessary, seek out a manual or a course that will teach you a method of safe restraint.

Do Not Take Points Away

No matter how much we warn parents not to take away credits when rules are broken, a few parents invariably jump to the conclusion that deducting points will logically work. *Don't go there!* We know from long experience that this will work against you, even if it appears to have a beneficial effect at first. Imagine your boss docking your salary for broken rules. It wouldn't take long for the gentlest of souls to start withdrawing energy from productive channels.

Also, a parent who combats a broken rule with "That's another 10 credits" is feeding the exact pattern she wishes to change by giving it her energy. When there are no more credits left to be lost, the child may exercise a certain amount of license, figuring there is nothing left to lose. *Give your energy to your child when the rules are not being broken.*

A related issue to be cautious about: adding more time-out when rules are broken on the way to or during the original reset. It is much more productive to say nothing and simply let the original time-out run a bit longer once the child has quieted down. No matter how outraged you may feel inside, don't let it show, and be purposeful in getting right back to positives as soon as the consequence is paid.

This concept seems to elude many parents. Although it isn't easy on an emotional level to move back to the positive once the consequence is over, it is extremely important to the transformation process. The child needs to see that once the consequence has been paid, even if it arose from an ugly scenario, in reality it has been paid and it's time to move on. That means that, unless it is bedtime or homework still needs to be completed or a similarly inappropriate time, the store is back open and credits can be spent. This offends the old school of thinking, but it is crucial to future successes.

As a way of illustrating the above, think of someone who winds up in jail after committing some sort of crime. Once the consequence has been completed, that person is free to spend his money any way he pleases. He can be out of jail for five minutes and go to a fine restaurant if he can afford to. It's the truth of the present "now" and it really resonates on a heart level in experientially giving a great lesson to your child on how to be present (not in the past and not in the future).

Parents are also particularly likely to be confused when a child breaks a rule just prior to an event to which she had been looking forward. Most parents have the reflexive response to ban the event, even after the consequence has been paid. However, in this new approach, it is ultimately more important to "help" the child get right back to life. This means that, if she has the credits or can earn them prior to the event, she can still go.

A Case Against Physical Punishments

Much can be said about physical punishments and the undesirable effects they ultimately have. We will try to limit ourselves to comments about why they backfire strategically. Although we are dead set against any form of corporal punishment, even the mildest spankings, we are certain, having worked with as many families as we have, that most families who use it are far from abusive in intent. Ordinarily, despite intending to parent well, they have progressed to a point of frustration and desperation that prompts them to try any intervention that might work.

When we give them a new strategy that works and that offers them the level of healthy leverage they and their child needed all along, they are all too willing to abandon the old techniques forever. Ordinarily there is no underlying desire to hurt the child or damage the spirit.

Once the child fully perceives that a parent is in charge in this new and appropriate manner, and she begins to trust that she'll be seen for positive traits and behaviors, much of the fear or terror in relation to physical punishments will begin to dissipate. Children predominantly want to get on with their lives.

Most parents are thrilled to spare the rod when they find out something works better. All along they were just seeking to have a powerful impact, and were merely trying to adhere to an interpretation related to family philosophy or faith.

Spare the Rod, Spoil the Child?

Some parents end up arguing in favor of physical punishments because of their interpretation of the Biblical phrase, "Spare the rod, spoil the child." Here's what we tell them: According to Biblical scholars, this phrase translates from Aramaic in a way that has nothing to do with physical punishments. It refers to shepherds and their style of herding their flocks. Biblical shepherds apparently would never consider hitting their sheep. The rod is only used to guide the sheep gently to keep them within the desired limits. In the Nurtured Heart Approach, we are using the rod of intensified recognition along with the rod of clearer rules and consequences to guide or redirect the flock.

One reason to not even consider physical punishments has to do with a possible progression in severity. Especially for the parent who feels physical punishments are working, what can be done for an encore if two spanks worked last week for one bad word and your child now offers up two new choice words? What do you do next week if it becomes two choice sentences? These methods ultimately leave the parent in a disempowered position.

When physical punishments of any magnitude are administered, the child is even more confused about whether he is being rewarded or punished. Children who are addicted to negative attention elicit a huge payoff in terms of the parents' level of reaction when the parent resorts to spanking. Of course they hate being hit, and they are frightened, but they still feel the rush of having pushed a button big time—with a big payoff. That "toy" has just clicked into a whole new level of animation.

At the same time, children sense when their parents are out of control, and will continue to test until convinced that their parents can maintain a calm and healthy level of control. Children need their parents to be powerful in healthy and balanced ways. It is a primary way in which they learn to have their own healthy power.

In addition, the commonly cited argument against physical punishments—that the underlying message is that it's okay to hit a person smaller than you—

holds up in our experience. Many young people who are spanked will behave aggressively toward younger siblings or peers.

Community Service

When a child commits a major offense that goes well beyond everyday rule-breaking, it doesn't make sense to give only a short reset. The dilemma is **how to issue a stiffer penalty without accidentally giving an emotional payoff by overreacting.** The trick seems to be in having several predetermined rules that carry additional consequences.

We feel **it is always wise to issue a reset initially, as a first step,** both to maintain consistency and predictability and as an aid to maintaining a neutral stance. Required community service, however, can be an alternative when deemed appropriate.

For example, a parent might have a star next to three rules: no hitting, no destroying things and no violating curfew. If any of these rules were broken, the child would understand that somewhere between 15 minutes to a few hours of community service would be added to the reset. Spending on privileges would again be on hold until the reset and the community service were completed.

However, the child would still earn credits (even if completing community service were delayed) for all the other areas of possible earning during this interim period while rules are not being broken. The spending of credits would simply remain frozen until the child chose to finish the community service. Strategic periodic verbal acknowledgment also should be continued.

Community service might include restitution services for lost, damaged or stolen property, doing a special project around the house or, ideally, some form of work toward helping others or the community. Parents and children have been very creative in this area. Some children have assisted an elderly neighbor or relative, swept the sidewalks or undertaken a beautification project. What we like about community service is the idea that the child is learning to channel energy in constructive ways. We have seen this intervention work beautifully in keeping the parent from reverting to frustration and punitive measures. It makes it easy to maintain the necessary neutral stance of a consequence.

Use your judgment as to how long community service should last. The amount of time should be completed with parental approval before the child may go back to spending credits for privileges. Community service offenses should, for the most part, be predetermined. It can also be arbitrarily declared necessary in an unusual situation.

In the event of these more serious transgressions, remember to still keep the Credit Review as positive in focus as possible. It is vital that the

Credit Review be a positive experience that your child looks forward to, especially if it has been a hard day. It is good for parents and children to have a special time to refocus on what has been good about the child's behavior that day. Even if children are not thrilled about the Credit Reviews, it is a vital time to confirm their efforts and to attempt to connect through acknowledgment and recognition. Even if he is grumpy, he deserves to be paid for the part of the day that went well. Stick to the truth of all that merits recognition.

Resist lectures, warnings or negative comments during the Credit Review. Resist talking about why your child didn't earn full points.

The broken rules usually comprise only a few minutes of a long day. Emphasize the control used the rest of the day. Continue your insistent plan to emphasize successes and nurture the spirit. Nurture the learning in process by insistently cherishing progress and movement in the desired direction.

The More Intense the Child, the More Intense the Intervention

Here's a true tale from Howard's therapeutic practice:

In my waiting room were two brothers, I was scheduled to see for the first time. Let's call the children "Rough" and "Ready." They obviously had not been clearly informed of what to expect in the office. They were bored, antsy and had already been pushing the limits. They were clearly frustrating their parents. An unsuspecting therapist might have escorted the family back to his office, spent the next hour witnessing chaos, and then might have had a lot to write up in a report of the shortcomings of the parents and children.

Since I am not at all interested in gardening anything other than success, I sized up the situation and quickly decided that I needed to be super clear. I walked up to the family, introduced myself and said to the two children: "Right this moment, you both are paying attention and you are using your self-control to follow the rules. I bet you didn't know the rules of the waiting room. They are: no hurting anyone or anything in any way, no yelling, no running around, no whining, no tantrums, no arguing and no disobeying. Right now you both are making the great choice to follow all those rules. I especially like that you're not arguing or whining and I appreciate the effort you are making and the power you are using to control yourselves right now."

"Now I am going to say something that you may think is weird, but it's true. If you decide to break a rule, it's okay, I won't be mad or upset at all. You will just get a short reset without any kind of warning. It will be a little like basketball. If you step out-of-bounds just a little bit it will be a consequence. I won't be bothered at all if you decide to break a rule. I know that at any moment it's your choice and right now you are making great choices not to break rules. Follow me to my office

and I'll show you where I keep some fun things to entertain yourselves. If you choose to need a reset, you can play with the toys again as soon as it is over."

They followed with their parents and it was clear to me that "Ready" was cruising to push a limit. So, I got out of the way and let him. His father told him that he needed to ask permission to play with my toys. "Ready" whined. I told him that he had a reset for whining. He did it with a fuss, but eventually finished his reset well.

I needed to be fearless here. I was obviously choosing to be picky. Most people would have let that go. They may even have fueled the incident by discussing the problem in some way. I wanted the opportunity to establish the line.

"Ready" came out of time-out grumpy but thinking. Within a minute, he thoughtfully asked permission to play with the toys. Permission was granted. Compliments were given for good manners, good choice in thinking it over and asking, and so forth, and "Ready" proceeded to spend the rest of the hour carefully and vigilantly observing the rules and enjoying his play and the wealth of success for which he was acknowledged. He apparently trusted me and needed no more evidence as to whether he could depend on me for limits. He showed a lot of respect and even some affection.

It turned out that an issue for his mother was the fear that, if she enforced the rules, the kids would dislike her. So, she let a lot of things go until, out of frustration, she exploded. The children would then get a major dose of negative reaction and animation that inadvertently reinforced their habits of pushing the limits. "Ready" operated successfully in the clearly defined circumstances that I set up in an ad hoc way. He left the office feeling like a million dollars.

His older brother "Rough" carefully studied this whole situation unfolding and made some wise decisions. He calmed himself down and chose also to use his self-control judiciously. He restrained his obvious impulsiveness and, on several occasions, held on tight and managed to contain strong feelings that in his past, according to his parents, had led to explosive outbursts and aggression.

"Rough" wound up leaving the session with a wealth of compliments and new information about his abilities. He was a child who could indeed make an effort to control himself and his intense feelings. He wound up feeling very successful. His parents, who had come to complain, saw both children's ability to behave and wound up giving them many detailed acknowledgments. Both boys, within the safe limits of the office, wound up playing cooperatively and sharing, which apparently was something they rarely did.

This family wound up doing quite well, but because of the higher intensity of their children, they most certainly had to play hardball both with the positive interventions as well as with the limits. "Hardball" simply means being straightforward and clear. It certainly doesn't mean consequences that are longer or sterner.

153

Chapter Ten

Consequences: Critical Points

The consequences phase of The Nurtured Heart Approach is the final leverage that stabilizes the structure you have created and provides a safe, predictable container for your child's need to test. It is the phase where children often demonstrate the most testing of parental stands. For this reason, it is often the most challenging phase for parents.

Giving resets is sometimes very emotionally painful for parents, especially parents who never have taken a firm or a consistent stance on behavioral issues. **This is the phase where your child will try every manipulative behavior that has ever worked to get a reaction from you in the past. Be mentally and emotionally prepared for this.**

A relatively small percentage of children's behavior appears temporarily to worsen in the first week or two of this strategy. Among challenging behaviors at this juncture might be the child's attempt to pull you back into old, unproductive patterns where the child had the illusion of more power and control, albeit negative. At this stage of the transformative process, the child absolutely needs to see if you can truly handle him or her under a variety of circumstances and to determine that you will stay with the plan consistently.

Before moving solidly into a new pattern of success, the child makes a final assessment of your skill and resolve through challenging behaviors. This should occur and is actually desirable.

Cultivate your firm and neutral stance to an art. Be prepared for the flurry of drama that could come as your child attempts to garner your sympathy or reach your soft "give-in" spot. "You didn't tell me about that rule!"…"I'm not going to take a time-out. You're mean. I'm calling Child Protective Services to report you!"…" I hate you… you're the worst dad in the world!" Ignoring the drama and calmly adhering to the plan to see the consequence through in the most neutral way possible is what transforms this into a powerful intervention.

- **It is desirable for the child to realize that time-out/reset is no big deal**—that it is worth doing and getting over with and that it really cleans the slate when the consequence has been paid.

- **A completed reset is a success.** Limit-learning is the hallmark of a successful person. It allows him to focus his energy a great deal more directly than if there were no defined limits. Excellent limits help a child be far more successful and waste far less energy and intelligence on the muck and mire of negativity. By being persistent you are cultivating a priceless internal skill.

- **Practice fearlessness** when your child is resisting taking or remaining in reset. This resistance is often an attempt to test your resolve. Looking and

154

acting fearless (even if that's not the way you feel) will pay off in a big way.

- **Consistency is the key** to letting your child or children know that you mean business and have clear expectations and predictable, nonthreatening consequences for any rule broken. It helps both the parent and the child to know exactly what happens if a rule is broken.

- Most parents ultimately opt to apply the consistency and predictability of the Nurtured Heart Approach to consequences to all children living in the home over the age of three.

- Make use of the rule "No Disobeying." If you make a request and your child doesn't respond quickly, give an immediate reset. **Resist the temptation to repeat the request or worry whether your child actually heard you.** Move right to consequences.

- Consequences for noncompliance do not excuse your child from doing any task they may have refused or blown off prior to time-out. **Expect your child to correct the uncompleted task immediately after the reset.** The willingness to do the request makes it possible to still earn credits for that task. However, resets should be given in succession if the child continues to defy completing the task, until such time as the child takes action and complies. Each time neutrally state: "Thank you for doing your reset. Now I need you to do your chore." **Follow this immediately with appreciation if she does it or with another reset if she doesn't.**

- **Give credit for consequences well done if you do the daily Credit Review**. You can give further incentive to improved behavior by giving major bonus credits for days with no resets, as well as lesser amounts of extra credit for days with few resets. Use your judgment and customize this concept for your child.

- **Avoid comforting or hugging the child during the time-out.** This confuses the child regarding whether the experience is tinged with affection or is really a consequence. It is fine if you or your child feels the need for comforting or affection after the time-out, but if this is the case, make sure you give a far greater amount of comforting and affection at other times when rules and problems are not an issue. You don't want your child discovering that resets are a way to get affection.

- **It's often a good idea to practice resets** so you and your child can see in advance how simple and easy it is to move through a consequence and back to positive moments. Practice until you feel confident you will follow through every time. In any case, definitely prepare the child at least verbally for how things will proceed when a rule is broken.

• We really want to underline one more time the distinct advantage we feel the new time-out offers. The biggest reason for us is that it seems to by-pass so much of the resistance and help a child settle into taking his consequence well so much faster and more easily.

However, if your family values precludes this simple version and you insist that going to a time-out chair is needed to satisfy your requirements of completion, then here is one further tip for the child who resists. Some parents have had success with sending a child to her room, telling her that all privileges are on "hold" until she has sat in the chair and completes her time-out. This option is useful when a child is particularly noisy or resistant during the initial phases of time-out. We would keep this as a backup plan rather than a primary strategy since it seems not to foster the same loss of freedom and sense of missing out on "time-ins." Children's rooms are usually their most stimulating environments, and even sitting in the middle of the bed will not restrict an imaginary sense of play. Also, associating the safety, security and sanctity of the bedroom with a consequence is in our experience an undesirable link to foster.

Consequences: Prescription

Having decided that it is time to initiate consequences, immediately begin the use of resets as the sole consequence for any rule broken.

• Inform your child of the reset procedure, and the reset rules. Some children benefit from a "trial run" reset so they understand exactly what will happen. (This may better help children who have experienced previous abuse to avoid panicking, since they now will know what to expect. This is often particularly true for foster children)

• Remind the child that it is your job to enforce the rules and to help her to get the reset complete and over with. Remind him that he is now free to break rules since it's always his choice anyway, and that you will continue to be appreciative when rules are followed.

• Exceptions to using time-outs as the only consequence might be serious infractions such as stealing and damage to persons or property. In these cases, adding Community Service time in addition to the reset is appropriate. This models the experience of restitution, mirrors consequences used by law enforcement and is non-punitive. For some children, community service time has greater overall impact through its very nature as a hands-on, reality-based consequence.

- Resist giving the child warnings and chances. This communicates a mixed message about who is responsible and about the certainty that you really mean business.

- When the child breaks a rule, be quick and fearless about calling for a reset. It is best done in a mild yet clear tone. You are no longer ignoring broken rules. You are holding your child accountable every time she crosses the line by breaking a rule. Even a tiny bit of a broken rule counts. A little bit of arguing is still arguing.

- Short time-outs are powerful. It is not the length of the reset but its connection to the event and your clear attitude that matter.

- Resets begin as soon as your child quiets down a bit. And in some cases that is not even necessary as long as you feel okay about chiming in a short while later with an appreciation that brings closure to it. If you require going to a designated space and if the child goes directly and quietly to the time-out chair or designated area, begin timing right away. Remember that in any case there should be no consoling, lecturing or talking when the child is in reset. Keep siblings away.

- Award credit points or appreciation if the time-out goes smoothly and without incident. This encourages the child to learn that he can cope with negative consequences. It also demonstrates that positive behavior on the child's part is recognized, even in the wake of a negative choice. Completion of a reset is indeed a success.

- After the time-out, the child should be required to clean up any messes made prior to or during it. She should also complete any tasks resisted or unfinished before time-out. For example, Jeremy must pick up the towel thrown on the floor as he took his reset and finish the dishwashing task that resulted in the reset in the first place. If the new request is resisted, stay with the plan and issue another time-out. Stay with the plan until all requests have been completed.

- Remember to apply the rule "No disobeying," both for purposes of positive reinforcement and for situations where requests are met with noncompliance.

- Don't expect remorse or other displays of conscience from your child. Many children are removed from their feelings or adept at masking these feelings. Resist responding to this lack of affect. Trust that you are indeed having an effect despite the possible lack of immediate results or direct feedback. Continue the predictable experience of consequences—realistically linking choices and result.

- Don't request or require promises from your child not to break the rule again. It will continue to energize the original problem behavior. Don't discuss or mediate the problem once the reset is over as that too will be gas on the very fire you are trying to put out. What is very beneficial however is appreciating the absence of the problem in the present moment now that the reset is over. We find you can house the very same 'lecture' in the truth of the ensuing positive moments in a way that will have the great impact you desired all along. "Debby, I appreciate that you recovered so well from your reset. Even though you are still frustrated with your sister you are handling your strong feelings well and not calling her names. That's great power and great control. Congratulations on that great choice."

- If you are using the Credit System, be diligent about doing the daily Credit Review. Be neutral about negative behaviors and focus entirely on the positive, successful choices your child has made. At this point you should start seeing many more instances when new levels of self-control are exercised. Applaud as much movement in the right direction as you can. This will strengthen the emerging patterns and make the new positive behaviors and the feeling of success more predominant. An example might be:

"I noticed you restrained yourself when your sister teased you. It looked like you wanted to hit her and instead you walked away. I appreciate your effort in controlling your anger. Here is are some bonus credits for being wise and using your power well."

Lastly, keep in mind that this book isn't called *Transforming the Difficult Child: The Nurtured Heart Approach Plus Consequences.* That's because **consequences are an integral element of the approach and have a nurturing influence.** Consequences reflect the intention and art of "creating successes that wouldn't otherwise exist" (Shamu) and the intention and art of "it's all about how we choose to see things" (Tolltaker) as much or even perhaps more than the positive strategies. Many people believe that the act of setting limits is contrary to a compassionate heart. However, **clearly setting limits along with straightforward consequences is actually very much an act of compassion.** Solid consequences are truly compassionate in that they allow a challenging child to finally move through the emotional-psychological issues of limits and leave behind the convoluted behaviors associated with compulsively pushing those limits. Clear rules and consequences are also compassionate in that they ultimately lead to a much higher level of recognition and success.

When a child finally perceives that there is no longer anything to be gained by rule breaking she can finally retrieve her intensity and intelligence that has been literally stuck in the convoluted endeavors of playing out negativity and have the same now fully available for playing out success. The latter is so much more congruent and gratifying for all involved.

Chapter Eleven
Step 7: Extending The Success To School
Good Intentions Are Not Enough

I MAGINE TEACHING A CLASS OF CHILDREN conducted in Swahili, and all but five of these children understand this language. Those five children can communicate only in Hindi. For the teacher to proceed without some workable accommodation for those five would constitute a level of exclusion and the start of almost certain experiences of failure for the children involved.

These five children don't feel included. Nor do they experience success in an immediate way. Unless they are exceptionally bright and adept at picking up on the new language, they begin to lose ground and will continue to do so unless some interventions are made. Those students can be told to try harder all day long, to no avail. Their attitude about being in school is, over time, seriously affected. They lose interest and appear dysfunctional in academic pursuits. Some children in this small group begin to demonstrate manifestations of anger, despair and distractibility.

No matter how many notes of concern travel home, no matter how many pep talks transpire or how many consequences take place, the evolution of this scenario is certain to proceed in a downward spiral.

The parents of these five children might feel they are being blamed for their child's differences. "Why don't *your* children speak Swahili?" everyone seems to want to ask. Everything would be so easy if they did.

You, as teacher, experience a persistent progression of frustrations. You are fully aware of everyone's angst, and you are faced daily with the behavioral spin-offs of failing, frustrated children. As you try to help the Swahili-speaking children, you find yourself wishing for the other children to just go away. The Hindi-speaking children don't need an interpreter to translate the signals of rejection this situation is sending them.

This is an illustration of a scenario that happens every day in conventional classrooms that attempt to mainstream difficult children. Trying to teach or discipline them with conventional educational methods is no different than attempting to communicate in a language the child does not understand or relate to. If your child has been in the shoes of one of those Hindi speakers, you know how frustrating this situation is for everyone involved.

Whether your school is (metaphorically) speaking your child's language or not, you have established a new structure in your home to help teach your child's teachers how to interact with him in a way to which he can respond optimally.

You are now in a position to further affect your child's success at school, regardless of whether the school staff warms to your new philosophy and practice and regardless of whether the school finds effective new methods of their own.

Teachers Need New Tools, Too

Most teachers enter into the profession for all the right reasons. They have the highest regard for children and wish to do the best possible job—not only as teachers of academic information, but also as guides who help the child learn how to interact with peers and adults. Although most teachers receive considerable training relevant to imparting knowledge, most current teacher training in the latter category is in the context of conventional methodologies. Most teachers only come to their jobs adequately prepared to cope with discipline issues that commonly crop up with average children.

With challenging children, however, teachers try and try these traditional methods and wind up frustrated. Difficult children in the average classroom continue to lose ground despite teachers' best efforts using conventional techniques.

For every child who is acting out in a classroom, one or more additional children are under-functioning in less obvious ways. These children are equally at risk of falling into the 50 percent of children (in most cities) who don't finish school—and with conventional approaches, they usually get the short end of the stick when it comes to attention, intervention, and guidance compared with those who act out in more obvious ways.

One measure of student attrition is the infrequently cited high school graduation rate, which reflects the differential between children starting kindergarten and those finishing twelfth grade. This is the elusive rate of attrition that statistically represents children who may wind up costing society dearly later in their lives.

Teachers are quitting the field in huge numbers. It used to be that one in three new teachers left the field within the first five years of their careers; at this writing, that figure has risen to *one in two*. Why are teachers staging this exodus from their honorable calling? The single largest reason teachers look for another profession is that they get burnt out by the disturbances in their classrooms. They want to teach, not put out fires all day. They get tired of troublemakers who prevent the rest of the group from learning. We cannot afford to continue to lose teachers who come to the field ready to devote their lives to cultivating knowledge and character in the children in their classrooms.

Despite teachers' good intentions, even the newer methodologies and schools of thought often lack the structure and strategic rigor to shift challenging children into new patterns of success. Except in a few states where highly specialized additional training is mandated, it is a distressing reality that few (perhaps as few as one teacher in 20) have acquired the skills to guide the difficult child to consistent levels of success. This is true in our home town of Tucson, Arizona, where we have seen an endless parade of children who have been adversely affected by the lack of teacher training in this area. We have privately discussed this situation with several school officials, whose only point of disagreement has been that one in 20 might be an optimistic estimate.

This does not make the teachers blameworthy. They are doing the best they can with the tools they have. Teachers, like parents, have the best intentions for helping difficult students, but they don't have the right methods at their disposal. This is the legacy of university teacher education programs. Virtually everything teachers learn about helping difficult students is some variation of the conventional, upside-down approaches you are now moving out of as you apply the Nurtured Heart Approach.

The Nurtured Heart Approach offers a method that works beautifully to create a great learning environment in the classroom. Teachers who have gone to the trouble of acquiring the skills described in this book are truly amazing to watch. Challenging children in their classrooms almost invariably thrive and succeed, channeling their intense energies in more constructive ways. Their classmates thrive. Both average children and challenging children achieve at higher levels.

Inclusion is Really Exclusion

In the mainstream classroom, teachers are trying their best to teach intense and otherwise behaviorally challenged children using the conventional and traditional methods that are the tools of their trade. Every year, in the majority of classrooms, three to five children wind up out of the learning loop. Teachers perennially hope that next year they'll be able to simply teach and not have to deal with challenging children or the issues related to them.

Most teachers realize that this is more a fantasy than a dream. **They will not only continue to have energy-challenged kids, but—if current trends continue—they can count on having more, with more variations and growing intensity.** Properly prepared teachers are excited by the prospect of meeting more children with a strong life force. Unfortunately, most teachers do not share this enthusiasm. Many are despondent and disenchanted.

Much of the average teacher's school day must be spent managing behavior problems and following the protocol that goes with behavior problems—incident reports, documentation, telephone calls, meetings—or unnecessarily having to repeat parts of lessons that have been interrupted or sidetracked. **The** typical teacher only gets to actually instruct—the work for which he or she was trained—40 to 60 percent of the time, far less than the sought-after level of 80 percent.

Most difficult children cannot accommodate themselves to the mainstream classroom, no matter how desperately we urge them to try. Our educators wind up wasting much precious time working up individual educational plans (IEPs), creating special classes, putting out fires and dealing with student and parent problems, only because the language of the mainstream classroom fails to really include rather than exclude these children. We have seen how, with the right approach, much of the problematic issues can ultimately be avoided and how an entirely new positive side to the equation can be accessed.

A Precarious Position: No Turning Back

All this can put parents in what feels like a precarious position. Having learned to help your child therapeutically in a shift to successes, and having learned how this shift strengthens the child's positive orientation and ability to use self-control, it is now imperative to extend this orientation to other important environments. At this point, it may feel impossible to sit back and watch a disaster unfold when you know how to avert it.

When the child is comparably difficult at home and at school, it is very hard to give advice from a vantage point of strength. However, as a parent, once you have firsthand experience of the transformation that the Nurtured Heart Approach techniques and structure produce, there's no turning back.

Even if it feels far from your realm to convince anyone—much less the principal of your child's school—to adopt this new approach, bear with us as we make our case for Nurtured Heart schools.

At the very least, you can request a teacher most oriented to the interactive use of a strong level of recognition in combination with a strong level of limits. Look for a teacher who is most potentially receptive to your expert input. Remember, you have become your child's therapist, and now you are about to become your child's social worker.

If you are willing to ask your child's teacher to participate in this approach with you, read on. Later in this chapter, we will describe what we would call a reasonable accommodation, to which many challenging children are entitled by law. It is such a reasonable and simple accommodation that even the teacher who feels overwhelmed and feels he or she cannot—"because I have 30 other kids"—should be required to fully adopt. If necessary, this accommodation can be pursued at every district level until agreement to follow through is reached.

Nurtured Hearts In School

Conventional teaching methods, like parenting skills, have the payoffs of energy and animation in all the wrong places. Attempts to help difficult children typically make matters worse. We must support our teachers in their ability to use powerful tools in the classroom, so they can do what they were trained to do—teach, nurture and inspire our youth.

In classrooms that have adopted the new "language" we advocate using, all children flourish and teachers retrieve their dignity and time to instruct. Parents enjoy the progress of their children, and principals enjoy the successes of their teachers and students.

It is a dramatic experience to witness what happens in a classroom where the teacher moves freely around a calm, alert class. Free-flowing recognition, acknowledgment and appreciation create a palatable feeling of heart-centered nurturing. Even more inspiring is to see the face of a child who takes in this sustenance—glowing, breathing deeply and becoming even more deeply rooted in the pleasure of achievement and recognition.

Such a super-nurturing, positive atmosphere is interactive, with clear limits and clear consequences. Most educators fail to achieve sufficient intensity of either element and fail to get the two elements working powerfully, side-by-side and interactively. The Nurtured Heart Approach represents the required mix of structure needed in the classrooms of the present and future.

Teachers with an intense orientation toward being positive sometimes find it difficult to take a stand on limits. They fear being seen as lacking compassion, or think that strictness will negate their acknowledgments. Some have the false impression that giving warnings, sending a child to the principal, or calling in the counselor or parent is tantamount to taking a stand.

Other teachers have a hard time being positive and lean heavily on the side of limit setting. These are often teachers who harbor the illusion that a lecture, a browbeating or a call home is a consequence rather than the reward of energy that it really is.

Children who are easily stimulated or distracted can often be re-grounded when recognition and appreciation are given before such a child acts out and when a micro-focus on successful behaviors is maintained. A proactive stance conserves on the energies of both teacher and child as a positive connection develops between them. In this awe-inspiring dance between adult and child, the underlying rhythm is recognition, appreciation, affirmation, and the nurturing of all hearts involved.

Limit-Pushing Children Rule the Typical School

The biggest mistake teachers make is to allow themselves to be pulled into scripts of failure with a child, particularly when it escalates to where the child is sent out of the room. The child will always come back and is highly likely to graduate to stronger challenges. This is the only way children who need more structure can determine whether the teacher can handle them.

Other children in the classroom are adversely affected. At-risk children who haven't yet incurred the teacher's wrath internalize a sense of hurt and dread in relation to their classmate's "exile" and their own concerns about whether the teacher can handle their strong feelings and reactions.

Unfortunately, when a child is sent out of the classroom, the underlying pronouncement from the teacher is: "I can't adequately handle difficult behaviors within this environment." Intense children need adults in their lives who demonstrate an unflinching ability to handle them. When a child finally perceives that the teacher is in charge, the challenges come to a halt.

Why Some Educators Resist This Approach

Some educators fear that all this appreciation would make too much work for an already overburdened staff. Many, on the other hand, are under the impression that they are already being positive at an adequate level.

Another fear is that so much appreciation will contribute to the rise of a generation of kids who won't be doing the right thing for its own sake but rather to please adults. The sentiment is that children will lack the moral fiber to make good choices through their own inner processes because they instead will have adopted a process of projecting the imagined desires of others. This is a major tenet of a growing movement in education called constructivism.

Many constructivist teachers try to remove any emotion from their responses to avoid influencing students to do things to please the teacher. (Children have incredible radar for detecting what pleases the teacher, and can do so even when the teacher tries to remain neutral.) Some of these same teachers still give a tremendous amount of response to problems and problem behavior by design. Focused discussions are aimed at problem solving when behavioral issues arise. We have seen many such children—who are predisposed to draw negative attention in these settings—form an even clearer impression that the greatest amounts of teacher availability, interaction, and energy can be gained by breaking a rule.

Certainly it is hard for these children to gain the teacher's energy and response by doing well in these classrooms. It is held back by design. Approval of any kind is guarded. We've also witnessed children who are not ordinarily problem-oriented discover that it takes a problem to get a

continued next page

continued from previous page

response from an adult in this environment. Many of these same teachers have a negative view of behavior management, but what they fail to recognize is that focusing energy on problem solving is also behavior management. Unfortunately, it is a poorly conceived version. They are inadvertently reinforcing the very behaviors that are least desirable with the gift of their energies and relationship.

Constructivists seem to think that their theories are based on Piaget, a great developmental psychologist and learning theorist. The belief is that young children's intrinsic motivation to do the right thing can be cultivated in an environment that does not lead children by means of external indicators of what pleases us, like praise, appreciation and recognition.

According to Piaget, however, intrinsic motivation occurs during the advanced stage of development called formal operations. Even most adults are not functioning on a level of formal operations. It takes years of extrinsic reinforcement and motivation to crystallize the underpinnings of internal, intrinsic motivation.

The healing that transpires through the Nurtured Heart Approach is considerably in line with Piaget's learning theory. Kids surrounded by success will absorb an experience of success that at first will be external to them, and through a process of time, assimilation and integration, will come to be second nature. In the same way, children who are surrounded by a clear structure of heightened appreciation and limits will integrate their abilities to appreciate self and others appropriately. They also develop the ability to appropriately set limits for self and others.

Our society currently is deficient in these abilities, in case you haven't noticed. Self-help books offer a multitude of ways to appreciate ourselves more and to be more assertive. If you've gone on this quest yourself, you know how hard it is to acquire these skills as an adult. The Nurtured Heart Approach is a systematic way to teach these qualities to children, who learn them much more readily under the right circumstances.

Escalating energy and relationship to negativity leave the good children in the classroom anxious and upset about the classroom's inequity. It doesn't make sense to them that their positive actions and decisions get fewer payoffs energetically than the adverse actions of the challenging children. Meanwhile, the marginal children are understudies to the blatantly difficult children.

They're taking note of the actions that get that teacher "toy" hopping most energetically. They often jump into the fray of difficult behaviors to obtain the high-octane connection they feel they, too, deserve. And if a teacher dares to start being more positive with just the challenging children—and this is often the recommended wisdom—watch who becomes even more angered and more willing to jump into the fray as the inequities grow: the marginal children and the good children!

Principals make the same mistake in suspending a child or calling parents. The underlying message to the child is that the school cannot handle her. If the parent is commanded to take the child home, the pattern deepens and becomes further convoluted. Everyone loses. In order for the child to determine that the teacher or the school can actually handle her, she has to test at least as hard the next time. Even if there is a brief honeymoon period, the increased challenge is inevitable.

It is far more effective in the school setting to demonstrate that consequences can happen smoothly right then and there in the situation, wherever that is—in the classroom, the cafeteria, the schoolyard—wherever and whenever a problem arises. No energy, just a reset, then right back to positivity. That's the way to really play hardball. And we've seen this work best in schools that adopt the Nurtured Heart Approach school-wide.

Conducting the Educational Symphony

In the current school culture, principals are reluctant to dictate, school-wide, how discipline problems should be dealt with. As a result, many schools end up less than harmonious, with inconsistent messages to children depending on which staff member they are with.

Leonard Bernstein didn't give the string section a choice to play a piece differently than the brass or wind sections. He conducted the entire orchestra as a whole. Similarly, the best schools are those with principals who act as a conductor, bringing teachers on line with a school-wide plan. Very few principals have been willing to include all personnel from the classroom faculty to the schoolyard monitors in an entire-school plan, however.

In a school where difficult children are running the show, consistency must become part of the school's fabric. Personnel can no longer be allowed to do their own thing. Certainly teachers can have their own flair for instruction, but the language of success must be encoded in every interaction between students and adults.

Inclusion can work, but not without leaps in philosophy and technology. Seismographic rumblings in the world of education dictate a major shift in the next 10 years. When we look in our crystal ball, we see that every future classroom will need to be therapeutic as well as academic. The two go hand

and hand. Teachers are always dealing with therapeutic issues anyway, especially regarding behavior and character. These issues are windows of opportunity for the child to shift to higher levels of functioning. Why not do a great job of it instead of one that is less than fully successful? There's almost nothing that cannot be accomplished in six hours a day.

Why wait? If you have a genetic propensity for heart disease, are you going to wait until the heart attack or the bypass surgery to make important changes, or do you take steps proactively?

Conventional approaches cannot work with difficult children in schools any more than they can work at home. Inclusion—a desegregation of special education, where children with emotionally and physically handicapping conditions are integrated into conventional driven mainstream classrooms—has had too many debilitating repercussions. Until the mainstream classroom fully serves children with handicapping conditions, many of the current learning environments would be more appropriately termed "exclusion." Let's stop the bleeding and integrate a new level of real inclusion.

After all, teaching and parenting have remained two frontiers that have resisted evolution. Every other major field has made quantum leaps in technology. The transportation, communication and information industries have embraced endless generations of progress through improvements in technology. Parenting and teaching methods keep painting the Model-T new colors, but it is still a Model-T.

New horizons are ready and waiting. The question is, who is going to provide the impetus to change? Our guess is that change will occur on many fronts, but most notably when principals—the school's conductors—pick up their batons and truly lead: "Today, we're all playing the symphony in A sharp."

As a parent, you help decide what movement the school orchestra will play. You, too, write the music. Charter Schools, if their approach to setting policy is founded in the real world of teacher-child interaction and learning rather than a fantasy of inclusion that doesn't translate to reality, will help to push the shift. These and other forward-thinking public and private schools can prove to the world that energy-challenged children are not a curse, but a blessing, and that *real* inclusion can work.

The Override Intervention

The best-case scenario would be for the teacher of your difficult child to take a "best practices" stance and adopt the whole methodology we describe in this book, as many teachers have done with great success. Barring this optimal outcome, parents can initiate a fail-safe to override the teacher who is relatively unskilled in working with intense children. **The intervention you will suggest**

to the child's teacher will take the teacher less than 30 seconds a day.

Fortunately, in our experience, 90 percent or more of teachers who are asked to help do so willingly with a very positive attitude. They see the payoff within a matter of days in some cases, or weeks at most.

This intervention is designed to dramatically improve your child's performance regardless of whether the teacher knows the Nurtured Heart Approach or any other approach that has the potential for a positive impact. It is based on the system, the accountability and the philosophy that you already have in place. It is impossible to pull off, however, unless you have the previously designed strategies already rolling at home. Its basis is to override classroom strategies that aren't working and to propel your child into using his school-linked energies productively rather than in ways that get him in trouble.

The foundation: God is watching. As we all know, many people of varying faiths are able to walk the straight and narrow, so to speak, in connection with an abiding feeling and faith that God is watching. In a literal sense, they are able to translate their belief that God is present in their lives into a lifestyle that is guided by their faith.

Most translations of this faith are along these lines: God is aware of everything, and in the grand scheme of things, God will hold them accountable for their thoughts and actions, both good and bad. By way of this belief, people of many religious traditions conjure up the wherewithal to consistently do the right thing.

In a manner of speaking, we as parents are a temporary representation of God in the context of the child's life. We fulfill a similar role in that the child perceives us as all-seeing, all-knowing, all-wise, all-powerful and all-loving. Most children's accountability comes by way of our responses to what they do and say, not to their belief that God is listening and that they will be held accountable by that God.

Now shift gears and think for a moment about any time you may have spent in your child's classroom, observing or participating. Most children, knowing that a parent is present, are somehow able to conjure up an extra measure of self-control and resiliency that might be absent or underutilized if mom or dad were not in sight. Somehow, the knowledge of parental presence enhances and benefits a child's abilities to track and perform. We are not directly creating the improvements; our child's perception of being accountable to us gives her the extra edge of control and motivation.

If we can create a new scenario in which our child perceives a parent's benevolent presence in the back of the classroom without our actually being there, we may well be able to further enhance his ability to function successfully in the school environment.

Our experience bears this out dramatically. You can have a profound effect on our child's school performance by playing the role of omnipresent deity in your child's life. This will allow you to effectively extend the reach of the system you have already put into motion.

The methodology: written communication between parent and teacher. To move your hard work with this approach into the school setting, open up a daily line of communication with the teacher or teachers who are in a position to evaluate how the day went.

Our goal has been to devise a procedure that it is easy and quick for everyone involved. It would make no sense whatsoever to come up with a complicated system that would further tie up a teacher's busy day. We need a system that transcends considerations such as "I don't have the time. I have 27 other children to work with"—an intervention that requires less than 30 seconds daily and preferably half that time. An intervention effective enough to become a win-win joint venture.

You will create a simple note that the teacher marks in the appropriate areas with a checkmark, signs, and sends on its merry way back to the parent. It is what you do with the note that works a little magic.

The samples on the two following pages combine rules, goals and potential bonus areas that the parent or teacher feels are relevant for the particular child. The combination crucially needs to include several "gimme" listings that are likely to yield some level of success, along with listings that cover the areas of behavior and function with which the child is currently struggling. The note can be adjusted on an ongoing basis to include newly relevant areas.

Arrange a meeting with your child's teacher and explain that you have been using the Nurtured Heart Approach at home and that it has been recommended that a link be formed between home and school. You may want to explain how heightened recognition and limits have helped your child thus far and how you plan to give your child credit, acknowledgment and accountability at home for his or her academic and behavioral efforts at school. Show a sample note, ask for the teacher's input and reassure the teacher that this process will only take a few seconds at the end of the day.

Stress as most important the need to give positive marks to the aspects of the day that were *not* problems and the need to give partial credit to problem areas to the degree that effort was made. One instance of disruption does not seal the fate of a "bad" day. Credit must be noted for the part of the day that went well.

If the teacher's cooperation is not forthcoming, know that if you have been told that your child's behavior has interfered with his learning or the learning of other children, whether or not they have a formal diagnosis, your child by law is entitled to a reasonable accommodation. We believe that asking a teacher to fill out a form that takes 30 seconds or less is a reasonable accommodation.

If your child attends a public school, you are entitled to consult with the Compliance Office at the district to obtain the teacher's cooperation. Fortunately, the vast majority of teachers assist with this accommodation in a straightforward and collaborative manner.

Refueling and Accountability

A helpful frame of reference for using this system is to consider that each day he attends school, your child is away from his primary energy source for at least six hours. When you see him again, he will probably be in dire need of refueling. Unless we are super-aware and determined, we may well fall right into the trap of refueling through negative responses, which of course winds up being emotionally non-nutritious and counter to our goals.

A challenging and intense child may return from school with strong need for energized connection, recognition and acknowledgment. He or she needs to feel relationship. Typically, the first thing we say to a child returning home from school is "How was your day?" This is probably an effective question about 10 percent of the time, if that. Consider yourself fortunate if your child provides a comprehensive response. Most of the time, this question elicits a minimal response such as "I don't know" or "It was okay." At this point, a straightforward attempt to connect in a positive way usually comes to a screeching halt unless the parent perseveres with further interrogation. Further questioning can also be of dubious value and can occasionally backfire into a negative scenario.

After all of this interrogation, the child still needs connection—and may attempt to bring it about in roundabout and potentially self-destructive ways. In the negative scenario, the child is able to extract attention, reaction and focus from the parent in non-affirming ways.

The After-School Trick

Letting school exist as a separate sphere of functioning without the tie-in to home accountability, especially for the challenging child, is a big mistake. Assuming that the school staff can suitably handle problem behaviors without accidentally rewarding them through undue reaction is, unfortunately, betting against the odds. Only in the best of all possible worlds would every teacher be sufficiently skillful to make the home/school link unnecessary.

In the chapter on the Credit System, we told you that you don't have to use this kind of system to effect huge change in an intense child's life at home. **However: if you want to effect similar change on the child's school behaviors, attitudes and achievements, the credit system at home is the only reliable way we've found to do this.** You need a codified system of recognition at home so that you can award credit for the many hours the child spends

Elementary School Credit System   *(Sample)*

Name_____ Date_____ Initials _____

	Poor	Fair	Good	Very Good	Excellent
Paying attention		X			
Following directions			X		
Good attitude					X
Completing assignments				X	
No aggression or bullying					X
No teasing or name calling	X				
No bad words					X

Comments:

_____

_____

_____

Elementary School Credit System

Name_____ Date_____ Initials _____

	Poor	Fair	Good	Very Good	Excellent

Comments:

_____

_____

_____

Note to Parents: Use the teacher's rating to give your child credits and add them to the home Credit System.
A suggested conversion is:

Poor = 0   Fair = 10   Good = 15   Very Good = 20   Excellent = 30

Middle/High School Credit System   *(Sample)*

Name _____ Date _____ Initials _____

	Mrs. T	Mr. M	Ms. P	Mrs. F	Mr. W
Following directions	2	2	3	3	4
Good attitude	3	4	4	3	5
Participating	2	3	2	2	5
Completing class work	4	3	4	3	5
No aggression	4	5	5	5	5
No put downs or teasing	4	4	5	4	4
No swearing	5	5	5	5	5
Ignoring provocation	2	0	2	3	4

Comments:
_____
_____
_____

Please assign a number to each listed behavior as follows:
0   Poor: poor effort, persistent problem behaviors, poor recovery following consequence.
2   Fair: fair effort, some behavior problems, fair recovery following class consequence.
3   Good: good effort, minimal problems.
4   Very Good: very good effort, no problems.
5   Excellent: exceptional effort

Middle/High School Credit System

Name _____ Date _____ Initials _____

Comments:
_____
_____
_____

Please assign a number to each listed behavior as follows:
0   Poor: poor effort, persistent problem behaviors, poor recovery following consequence.
2   Fair: fair effort, some behavior problems, fair recovery following class consequence.
3   Good: good effort, minimal problems.
4   Very Good: very good effort, no problems.
5   Excellent: exceptional effort

Note to Parents: Tally the teacher's ratings and add to the home Credit System.

at school each day and leverage the impact to motivate a progression of improved choices away from home.

The trick is to have an effective, systematic way of accomplishing connection and refueling when your child gets home, while avoiding the trap of being pulled into negative payoffs.

Our recommendation is this: when your child arrives home with the filled-out note, instead of asking questions, say something like "It's great to see you. Let's take a look at how the day went." A lot of parents then give their child a bonus, right off the bat, for safely bringing the note home. Then, take the note and focus on every last opportunity to acknowledge and appreciate. First things first.

Make sure to give the credits earned on the basis of the rating system. School is a major chunk of your child's day and he deserves a commensurate degree of credit for his efforts. Be generous. Give credits and verbal recognition for every degree of success above the category of poor. Do not participate in any system that takes away points for unsuccessful or unacceptable behaviors. You will defeat your overall purpose.

Before sending the first note to her teacher, let your child know that you will be holding her accountable for rules broken at school, even if someone there has already given a consequence. Let her know that you will give as much credit as possible for all good behaviors at school and that she will be able to use those credits for home privileges. However, for every "poor" listed she will owe you a time-out, which must be completed before any after-school privileges can be bought. The rules of time-out would be those that you have already established. Your child already knows that time-out is no big deal and is over in a flash, so normally this is not an issue. **You won't even be asking her what the problems were about, but just moving on after the time-outs are complete.**

Rather than making any kind of big deal about a problem, stick to the plan of giving the time-out as a neutral afterthought following the acknowledgments for the successful, credit-earning behaviors. And, when the time-out is over, it's over. Life gets back to normal.

One possible way of administering accountability for a poor rating would be to say, after the positive points have been given, "Okay, let's get paid up on the time-outs you owe, and we can get that out of the way." Keep the time-out short. If a major problem merits additional community service, stick to your plan and administer the consequence with a continued neutral attitude. Again, don't be drawn into the trap of initiating an inquisition or discussing the problem or issue.

The reason we can recommend this intervention so highly is that we frequently work with children who have been referred to us primarily because of moderate to severe problems at school. Occasionally, school personnel have given up or have reached a point at which they are saying the child cannot return without being on medication, which is a completely illegal condition of return.

What we have seen as a result of our recommended intervention is astounding. Children with horrendous patterns of negativity at school, once approached with the school-to-home accountability of recognition for positives in combination with consequences for school transgressions, quickly begin to use much more control and subsequently come to use their energies constructively.

This happens because the child's previously confused world comes together in a clearer version of life that makes sense. They see for themselves how their school life is intrinsically related to their home life, as well as the extent to which they can choose from their menu of privileges.

Many parents have asked whether giving additional consequences at home is actually a form of double jeopardy that might have an overall adverse effect. This unusual stance turns out to be an extremely compassionate one in the long run. Within a few days to a few weeks, children will have reinvested their energies in positive endeavors and you will have little or no call to issue timeouts. It is just a matter of the child's learning to trust that there is really a wall where they need a wall to be.

The very intense children we have worked with have typically started out with either mixed reviews or rocky school reports for the first few days, followed by steady progress. The progress really takes off once a child determines that parents are really going to hold him or her accountable for school behaviors. To make sure of the meaning of this new factor, the child has to challenge the format and see its two primary features on an ongoing basis before pulling in the reins and proceeding successfully.

First, the child needs to trust that you will notice, credit and show excitement over all the degrees of positive choices reported, day in and day out. Second, he or she needs to see that every challenge will result in accountability, no matter what, and with the same neutral attitude.

In this way, you are providing structure that overrides any structural deficits of the classroom or the school itself. Children need to challenge the system to see if it will hold up under fire. Their job, at first, is to give you a run for your money to see if you can really pull this off. Once they pass through this inevitable initial phase, tests will come only occasionally to keep you on your toes. The outcome will be a child who is investing in successes.

Again, they must first see that the emotional payoffs—the verbal and nonverbal energy that you radiate—are far greater for the positive behaviors than for negative behaviors, to which you supply only a neutral reaction and a simple consequence.

Most parents become slaves to an inconsistent flow of information from teachers. Parents of difficult children typically only hear from teachers about problems and then only after the problems have stacked up to avalanche proportions. The daily note allows you to make a point of reinforcing good school behaviors.

Once the child is able to make the shift into "normal" levels of classroom behavior, the teacher's existing degree of expertise comes nicely into play. This is an excellent secondary payoff of this aspect of the Nurtured Heart Approach. By strategically using this note system, further adversity related to teacher-child power struggles can be sidestepped. Even a teacher who starts out unhappy about the note system is usually thrilled to share in the celebration and credit once he or she sees the positive impact on the child's behaviors.

The School Link-up: Critical Points

Crediting as many successful behaviors as possible in school and at home lends powerful support to any child. Without such a system, children typically under-emphasize how the day went, communicating only bits of specific information—usually, not enough for parents to utilize beneficially in this approach. It provides many more opportunities to verbalize appreciation and use positive efforts as incentives. It is also a way for hyper-needy children to refuel after many hours of separation from their parent(s). Not being thus re-energized dramatically increases the likelihood of negative acting-out as an alternative route to connection. This proactive aspect of intervention alone makes a huge difference in how the remainder of the day goes.

This basic, simple feedback system between school and home builds a new level of trust and certainty based on consistent focus and expectations across environments. When children are aware that feedback from school goes home to parents, they generally are more motivated to behave well. The feedback system encourages other care providers to adopt or increase frequent recognition and appreciation of positive behavior. Such a format can keep you informed about how well the out-of-home support and structure are meeting your child's needs. It often can be directly integrated into the school's individualized education plan, if one needs to be devised, to increase school support.

Similarly, it can have tremendously positive effects on your child's behaviors with baby-sitters, during visits with relatives or in any other relevant setting.

Linking to School and Other Settings: Prescription

- Identify one or two major care providers in places your child spends significant time.

- Develop a simple behavior checklist to give to the responsible person(s) in each of the settings.

- Let your children know they deserve credit for how they do away from home as well as at home. Advise them that a new responsibility will be to take the checklist sheet to the designated person(s) and to bring it home. Clearly communicate to all parties when and how often the sheet comes home (for example, daily or every Friday).

- Let your child know she will get bonus points for bringing the report home, no matter what is in the report. Point out additional bonus credit opportunities as you see fit or if behavior away from home showed special effort. **On the home report, include items with which you know your child is unlikely to have problems. Purposely include things she already does in acceptable ways.**

- **Emphasize that the child cannot get credit, no matter how well he did, on any day that he forgets the paper or that it hasn't been filled out by the key person.** Factor in exceptional circumstances such as substitute teachers or unexpected events of the day. After all, we still deserve to get paid if our boss is out of town or inclement weather blocks the supplies our company needs to complete a project.

- Explain that expectations and basic rules are the same outside of the home and the child will be held accountable at home for rules broken elsewhere (even after already having received a consequence in that environment). Explain that this means time-outs at home for rules broken in other places.

Here are some examples of possible school goals consistent with your home program. We recommend that your daily note include fewer than 10 of these related goals and rules:

> No disruptions
>
> Getting along with others
>
> Completing class work
>
> Following directions
>
> Good school yard behavior
>
> Good lunch room behavior
>
> No put downs
>
> No aggression
>
> Good participation
>
> No angry outbursts

No arguing

No teasing or distracting others

Good attitude

Good self-control

Being respectful

Showing responsibility

Sharing or cooperation

Good problem solving

- **Tailor your child's list to his specific needs and situation.** Don't forget to include several items that are not a problem and therefore will tend to be consistent successes.

- In conjunction with a home credit system, offer school-based incentives clearly: Let your child know exactly how many credits are potentially available for each level of success. We recommend clear gradations with bonus credit available for special achievements. **Keep in mind that your child is at school for six or more hours. Make the total credits available proportional to the overall size and importance of the job.** School is one of a child's biggest and most important jobs. Be generous. The total credits available could even be approximately equal to the total number your child can earn for a good day at home. Let school or day care credits earned roll into the home credit system.

- With the addition of school credits to the child's credit system, some parents slightly increase the prices of privileges to balance their child's newly increased credit income. Other parents create a few new incentives to inspire their child to save up for larger privileges. It is also perfectly fine for a child to simply become rich in terms of saved credits.

- If your child has broken rules at school, as reflected by indicators of poor performance on the report, hold her accountable in the same neutral manner that you have developed for home use. Use a short time-out, unless additional community service is merited by the magnitude of the problem behavior.

- Do not get punitive! Scolding, lectures and such are really rewards. Do not take additional points or privileges away or add special grounding.

- When the time-out is over, resume regular activities and family life. Get right back to recognizing all the positive behaviors that you can.

- **Be generous most of all with your deep and authentic verbal appreciation of your child's choices and efforts.**

Share Your Successes

By this time, you have worked hard through trial and error to know what words, strategies and support best help your child. Share these strategies with teachers, daycare workers or other after-school personnel. This builds additional support for both your child and a caregiver in your absence. Offering to meet with or scheduling a phone consultation with those who are having difficulties giving your child the support and structure he needs can really help encourage willingness to support both you and your child. You now know your child better and have gained much shareable experience and wisdom in the area of supporting your child's successful behaviors.

Noncustodial parents should also be included in this powerful feedback loop when possible. Most parents will provide extra effort if it is clearly sought for the child's benefit rather than as an attempt on one parent's part to control another. It is vital that as many as possible of the significant people in your child's life use the therapeutic strategies of recognition and appreciation along with clear limits.

If the noncustodial parent refuses to adopt any level of these strategies, all is not lost. Even though your child may have difficulty making the transition back into your home following a visit, let him know that your system, in its entirety, will be in effect the second he arrives back home—and stick to this plan. Hold your child fully accountable even though you may privately lament the other parent's negative influence. Excuses now lead to a life of excuses on the part of the child later in life.

For many parents, the conflict is heightened when they know that the child had few or no limits while visiting and had been given everything she demanded, without having done anything to earn the privileges received. Such parents may fear that their children will ultimately resent them and admire the Disneyland parent. This fear is understandable. Our experience is this: **The determined parent who sticks to his or her plan will wind up having by far the strongest effect.**

We know this from our experiences in group homes and residential treatment centers. There, we have met many children who, once the initial testing is over, wind up respecting most the staff members who resolutely have given plentiful recognition and enforced clear limits. The staff person who attempts to win a child over by catering to her or by feeling sorry for him is at risk of attracting all kinds of manipulative behavior. Often, the first time a child shows love for another is for a staff member who holds him accountable.

Chapter Twelve
Later Stages of Treatment
Pulling It All Together

M ANY FAMILIES WE MEET have already tried several parenting formats, therapies, or other treatment avenues on their own before coming across the Nurtured Heart Approach. This is especially true of families dealing with behavior diagnosable as ADHD. For these families, most new attempts yielded at least some initial changes, if for no reason other than that, especially for an ADHD child, new is novel. Thus, new has some temporary impact—emphasis on the "temporary."

In the families that we have met who are frustrated and are seeking further help, no matter which conventional methods they apply, the benefits are short-lived. New problems crop up... always. Often, the parent does not receive clear instructions on how to adapt the new parenting framework to new challenges, which are inevitable. In other cases, the framework in use is simply not intense enough to meet the child's unique challenges. In still other instances, the child's challenges have evolved beyond the effect the parents can muster with the tools they have.

We are describing a crucial stage in the transformation process. Do not throw in the towel. Your new tool kit includes everything you need to adjust to new and difficult circumstances.

Increasing the Therapeutic Tension

The structural brace can be tightened. The first time around the block, the generic version of the techniques described in previous chapters works for many families. However, two factors are clear:

- **Even in families for whom this version seems perfect, there will be new challenges in the future.** You must be prepared for these—even if they are simply the result of the relative destabilization that comes with new stages of child development.

- **In approximately 20 percent of the families we work with, the generic version is not enough, even from the beginning.** We must go back and apply some torque to both recognition and limits and increase therapeutic tension to meet the needs of the child adequately. Increasing the degree of structure increases the therapeutic tension.

Fortunately, our system is designed for this very maneuver. The more intense the child, the more intense the application of the intervention. Fortunately, this model allows a lot of room to meet the challenges of the super-intense child. This is crucial, because if parents had to abandon yet another system and yet another attempt to parent, the message to the child would again be, "We just can't handle you."

This stage is not to be taken lightly, for a child must perceive that his or her parent can, in fact, handle him or her. The child's basic trust of the world rides on the parents being able to move past the stages of temporary impact to a period in which the child can abide safely in the parents' consistent, predictable, benevolent control over an extended time. The child's eventual ability to apply consistent internal control depends upon this happening.

More Big Bang

We worked with a mom and dad who were trying very earnestly to give their eight-year-old son all the recognition they could. Some improvements were evident. However, the main problem was that the child continued to steal on a regular basis. On closer study it was evident that, although the parents were making every effort to follow our advice by providing recognition for a greatly expanded version of positives, the father, in particular, was still emotionally in the thick of things. He still had his emotional payoff aimed primarily at the problem behavior. His son was hell-bent on connecting with his dad emotionally, and the only way that emotion was available was to do the things that drove Dad wild. This child was very confused. He might even have thought that his dad loved the thievery because it was the only thing aside from football that he seemed to get excited about.

The dad had started each of the previous three sessions with heart-wrenching litanies of the latest challenges that his son had posed. Special emphasis was placed on the child's acts of stealing. When we shifted the conversation back to wanting to hear about gains made during the same time frame, they were typically described in a muted, low-key manner, even though there were significant overall improvements and a lot of positive behaviors to be excited about.

Therein resided the problem. Despite the parent's shift to a lot of positive comments, the heavy payoffs in regard to affect and emotion were still for a small array of negative behaviors. This, of course, continued to be well advertised. The trick was to change the venue of the payoffs.

The parents were advised to have a response to a broken rule (a consequence), but to be sure it was accompanied by *no energetic payoff* (negative attention) whatsoever. "Put the core payoff, your energy and your emotion, into your positive acknowledgments, not your disappointments," they were told. And they were reminded that this kind of emotional investment inspires a healthy and balanced spiritual nutrition and a fulfilling enjoyment of the child's life. It teaches aliveness. Holding a child in increasingly greater esteem while holding him accountable for unacceptable behaviors is the simple formula for success.

New issues will surface; old issues may resurface. New rules may have to be added. Inspired emphasis on recognition may have to be rekindled. The natural tendency as things improve is to ease up on what may have been working. The credit system may slide out of sight or the initial level of appreciating positive traits or appreciating when rules are not being broken may become negligible. Be vigilant. It will take a lot of conscious determination to stay on track.

Think about world-class athletes in any sport. If they discover something that works, the last thing they'll do is let it slide away. They'll work even harder to develop and deepen that part of their approach. The same is true in this adventure we call parenting.

It takes a lot of conscious determination to up the ante if the need arises. Here are a couple of scenarios where this might prove necessary:

Scenario 1. *Your child has been doing fairly well, but enters middle school and is exposed to a quantum jump in peer pressure. She child succumbs to this pressure by ditching several classes and by importing a few choice expressions, attitudes and behaviors into your home.*

Although you know to anticipate and therefore be prepared for such contingencies as the one described above, you are not overwhelmed with joy at this new development. You can see that it will take a lot of determination to stick with your plan, matching your child's new intensity with renewed efforts to maintain this intervention model—especially since things have been going fairly well until now.

So, what do you do? Is your first response to revert back to lectures, warnings, threats or outrage? The tendency to overreact may still be lurking in the shadows. **The answer lies very much in *sticking to the plan*.**

No energy other than a neutrally issued consequence goes to the new problem behavior. It gets the smallest amount of payoff possible. No inadvertent reward for breaking the rules. Make new rules on the spot if necessary to cover the issues that surface. And when rules aren't being broken, show your appreciation. Watch out for the tendency to soften your hold on recognition.

Scenario 2. *Your child is simply not responding to the techniques. Maybe just a tiny bit of response here and there, but the challenges continue to be strong, particularly in regard to your child's emotional reactivity.*

This happens in a modest percentage of children who are at the high end of the scale of intensity. They are either constitutionally more intense or life experiences have given them such strong emotions that they are simply on overload. These children absolutely need from within a far greater ability to control than the average difficult child. They need to develop trust that they can handle their strongest feelings without folding.

They're already overwhelmed by their intensity and they certainly do not need to have their emotions explored or mobilized. They do, however, need to be reassured that their emotions are okay and that they are capable of handling them.

This can be achieved in several ways:

- **By frequently emphasizing self-control in positive recognitions.** Constantly create instances when the child is having the experience of self-control. Opportunistically find moments, even if they are random and short-lived, when your child is not breaking rules. Strongly emphasize the effort made and the self-control used to avoid whatever problems could potentially be happening. Lay it on thicker and thicker, as if you were fighting for your life. Search out and seize moments where self-control is being used, even if they are sparse at first. If necessary, get out the magnifying glass or get a bigger microscope. "I see the control you are using right now—(elaborate)." "I like how you are handling your strong feelings right now." "I see how you are using your power to handle your intensity in this frustrating situation." Power is a key word to help heighten the trajectory of this intervention.

- **Take a stronger and clearer stance in relation to your child's strong feelings.** Let go of trying to fix the child's hurt or anger. Stop trying to get to the bottom of it. Appreciate your child for expressing his feelings appropriately if that occurs, but don't hold your breath waiting for that to happen and don't try to facilitate it. With an intense child, exploring and mobilizing emotions is yet another trap. You'll ultimately wind up giving way too many payoffs to aspects of your child that you would prefer not to energize. A better tactic is simply to acknowledge whatever it is you see:

  "I see that you're furious and I appreciate that you're handling it as best as you can. You're not yelling or fighting. I appreciate your effort. I'm willing to hear you when you're ready to talk calmly."

If this furious child crosses the line by breaking a rule, keep it simple by giving a time-out without payoff. Get better and better, if necessary, at recognizing rule violations as soon as they happen—even a little bit of a broken rule is a consequence at this point - and get better and better at handling them neutrally. And even more important, get better and better at being proactive. If you can recognize the moment when a rule is broken, then you can also get better at anticipating problems and at giving all kinds of recognition *before the rule is actually broken.*

Think of all the great plays in sports where a player was excruciatingly close to being out-of-bounds but managed to stay in-bounds and score. Some of the loudest cheering comes at those moments.

For the very intense child, the magic is in giving a lot of appreciation *before* the rules are broken.

Amp up the attitudes embodied in the Shamu story and the tolltaker story. The answer is always in how you choose to view the world and in how you choose to employ your expectations strategically. These are the essential attitudes to refine. We have found that with each measure of improvement there are always new levels to attain and a new harvest to reap.

Once your child finally links the internal feeling of success to your energy and emotional payoff, she will begin to integrate success into every aspect of life. Children who feel successful on the inside do not create or attract havoc in their lives. On the contrary, they attract and perpetuate the best life has to offer.

Pointing Out Your Child's Greatness

One additional way to heighten the trajectory of the positive side of the equation is to occasionally make references to your child's great choices, great wisdom, great judgment, and other qualities of greatness you can discern and verbalize. This is a very powerful form of recognition that in our experience reaches a child on a heart and soul level. We highly recommend trying this on for size. The concept of greatness is addressed in more detail in Chapter 15.

Some children are simply harder to sell on this new connection, especially if they have had a long prior history of negative hookups. This is also true for children who have had major adverse life experiences. They frequently believe the world is a chaotic or crazy place or that life stinks. If a child is strongly accustomed to being rewarded with a lot of attention and reaction to negative behaviors, you have a greater degree of patterning to overcome. Be convincing. Work the techniques with more zeal.

A perfect example of applying this approach with more zeal happened at Reynolds Elementary in Tucson, where an extraordinary and imaginative staff counselor, Bob Scheuneman, had a magical effect on the most challenging children. Somehow he found a way to connect the tone in his voice to his heart. Kids readily picked up on his zeal; his comments to children seemed to resonate at a deeper level. This is something you can achieve, as well, as you seek out deeper, more compelling ways to send your energy out to your child at the appropriate times.

The great news is that simply staying with the positive and choosing to believe in the truth of that in each new moment will bring your heart increasingly to your voice. You will be astounded at the power your voice will take on and at the impact you will see from your words and intentions.

Opposition and Defiance in Children Who Have Witnessed Abuse

An unusual dynamic often exists in families where a child has witnessed his or her mother being physically or emotionally abused. In these families, even if the mother has already found the inner strength to send the offender on his way, the child attempts the offense himself against his mother to see what will transpire. Children of domestic violence will often live this out, even though witnessing the original event had been painful and traumatic. This can happen even if the spousal abuse was rare. It's almost as if a computer file has been opened that can only be deleted once the child sees for herself that her mother is now strong and won't be drawn into putting up with abuse again.

There seems to be a need to challenge Mom, adamantly and defiantly, to assess whether she is truly in charge, or will ultimately give in as she has in the past. In these situations, the child will test hard to try to make certain the parent is strong and reliable. The child psychologically needs to do this in order to begin to trust the world again and to move on with her life. Verbal reassurances alone will not suffice.

Many women who find themselves in domestic violence situations give unusual deference to men. Many of these women have grown up in homes where they saw their mothers dominated by their fathers and where undue heavy-handed control was used in the parenting that they experienced. This is one of several surefire formulas for disempowerment. Even though the mother in this dilemma may have begun the journey of finding her own power by sending her offending partner on his way, she may still be afraid to take a stand with the "offending" child for fear of not being loved. So, typically, her child will push the limits. It is extraordinarily hard for mothers in this situation to feel fully comfortable taking charge.

It is crucial for women in such situations to realize that, even though their prior experiences with control as a child or as an abused spouse may

have been ugly, control itself is not an awful thing. To help a child eventually become empowered in a healthy way and move toward self-control requires a parent's healthy use of control. In particular, children who have witnessed or experienced domestic violence in any form especially need healthy parental control. This is primarily achieved by having very clear rules. The next step is to generously credit the child for instances of exercising self-control.

"I like the effort you are using to control your strong feelings."

"I like that you are using your power in a positive way. You were told no when you asked for more TV and you used your power to keep from having a strong reaction. Keep up the good work."

Extend your appreciation strongly when rules are not being broken. Use obeying the rules as a frequent source of success. Keep the theme of pointing out when self-control is being used.

"I like the control you are using right now to not use bad words and aggression."

"I like the control you used today to not break rules at school and to get home before curfew."

Credit systems help dramatically with these children, both by demonstrating the consistency they desperately need and by fostering experiences of healthy parental leverage and power. Having seen abuses of power, they want to experiment with power themselves. They desperately need role models of healthy empowerment.

Also be creative in pointing out moments when the child is using power in acceptable, healthy ways. Sometimes it is simply a matter of re-framing ordinary moments in an extraordinary manner. Examples might be:

"I appreciate how you just used your power to be helpful. Putting your plate in the sink is thoughtful and responsible."

"I noticed that you stopped yourself from reacting to what your sister said. That kind of good attitude is a great way of using your power."

The last step that is vital to transformation is the clear and predictable enforcement of the rules. The child will often go to great lengths to derail a parent's efforts, trying every manipulative behavior at his or her disposal to attempt to throw Mom off course and thereby avoid the consequence. There may be physical resistance as well as ruthless use of tactics of wit, cunning and guilt. **Do not buy in for even one moment!** Do not show your child that these ploys have had any effect on you, even if what has been said has caused you a great deal of pain. Don't even think about trying to get your child to feel sorry for you. It won't work in the long run, even if it appears to work on occasion.

Most importantly, if you are a parent of an intense child who has witnessed or suffered from parental abuse, let the child see that any attempts to throw you off will not result in getting out of doing a consequence. Don't apologize for giving a consequence. If the child tries to use apologies to avoid consequences, keep in mind that you do not want your child to link being hurtful to loving moments of closeness. Believing this is a precursor of being a perpetrator of even more violent action. We want him to see that true closeness is only accessible by way of positive choices and actions.

You do not have to give reassurance of your love. Every time you give an appreciation or a consequence, you are giving your child love. If the recognition is happening regularly, your child already knows that you love him.

Stick to the plan of short but decisive time-outs when rules are broken even a little bit. Then, hold the course, because it will take significantly more testing before a child who has experienced domestic violence will stop testing and reinvest her enormous reserve of energy into successful endeavors. Stay the course. Stay the course. Stay the course!

You're in for a wonderful surprise: the level of satisfaction you will find in your therapeutic role when eventually you change the course of your child's life. If you see this through, you will not only enjoy a positive relationship with your child, but you will not have to worry about your child becoming an abusive spouse or parent. Those who work this issue out in relation to a child also become much clearer in all their other relationships.

History Lessons

In our clinical practice, it is very rare that we spend time discussing family history. Yes, we are aware that other therapists deeply value history and the challenge of unraveling the past as a segue to a more inviting future; however, we find that there are equally exciting and quicker ways to set the stage for a healthier now, without dredging up the pond.

People come to therapists because they desire change. They would like change to occur both as rapidly as possible and in a way that has lasting effect.

Imagine you've called a plumber about a sewage problem. When he arrives, do you want him to spend the entire "treatment" period discussing the history of the system rather than fixing the leak? What would it be like to have him return and continue the inquiry on subsequent visits? You might well begin to understand your plumbing better, but unless the repair actually got underway, you might become anxious to see some results.

Discussion of history can easily make a parent feel blamed for past transgressions. No matter how delicately one explores factors such as broken relationships, past parenting styles, use of substances or family mental health background, a connection to the present problem is implied. Since history cannot be erased, this approach implies that we are stuck with the burden of the past, with little recourse—the last thing we would ever want to imply.

Getting to a level of real acceptance and letting go takes substantial time and work for most people. There's nothing wrong with moving in that direction, but **this intervention is designed to work *right now,* without extensive processing of past events.** The only time we occasionally find exploring history useful in the context of this approach is when treatment has ground to a halt because the parent is stuck.

For example, a parent might have a tough time giving recognition to a child because of resentment or grief about not having been given recognition in childhood. In cases like these, it might be helpful to review the parent's experience as a child as a lead-in to what she would like to see in her child's experience. How can she bring herself to deliver emotional nutrition to her child despite her own deprivation? Often, the positive steps the parent is already taking ultimately transport her to the next level of helping the child. **A parent's success in this venture enormously helps her own healing process.** We've seen so many examples of this. Applauding and appreciating a parent over and over for her new, extraordinary efforts propels this new world of success for her. In this regard, please be appreciative of the great efforts you have made so far and the great wisdom and determination you are exercising every step of the way.

Trust and Success

When basic trust is established with the very intense child, many things fall into place. The child can relax, as if for the first time. His shoulders drop. His basic way of being in the world, his way of relating to self and others, and his style of having his basic needs for attention met are transformed and consequently blossom. He moves to a higher level of functioning.

Learning to trust allows a child to abandon habitual failure and reinvest her energies in success. A world of possibilities opens up. She can safely resume both childhood and childlike qualities; and at the same time, she comes to enjoy the intrinsic and external rewards of responsibility.

Trust comes when a child feels able to rely on his caregivers. The child comes to trust when he senses that his structure can be counted on and that it will exist, come rain or shine. The structure is trustworthy when it is an anchor—when the child can count on being noticed, enjoyed and recognized for the good things he is doing, and when he can count on being held accountable in a predictable and neutral manner for any rules he breaks. **If the basic structure is not consistent, the child remains guarded.**

A child does not learn to trust through a discussion of nine good reasons to trust. Your child does not come to trust you just because you claim you are trustworthy. True trust is a product of actual life experiences. These experiences must promote the reliability and consistency that lead the child to the feeling that life is safe and trustworthy.

We've met hundreds of young people who were out of control, sometimes gang- and drug-involved, who resumed their healthy and appropriate childlike qualities when their parents got back in charge. A child can give up the urge to act "cool" and 10 years older than she really is and, instead of seeking attention by smoking and dressing to meet peer codes, learn to trust and draw on an inner sense of worth and self-respect. As worth and trust grow, risk of acquiescing to peer pressure falls.

Children can withstand the pressures exerted by peers when they begin to trust who they are and when they feel truly stronger on the inside. They cannot go out and lift weights to make themselves stronger on the inside. They need a different sort of personal fitness trainer—someone who helps them to feel progressively stronger on the inside through repeated exercising of recognition and appreciation for the successful choices they are making.

Existing models of parenting barely accomplish this for the average child. More often than not, they serve to actually weaken the at-risk child. They accidentally give overwhelming evidence of more recognition when things are going wrong. If the child is only recognized when he is acting out, he comes to trust that he is worthiest for his negativity.

Power, Structure and Freedom

Children's attraction to and fascination with the power struggles depicted in action movies and TV is really about power over their own lives, not power over others. They are attracted, at their core, to this internal power—a power that comes from the freedom to make choices. Real freedom comes in not being a slave to locked-in ways of acting. Trusting the external structure leads to trusting one's internal compass and one's ability to make good choices. This leads to ever-deeper levels of true empowerment.

Intense and challenging children desperately need help in getting their inner power on line. They need to be noticed for all their efforts and instances in which they control their impulses, emotions and actions in approximations of healthy ways. These are the rudimentary beginnings of personal power and are an early movement toward being empowered to appreciate their many-faceted selves. **They need our help in seeing the glory of these new choices and the resultant new "portfolio" of who they *really* are.**

Success has a life of its own. It becomes second nature, like breathing. The child who begins to feel successful deepens his positive experiencing of self as someone worthy of attention for positive actions and attitudes. He begins to see himself as worth acknowledgment for his ability to control impulses, emotions and intensity in healthy and balanced ways. This beautifully brings the child to higher and higher trajectories of manifesting successfulness and greatness.

Pulling the Rug Out

When a child acts out as a way of temporarily resuming his previous comfort zone of failure, we say that he or she is "pulling the rug out." Expect this, and know that persistence in your stands will make all the difference here.

As your child begins to trust that your recognition is predictably and reliably available in response to positive efforts, she begins to experience recognition from the inside out. As she absorbs recognition externally, she begins to feel worthy of the esteem in which she is being held. She will be able to handle increasing levels of success before becoming uncomfortable and pulling the rug out. Her threshold of tolerance for positive acknowledgment will rise.

In time, with your perseverance in the face of these kinds of challenges, the child will reach a place where the danger of self-sabotage is minimal because he has become used to higher and higher levels of success. This is somewhat like acclimating to a higher altitude. It takes adjustment.

Remember that self-esteem is a product of holding one's self in esteem. This is absolutely born out of an inner experience and perception of having been truly and reliably held in esteem at a level of basic trust.

Having arrived at this crucial juncture of trust in her positive opinion of herself, a child can perform the miraculous. She can not only demonstrate more love for others because she has much more to give in terms of recognition and appreciation, but she also can give recognition and appreciation to herself. She is emotionally nurtured.

You have been massaging your child's heart with a powerful level of nurturing. The payoff is an intense child who can use her intensity well…to be constructive, productive and more loving of self and others. The payoff is a child with *inner wealth*. We have found that almost all children can ultimately be inner billionaires.

Chapter Thirteen
The Energy-Challenged Child
Emotions and Therapy

F LYING A PLANE IS SIMPLEST when the sky is clear and visibility is distinct. When the sky is pitch black or when the weather plays havoc with flying conditions, the pilot must rely heavily or entirely on the plane's instruments.

This is similar to our own plights in navigating through life. When it's clear sailing, we need very little from our instruments. But when situations are unfamiliar or more intense or when obstacles loom, readouts from our emotional indicators are needed to provide vital information.

Our repertoire of emotions—anger, sadness, joy, fear, frustration, satisfaction, excitement, rage, indignation or anxiety—can help define what we wish to pursue or avoid. Emotions are vital for providing guidance and direction. The more fine-tuned our sensitivities and the greater our facility in reading emotions, the greater the possibility of making positive, reliable decisions.

Back to the airplane metaphor for a second: We surely want to refuel before absolutely necessary and we want to avoid losing altitude when we cross a mountain range. We also want to avoid lowering our landing gear until we're approaching a safe landing. Similarly, in our lives, many outcomes of actions and relationships rely on accurate access to information.

Emotions are energy. They not only give us vital information, but can provide the fuel that powers our pursuits, shapes our purpose and clarifies aspects of who we are.

We evolve in our ability to handle our emotions. Children are not born with the ability to decipher their feelings or contain their intensity. Life events that stir up strong emotions can easily be overwhelming to children. Intense feelings can have detrimental rather than positive results, especially for children already troubled by elevated levels of energy.

Most energy-challenged children do not have sufficient wherewithal to contain and utilize their emotions to their advantage. Instead, strong emotions can throw them into a tailspin. For example, a child who is reeling from a traumatic family event, such as exposure to inordinate family stresses, trauma or violence or to some form of abuse, may not have the inner resilience to handle her subsequent strong feelings. The extra energy produced by the strong emotions, without the matching inner structure, could very likely spill over into problematic behaviors.

All children need multifaceted coaching in learning how to handle strong feelings. If a child is not comfortable with his own inner boundaries in regard to appropriate emotional expression and lacks the skills of self-control, then his inner emotional agitation or discomfort can easily lead to acting-out. From this perspective, negative behaviors and depressed life activity, which are flip sides of the same coin, are both forms of energetic acting-out.

Anyone who has ever tried to make a feeling go away—by denying it, sleeping it away, distancing, stuffing one's face, going on a shopping spree, drinking or drugging, or by taking it out on another—knows that feelings can be scary.

Even adults struggle with how to handle feelings. Even those who know why they are experiencing strong feelings may not have the wherewithal to contain them. Adults who consciously work hard on figuring out their emotions are often left in the psychological dust for their efforts. Adults who ventilate their emotions with great determination as well as those who keep their emotions buried may still find a path strewn with difficulties and may still act out in various ways.

Emotions are complex and there are few, if any, simple answers. How many people are under the impression that there is a little bag of anger or sadness within and that "getting these emotions out" provides relief? How many therapists operate on this principle?

How many people have the belief that knowing what feelings are beneath their actions will lead to emotional health and solutions? How many therapists try to apply this principle as an initial means to help the out-of-control child?

We cannot tell you how often we have met families whose children were receiving treatment based on the above principle but continued to tear their hair out because the child was doing distinctly worse. The negative acting-out continued while the therapist recommended more of the same treatment. The parents were feeling progressively more out-of-control as they waited for something good to happen. These children had been labeled with ADHD, Oppositional Defiant Disorder, Post-Traumatic Stress Disorder, Reactive Attachment Disorder, adjustment disorders, depression and more.

What makes us think we can we can apply therapies that are so ineffective with adults to children? How many adults have the wherewithal to handle very intense feelings? Some children are actually re-traumatized when therapy turns to an excavation of awful feelings. Most children simply want to get on with their lives with order and predictability restored. They are not invested in revisiting hurtful times and places.

Most children are not ready to do the scary process of emotional

exploration, which frequently further overwhelms them with the feelings that they already can barely contain. Often this leads to further acting out, increased confusion and lower self-esteem.

A child's acting out negatively often leads to situations in which the child is over-empowered. The child ends up with the illusion that he's in charge, whether he perceives that he has a parent over a barrel or that he can put one over on a parent through cunning or confrontation. **We have yet to meet a child who is over-empowered in this way who is happy.** However, we have met many unhappy children who made remarkable recoveries when their parents began to reshape a safe structure and to regain benevolent control.

Children begin to experience healthy control of their own lives as they experience, assimilate and integrate the healthy control exerted by their caregivers. They do not learn it from lectures, books, reasoning or other attempts at therapeutic implant. They learn from the overarching processes and experiences to which they are exposed.

Creating clear boundaries around what's okay and what is not by actively reinforcing positive efforts and assigning consequences for errant behaviors goes a long way to helping these children feel safe with their strong emotions. If the lines of demarcation are clear, your child will learn faster. If boundaries are fuzzy and your active recognition and limit setting are weak, learning will falter.

We see this situation frequently with children who have intense feelings as a result of a medical situation. Out of compassion for a child who is suffering, it is often the reaction of adults to modify the existing structure, softening the rules because they simply do not have the heart to hold this child accountable. Unfortunately, the child needs structure more than ever and will escalate efforts to obtain it by pushing the envelope even more. This is a deadly combination of factors that can easily produce a tyrant. We have seen this in children with cancer, heart disease and various forms of autism.

Even with a grave medical situation or disability, it is more compassionate to provide a safe container by upholding a strong level of rules and appreciation than to let go of the reins and allow the container to dissolve. We know this because we have seen children in these situations resume well-adjusted lives when their parents step up the level of their parenting, despite the emotional pain of the medical situation.

This is true of any situation that generates feelings that are stronger than the child's fragile ecology can handle. **At times when a child is emotionally overwhelmed, rather than relinquishing rules out of compassion, you may well find it more compassionate to add a few.** This simply creates more opportunities to appreciate the child when these rules are not being broken.

The Upswing

Emotions are not the bad guys. They have the capacity to deeply enrich our lives if we get to the point where they don't scare the heck out of us. In fact, emotions can be a tremendous source of energy, courage and determination. If we don't get lost in our emotions, they can deepen our resolve, give us vital information and inspire us to great accomplishments.

Look at many of the great artists, poets, dancers and authors who have used their strong emotions to create great works. Look at great leaders like Martin Luther King who have employed strong emotions to better the world. They did not use their emotions in self-destructive ways. However: think about how many people make themselves or others miserable with their intense emotions, creating strife, misery, war and insanity. And these are the very same emotions experienced by people who manifest greatness. The key is in how these emotions, and the energy they represent, are directed.

Emotions are strong waves of energy. Without internal structures to channel this energy into successes, emotions and behaviors related to those emotions become the downfall of many. Just as electricity, fire, water or wind can be sources of great power or great destruction, the bottom line is in how we use them. Until we learned how to harness these natural energetic forces, we had to use their power tentatively. A stronger force like atomic energy comes along and we have to exercise extreme caution until we possess the structure to handle it safely while putting its tremendous power to work.

This does not entail in-depth exploration of emotions. For children who are overwhelmed by their natural forces—their energy and their emotions—we must question the wisdom exploring their emotions in an attempt to get the children to get these feelings out of their system. We must question the wisdom of inadvertently giving children the underlying message that these powerful emotions are bad, as if they were a malignancy that had to be surgically removed. How many children in foster care wind up having disrupted placements and further trauma because therapy has pushed the process of opening up feelings? A child's way of letting us know she cannot handle something in her existing internal structure is to act out in escalating ways.

Many parents have come to us for treatment and have subsequently helped their child to quick and solid recoveries after years of worsening problems while the child floundered in individual therapy. The therapist might have been under the impression that treatment was proceeding well, but at what expense? Often the child was falling apart at home and school and the parents were completely stressed out by trying to pick up the pieces.

In many such cases, the acting out continued while a marriage faltered or went by the wayside due to the added stress. Many children went progressively down the tubes. While the therapist was busy building what he or she deemed to be critical working rapport, the child was being further traumatized by the continuing saga of negative life events largely related to his out-of-control behaviors and the overwhelming self-perpetuating spiral of consequent emotions.

As therapists, we question whether an hour spent to discuss a problem with a child might accidentally wind up as further convincing him that the most reliable way to obtain a connection and payoff from others is through problems. A child in individual treatment because of behavioral issues could well conclude the animated interest in him would go away if his willingness to create a flow of problems ceased to exist.

Let's stop imposing models of therapy that inconsistently work with adults onto our children while waiting and waiting for something magical to happen. We've known so many foster children with long strings of broken placements where the waiting is still happening. We've known so many emotionally intense children who had to endure broken lives while individual therapy remained the only route of treatment.

Foster children are often burdened with past traumas that bring up frightening emotions. We are thrilled to report that entire foster care agencies are using the Nurtured Heart Approach. A great program in New Jersey chose to require foster parents to use the approach and they have quickly reached the amazing plateau of no longer having any broken placements—a huge change from an average of 20-plus percent of placements broken in prior years. **When the safety of structure is in place, these children who carry strong emotions are as capable of success as anyone—possibly more so, because strong emotions are gifts as long as their energy is properly channeled.**

Exploring the past and the emotions linked to it in therapy isn't out of the question with this approach. It's just not the best *first* intervention. First, get the proper structure into place so that a child can achieve an inner sense of being able to handle strong feelings. Then, when she is more self-motivated, she can utilize exploratory therapies to advantage.

A great poet once said that we can live by our fire or die by it. One dies by his fire when he does not use his gifts. If a child grows up scared of strong feelings and under the impression that strong emotions always lead to problems, then it is unlikely that he can use his passion to fuel his life. This is the death of spirit.

Let's focus on helping to make children's emotions useful and purposeful instead of random, chaotic and overwhelming. They desperately need our external models of structure to create their own inner structure as they move toward adulthood.

Here are some examples of ways to lend structure to emotions, which will help your child find her comfort zone with stronger feelings:

- **Your child is very disappointed after asking permission for something and being told "no."** Before he explodes you can help him enormously by describing what you notice with active recognition:

  "I see that you're very disappointed. I appreciate that you are controlling your strong feelings. You are not yelling or screaming or throwing a tantrum. I'm going to give you some credits for handling your feelings well."

- **Your child is very angry about not being allowed to go somewhere.** Before the blowout, let your child know in an excited way that you notice the frustration and you are very proud she is handling strong feelings well. You might mention that she is using a good attitude or being responsible.

  If your child disagrees with your comment, do yet another Video Moment:

  "I can tell by what you're saying that you disagree. I want you to know it's okay to have strong feelings and I really appreciate that you're making an effort to handle your feelings without breaking rules. You're mad, but you're not arguing, fighting or breaking things. That's exciting to me."

The key is in catching the strong feeling before it spills over into unacceptable behavior. Anyone can do it, no matter how intense the child. You just have to stay on your toes. See the cup as half-full. Create the moment. Once the connection is made, that much more of your excitement can be had for the positive aspects of handling emotions. At that juncture, a great deal of skill-building can be accomplished.

Let your children have their feelings. It's their right. It's so easy to imply that something's wrong with a child or his feelings if we question or pry or try to "fix" a feeling or by trying to "help" it go away. It's ultimately empowering to the child, in a healthy way, if he sees that he can handle his own feelings. He will share them increasingly as he is ready. You're cutting a helpful path simply by pointing out what it looks like he's feeling and letting him know you appreciate his efforts.

The Ripple Effect

The Ripple Effect refers to a phenomenon in the world of family treatment where the family is viewed as a system and where all actions within the system affect all the other people in that system. Therefore, **it's very possible to work with just one person who is motivated and determined, regardless of the presence or absence (or cooperation) of a partner, and produce dramatic effects quickly.**

Frequently, we'll work with a parent whose partner is part of the problem. One parent may show up with wonderful determination, but cannot begin to imagine that the spouse will ever be affected. Sometimes, the spouse is out of control in some way (habituated to alcohol, drugs or other self-destructive patterns). Other times it is more a case of resistance to new ideas or loyalty to what worked in his or her culture or family of origin.

Once the determined parent realizes the power of taking stands with a child, sees the positive effects and recognizes the powerful scope of the tools she is using, the power spills over to every aspect of her life.

If a parent feels inadequate and overwhelmed by the behaviors of her child, she is in no position to tell her spouse how to do it any differently. Her voice will have no power. It will be virtually impossible to have an impact. However, once the parent begins to feel competent and expert in parenting her child through actual experience, and she sees the change that her efforts have created, then that parent finds her voice… with her spouse, with the extended family, with the school, the sitter and anyone else involved.

When you reach this point, you know exactly what your child needs and what you need. That is true power. It will exude in the clarity of your voice and you will likely get what you want or be able to clear away people who are not contributing to the solution. The most frequent outcomes are that the nonparticipating or sabotaging spouse comes around or is "fired." **Ninety-five percent of the time, the nonparticipating spouse takes note of the positive changes and comes around voluntarily or when asked to contribute to the new solution**. Occasionally, the nonparticipating parent continues to resist change. The active parent is able to fully experience, from her new vantage point of skillfulness and positive effect on their child, how the partner adversely affects the progress. When this cannot be worked out, the new scenario sometimes leads to a parting of ways—which, under some circumstances, turns out to be the best thing for everyone involved.

Here is a real-life example of the Ripple Effect. A few years back, we worked with a family in which the mother came in for treatment, ostensibly because her daughter was getting out of control. The mother was on a leave-of-absence from work. Her supervisor found her in tears over her computer terminal several days running and moved her through the company's health service program. Initial consultation and evaluation found her to be depressed and they sent her to a psychiatrist for medications and counseling.

She was depressed because she cared so deeply about her two children and her stepchildren and felt she was losing them. The older kids were being extremely defiant and the younger ones were taking notes. To make matters worse, her husband was very uncomfortable coming home to chaos and having to play the role of the heavy. He flipped between coming on too strong in his parenting and his negative response to his wife and withdrawing and disappearing for increasingly longer periods. His wife suspected he was stopping at friends' homes or going to a bar. He started coming home drunk or stoned and belligerent. The marital tension mounted.

The Employee Assistance Program wanted therapy for the kids and wanted the father to have treatment for both substance abuse and domestic violence. She felt like no match for her husband and withdrew rather than confront him. When she attempted to speak up, she wound up feeling worse because she had no impact and he was withdrawing further. She felt isolated, abandoned and alone, with four kids who were beginning to believe she was driving their dad away.

Here's how that ball of wax unraveled, rapidly. This mother was a quick study of the Nurtured Heart model. Her husband had shown up for only the first session, and when he then dropped out, she decided to implement the techniques on her own. Within five weeks she had the "problem child" and the rest of her kids on the system and observed an enormous impact. Her children, with the added structure, were beginning to feel very successful despite the problems with their dad.

The defiant daughter, who had been very unhappy, was now tickled to be successful and finally to have a parent in charge. Again, we have never met an over-empowered child who is happy. You can make a million attempts to entertain him and get him things and he will remain unhappy. He is making desperate attempts to get his parents to take back the reins, and when this occurs, he will become happy again in record time.

Of equal importance was that the mother was no longer depressed. In fact, she was thrilled by the impact she was having on her children. Parenting is a huge part of who we are. When it's not going well, it's hard to not feel depressed or stressed. She was now prepared to return to work and no longer needed medications or therapy. And, without any direct input from us, she had told her husband what she needed from him if he were to remain in the home.

She made her expectations of him in relation to the children and herself perfectly clear. She now had a voice and was heard. Her partner initially decided to stay away from the home for a few weeks. By now he had gotten heavily into cocaine. The mother took a stand with him and her in-laws.

On the occasions when he visited the children, he now witnessed a well-organized home with a composed parent enjoying her children. After a few weeks of self-imposed exile, he agreed to the terms of return.

On his own, he then rapidly cleaned up his act and returned to enjoying work, wife and family life. He needed no further treatment for substances or abuse and, although the system would have had her on three medications for depression along with therapy, his wife absolutely did not require any additional treatment. Many professionals viewing the defiant daughter at the beginning of treatment would have recommended individual treatment. She too required no further treatment. The debacle of piecemeal reactivity to each and every separate issue in this situation was avoided by the positive rippling effect of one person's determination.

Both spouses started feeling and expressing appreciation of the other, the children and themselves. They could now set limits when they were needed, although the need grew rarer and rarer.

Healing Depression

Parenting is a big piece of who we are. It makes total sense that a parent tends to be depressed when a child's behaviors are out of control and when the school and the neighborhood are offering complaints without solutions. That is a scary, depressing situation. However, depressed parents can make remarkable recoveries when their child begins to thrive.

When the child begins doing better, especially through the skilled work of a parent who is now having a therapeutic effect, both the child and the parent have reason to be proud. Our experience is that, more often than not, whatever parental depression previously existed miraculously dissolves—an outcome that springs from the aforementioned ripple effect. The holistic interrelatedness of child with parents and parents with community triggers the benefits enjoyed by the child to flow outward to those who support him. This sounds simplistic but it's true. This result contradicts a lot of old theories that say that one must painstakingly work out every last molecule of disdain and depression in a therapist's office.

Depression is also a frequent visitor in the lives of our challenging children. It's hard to imagine a more depressing scenario than the one lived by a bright child with intense energy who sees her world crumbling. She notices how distraught she can make parents and teachers and feels addicted to pushing the limits and frequently gets into trouble; yet, she often can still manipulate her way to privileges. She hates being a problem and hears the urging to do better, and she knows she can do better. Still, she habitually feels pulled toward the high payoffs of negative behaviors. For this child, life stinks, and it's confusing to boot.

If we treat this intense child for depression, we might have to wait years to see change occur. The issue is not some biochemical balance within her brain; it's the fact that her life is systematically depressing. She leaves the therapist's office and goes back into a depressing, confusing existence. She may, over time, become more resilient and learn to handle it better, but a far better solution exists. That is to use new techniques of parenting that draw the child systematically into a new way of life that is clear, fair and predictable. As the child experiences the joy of using her intensity in positive ways, depression typically dissolves. Then, both the parent and child have a firsthand experience of mastery and accomplishment. Depression may still exist, but not in the same old significant and debilitating ways.

In case you haven't noticed, this planet has several built-in depressing features. Despite the fact that some people are portrayed in the media as having perfect lives, most lives are less than perfect and sometimes messy. Everyone is depressed at times, to differing degrees. It's how we handle the depressing features of life's imperfections that makes all the difference in the world.

There's a term in family therapy parlance called "detouring," which refers to attempts by a child to distract a parent from his or her pain. A common manifestation of detouring might occur when a child feels uncomfortable with a parent's stress, anger or depression and attempts to distract the parent by acting out. The acting-out is the child's attempt to divert the parent long enough to deal with the negative behavior. In the child's mind, it is often worth the trouble to get the parent activated. Such a child is truly worried about the parent and may feel powerless to affect the situation in any other way. He also senses that, as long as the parent is self-involved with her own stresses, she is otherwise unavailable.

It becomes even more imperative that a parent in a funk, for whatever reason, does whatever it takes to parent, despite the strong emotional influence of depression. Given this prescription, most depressed parents not only manage to rouse the extra effort necessary, but find, ironically, that the effort and its effects contribute significantly to feeling much better themselves.

Chapter Fourteen
More on ADHD
Symptoms, Medication & Diagnosis

"MY CHILD HAS ADHD."

As therapists who specialize in helping intense children, we have heard this often in our offices. Although some parents come to us fairly well-informed about this diagnosis and the ways in which it's commonly treated, most only pick up bits and pieces of information from the media or the neighborhood. Some parents whose child has not been diagnosed will ask the therapist, "What is ADHD, anyhow?" to try to come, in a roundabout way, to solutions for dealing with their child's frustrating habitual behaviors.

This question is harder to answer than many parents expect. Many myths have been generated regarding ADHD. Even as diagnoses have become more and more common, with a prevalence rate of up to 20 percent of male children in some communities, parents are becoming increasingly wary of the stimulant drugs commonly used to treat ADHD. Many come to us in search of an alternative, and we are glad to report that the Nurtured Heart Approach is exactly that.

Although so many parenting books feature ADHD prominently, we have purposely saved this topic for the tail end of our work. We do so because we take a dramatically different view of the significance of this diagnosis and its relevance to the course of treatment.

What Every Parent Should Know About ADHD

ADD or ADHD (Attention Deficit Disorder, with or without hyperactivity), as currently diagnosed, is not much more than a laundry list of 14 descriptive symptoms, which to differing degrees describe virtually every person who ever walked the planet. Everyone is distractible sometimes. Everyone seeks attention sometimes. The formal diagnosis of ADD or ADHD is proffered when a child shows significant manifestations of any six of the 14 descriptions on a consistent basis over a six-month period.

These "symptoms" thus become the disorder. This is the fundamental model of biological psychiatry, where we are encouraged to pathologize certain inconvenient behaviors and "treat" them with pharmaceuticals with dubious safety records. Parents are encouraged to see this disorder as some sort of biological imbalance that requires re-balancing with a drug to make the child "normal." The hard truth is that this practice is tantamount to drugging a child into submission when what he or she really needs is a different way of interacting with adults.

Many of the people making the ADHD diagnosis— school nurses, teachers and other school personnel, as well as neighbors, relatives and family members who do not hold a license in a related subject—are unqualified to do so. Even qualified professionals may be limited in their ability to see the child with these symptoms in a light that is beneficial to that child and his family.

Instead of labeling a child as disordered and her parent as dysfunctional, isn't it possible that both manifestations are a function of how we choose to view the things we see? Take a trip to your local museum of natural history and look at a slice of life from the past. Look at the tools of 50, 100, and 150 years ago and then imagine the tools that will be in use that far into the future. Those old tools don't work anymore. The same goes for traditional parenting tools.

Moving from the parenting tools of the past to those of the future requires changing entirely how we look at energy-challenged children and the way in which we work with them. As we make this shift, we see that the malfunctions of the intense child have been more a result of the tools available than a result of a disordered child or a dysfunctional adult. Given the right tools, children with ADHD-like symptoms are by far the easiest to transform.

Treatment through Medication

If you go to a golf instructor, the parameters of what you are offered are going to be fairly limited to ideas and interventions related to golf. If you show up with a tennis racket, the instructor might respectfully point out that, although there are some similarities in the weight shift, he is not in the business of teaching tennis. You'll be directed elsewhere or invited to drop the racket and to try using a golf club.

In the conventional scheme of things, families faced with the thought of dealing with ADHD are frequently directed into the narrow perspective of conventional medicine for the initial official assessment and treatment. Child psychiatrists, pediatricians and family medicine practitioners, although well-intentioned in their desire to help, are sometimes bound to a menu as limited as that of the golf pro when it comes to possible interventions.

If a child's intensity is viewed as a disorder, and disorders are bad and need to be fixed, then if you are a medical professional, you will probably try to alter the disorder by looking within the current medical bag of tricks to see what can best alleviate the intensity of the problem. This frequently translates to one medication or another. If a parent comes to a physician frantically pleading for a solution, what physician wouldn't want to provide a solution to the best of his or her ability?

A more holistic point of view, however, sees intensity as inherently a good thing. It may be annoying at times and of great concern when it escalates into a pattern of problem behaviors, but those who are willing to look outside of the medical/pharmaceutical box can find a way to redirect that intensity into a new pattern of success rather than medicating it into oblivion.

Current wisdom in the field is to recommend a "multi-modal approach" in relation to ADHD treatment. This is an allopathic (mainstream medical) concept. It almost always means that medication is front and center in the regime. If the holistic view—that the intensity and energy are positive—were in effect, doctors would be more cautious about prescribing medications. **Why would physicians want to tamper with the energy system as a first-line intervention, especially if energy is viewed as a gift?**

Our Informal Study

Don't let anyone tell you that medication isn't still a first-line intervention. Some years ago, a referral system change brought a change in the kids who came our way. Up until then, we were getting only the most difficult children, those who had been in the public mental health system for years and in most cases were already on medications. Then, suddenly, many children were referred to us who had the very same kinds and degrees of presenting problems, but who had not yet been sent to a primary care physician or child psychiatrist for an evaluation.

There is no doubt whatsoever that a high proportion of these new referrals would have been given medications as a first-line intervention had they seen a psychiatrist first. As of 2003—the most recent year for which data could be found—between 64 and 70 percent of the 7.4 million children initially evaluated for ADHD were given medications right away.[4]

We devised an informal study to monitor the outcomes of 50 consecutive cases of this nature. In the families that entered into and completed the two- to three-month course of the Nurtured Heart Approach (we were required to keep a child in treatment for three months even if the case was ready for closure in one month), 85 percent of the children were able to leave treatment essentially symptom-free, without the need for any medications. The primary exception was a relatively small percent of children who had improved but were still hyperactive to a detrimental level. It was decided that these children could potentially benefit from medication, and they were referred to a physi-

---

4. Toh, Sengwee, B. Pharm., M.Sc., "Datapoints: Trends in ADHD and Stimulant Use Among Children, 1993-2003," *Psychiatric Services* 2006 Aug;57:1091.

cian. Tracking of the many hundreds of children seen at our clinic revealed that six percent of these children ended up being referred for an evaluation. Ultimately, only three percent were deemed to need medications.

We are actually much more cautious, at the time of this revision (in 2013) of the physical, emotional and psychological side effects of stimulant medications and we rarely feel there is need for it after treatment by way of the Nurtured Heart Approach.

Based on what we have seen, we exhort any parent who thinks that their child requires medication for ADHD to try this approach first. Although we are very glad that medications exist, we see the need to re-examine their wholesale use, as many children who are prescribed these drugs do not need them. Considering the use of any drug involves careful consideration of benefits versus risks, and with ADHD drugs, risks have been underplayed and underexplained in many cases. Below, find the short version of the argument against using ADHD drugs unless absolutely necessary. If you want a much more detailed explanation of these risks, please refer to my book, *101 Reasons to Avoid Ritalin Like the Plague* (Nurtured Heart Publications, 2005).

The Hazards of ADHD Drugs

When a doctor prescribes a psychiatric drug to your child, there's no way to know ahead of time whether 1.) it will have the desired effect, or 2.) it will cause side effects that prove either unmanageable or that the doctor will want to treat with an additional drug, which could in turn cause side effects or be ineffective. Any psychiatrist or psychologist who is willing to level with patients will tell you that psychiatric drug prescribing is more of an art than a science.

Here are some of the side effects that have been reported for the major classes of ADHD drugs:

Stimulants (including Ritalin, Adderall, Concerta, Dexedrine, and Metadate): Blood pressure and pulse changes (increased and decreased), rapid heartbeat, angina, irregular heartbeat, palpitations, dizziness, headache, inability to sit still, drowsiness, Tourette's syndrome, growth suppression, toxic psychosis, anorexia, nausea, abdominal pain, weight loss (during prolonged therapy), hypersensitivity reactions (skin rash, itching, pain, dermatitis), rebound hyperactivity, nervousness, insomnia, abdominal pain, hallucinations, aggressive behaviors, and vision disturbances. May mask symptoms of fatigue, impair physical coordination, or produce dizziness or drowsiness severe enough to impair driving ability.

Most frightening—if most rare—are the possibilities of psychosis or sudden death related to heart problems in children who use stimulants long-term. Between 1992 and early 2005, 27 children (18 and under) who were taking stimulants died suddenly. About half were found to have underlying heart defects or ailments. Package inserts for stimulant ADHD now include patient warnings about increased risks of hallucinations, delusions, manic or aggressive behavior, as well as cardiovascular problems.

Atomoxetine (Strattera), a non-stimulant ADHD drug: Abdominal pain, vomiting, nausea, fatigue, irritability, decreased weight, decreased appetite, anorexia, headache, sleepiness, dizziness, rash, mood swings, heart palpitations, dry mouth, constipation, insomnia; in adults, urinary hesitation or retention, erectile dysfunction, priapism (an erection lasting four or more hours), irregular periods, sweating, hot flashes.

Beyond the many physical risks and side effects of ADHD medications, there is a compelling psychological side effect that is rarely spoken of: that **a child who is medicated comes to feel that his intensity is a bad thing that must be made to go away because it scares people and causes problems.** He also may infer that **he cannot possibly be in charge of his strong feelings and energy—that he needs a pill to gain self-control.** This is not a message that will help the majority of children in the long run. With the right tools and plan, children can easily learn to handle their intensity well.

When we tell a child she needs medications we essentially are saying she can't handle her life force, and neither can anyone else. We contend that when a child comes to be afraid of her intensity/life force she comes to feel a huge void in her life. On the heels of this shift comes an enormous sense of loss of impact and accomplishment.

When we put a child on medications, the commensurate unspoken message to the parent is, "You are having no impact on this child and there is no hope that you will in the near future." Any big-picture look at the use of ADHD drugs is incomplete without a clear look at the danger posed by these debilitating underlying communications.

The "Brain Disorder" Misconception

People who are proponents of "brain disorder" theories may not be considering that a child faced with living with this label may feel a lifetime of shame, as well as a lifetime of issues related to responsibility.

If a child comes to feel that there is something wrong with his brain, it stands to reason that our courts will be clogged with people who have acted out and who argue that they lacked the control to act responsibly. Some paid professional witness will argue on their behalf that a brain disorder was responsible, not the person. It is time to get off that train. It only goes downhill.

Juvenile correction facilities are full of children who are and have been on medications and are still out of control. Medications inherently do not solve the control problem. On the contrary, they inadvertently teach kids that we've given up on our ability to control them and their ability to control themselves.

Was it really ADHD and worth medicating if, four sessions into working with the Nurtured Heart model, the child is doing incredibly well and his intensity is well on its way to becoming jet propulsion for his greatness? Was it worth giving a diagnosis that will stay in a child's medical files forever, and might interfere with future insurability or acceptance into programs requiring a clean bill of health?

It is not an uncommon psychiatric position to believe that most behavioral disorders are physiologically based brain disorders, and that treating these conditions through medications is comparable to treating diabetes through the use of insulin.

There is an internal logic here, but neurotransmitter balance—the parameter affected by ADHD drugs—is a far less clear-cut parameter than insulin and blood sugar balance. Insulin injections never stop doing their job, but a child's neurotransmitter levels can change and shift in ways that alter the effectiveness of the ADHD drug over time. Type 1 diabetics need insulin for survival, and so must accept whatever risk insulin injections might pose; but how many children with ADHD are facing life-threatening consequences from this disorder?

We could go on, but you probably have heard enough to go with us on this point—that this comparison doesn't bear out; that obviously, we're looking at a different risk-benefit equation here.

Of course there is an interrelationship between the brain and behaviors. It works both ways, though. As the behaviors move to a new realm of success, the concurrent brain functions move to a healthy place. Doctors are only beginning to discover the biochemical basis behind this seemingly miraculous shift. No one knows for sure whether any alteration in neurotransmitter activity in the ADHD child is a cause or an effect of the disease; it's beginning to look as though you can change that balance not only with the blunt tool of medications, but also with the delicate, un-invasive tools offered by behavioral interventions such as the Nurtured Heart Approach.

Fortunately, many families don't have to take the risk of giving their child ADHD medications. Having treated as many children as we have, we have come to realize that what appeared to be brain-related when treatment began no longer seems so as treatment evolves.

All this having been said: medication is a needed fix in some cases. But keep in mind that even if medications give an initial illusion of improvement, the problem-oriented parent-child relationship still leads the way. The parent is none the wiser on how to best help the child without that little bottle of pills, and the child is none the wiser on how to best help himself. In this light, the "improvement" so fervently desired by adults pales in comparison to *transformation*.

What is this transformation, exactly? **It's an outcome in which the child moves fully forward to the magnificence of using his intensity in beautiful ways.** The child that makes this passage isn't just an ordinary child or an intense/difficult child, but flowers into an *intensely great* child. The same intensity that once created a seemingly exponential level of problems now propels equally exponential explorations of living life in great ways. Now you have the best child on the block – a much sweeter outcome than inconsistent medication-related improvements that often come packaged with side effects.

We think that in the heart of most every parent we have worked with, this sweeter outcome is what has been most wanted all along. Even if they opted for the illusion of a quick, medication-induced fix at some point in the downward spiral, their heart's desire has been for a child who believes in herself rather than in medications. They have wanted a child that could come around without pharmaceutical help.

Fortunately, we have heard of many child psychiatrists, pediatricians and primary care physicians who have reversed the old procedure by deferring prescriptions until parents have tried interventions like ours first. By taking this tack, even if they ultimately need to medicate, they have a truer clinical picture of the situation.

We believe that our informal study has held up over the years. At the very least, 90 percent of those who work with our model are able to avoid the need for medications completely. In 1998, The Tucson Center for the Difficult Child had 212 referrals. Sixty-one were already on medications; of those, 15 were taken off of their medications because of their good response to the methods we used. Of the 151 children not on medications, we only needed to refer eight for evaluations; only four of these ultimately needed medications.

It should also be said that pioneers in holistic medical health such as Dr. Sandy Newmark, Dr. Scott Shannon, Dr. Brian Cabin and Dr. Andrew Weil have demonstrated a strong impact of nutrition and other alternative interventions on the outcome of children with behavioral problems, disputing the beliefs of conventional medicine that foods and food allergies have no proven effects on behavior. Our nonmedical experiences confirm this and also confirm that, in addition to innovative ways of providing emotional, physical and spiritual nutrition, issues of food intake, exercise and lifestyle have an enormous overall effect on us all. This is particularly relevant to intense, energy-challenged children.

Left to her own devices, the energy-challenged child may make poor nutritional choices. Just as adults can easily form patterns around ways of self-regulating their energy level—perhaps by drinking coffee or alcohol, eating sugary foods, or smoking cigarettes—children begin self-regulating patterns through the intake of substances that affect their energy level. A child has plenty of energy-altering influences to choose from, including the subduing/stimulating effects of sweets and the subduing/stimulating effects of television.

While sweets and TV may not inherently pose problems, there are healthier ways for children to affect their energy level without becoming a slave to an outside influence. They can find stimulation in their excitement for sports or involvement in art, music or other focused endeavors. They can achieve quiet control over their intensity through calming activities such as reading, walking, meditation, yoga and other soothing endeavors.

For a fantastic treatise on a holistic medical prospective by a leading Pediatrician read *ADHD Without Drugs – A Guide to the Natural Care of Children with ADHD* (2010) by Sanford Newmark, MD. He conveys a brilliant and extensive command of the effects of environmental toxicity and influences, foods and supplements, alternative practices and exercise, as well as his sense of how the Nurtured Heart Approach dovetails with all of the ways he describes of moving your child toward robust and resounding health.

Chapter Fifteen
On Greatness
Tilting The Trajectory To The Top

O VER THE YEARS, the Nurtured Heart Approach has evolved in a number of ways. One of the most exciting developments since the first printing of this book in 1999 has been the experimentation of Howard Glasser and other practitioners with bringing forth the concept of greatness.

The question became: *how does one take appreciation, gratefulness, recognition and acknowledgment to the next level?* Howard came to feel that *gratefulness* was intrinsically linked to *greatness.* It seemed that at the deepest levels of gratefulness, the greatness of another person, oneself or a situation was revealed. And it seemed that a different level of power was unleashed in seeing and denoting greatness.

With this shift to recognition of greatness, we saw a change in the trajectory of ordinary appreciation. Children and adults being told about their greatness stopped in their tracks. It appeared as if their aliveness quickened; they got a glimpse of a dormant side of themselves that awakened in response to something they knew about themselves all along but had simply forgotton. It seemed like they were responding on a different level–a heartful, soulful level.

So how does one go about tapping into this higher level? **How do we confront a child with her greatness?** How do we ignite the greatness of a child and have it become a vital force in her life, so that a more magnificent side of her true nature is illuminated?

Our experiments in the past few years have led us to two simple yet amazingly powerful ways of acknowledging the greatness of another person.

1. The e-mail attachment. Think about the messages we send to children by way of the Nurtured Heart Approach as an e-mail. You verbally send a message of recognition, appreciation or acknowledgment, just as described throughout this book; then, send an additional message pertaining to greatness just as you would add an attachment to an actual e-mail. Here's an example:

"Billy, I really appreciate how you are getting along with your sister. You've been so nice to her this entire trip home and I love that you are using your sense of humor to keep her entertained."

And then you might add the 'attachment:'

"Your wonderful sense of humor and your style of being nice are qualities of your greatness that I love to see."

Another example:

"Jessica, thanks so much for keeping an eye on your brother in such a respectful and responsible way. These are great qualities that you have that I appreciate so much."

2. Get feedback from others in the room or from the child himself on how he is being great. After initiating a statement of appreciation or recognition, we ask whoever is in the room, "What does this say about her greatness?" When we first tried this, we were amazed at the answers we started getting from the children and adults we worked with.

For example:

"Bradley, I am grateful for your choice to come forward and tell the truth about this situation. What does this say about your greatness?"

Bradley might answer; the others in the room might answer; or you might fill in the blanks. Usually, everyone jumps right in. In this example, they might come up with:

"Well, first of all, it says you have great courage to reconsider your first response and to dare to change your mind. It shows you have great power and great judgment. It shows you can stand up to peer pressure; that is a great quality. And most of all, it shows you really care about the ethics of doing what is right, and that you wish to be helpful, to bring clarity and resolution to the situation…these are all qualities of your greatness."

As you can see you can go on and on, in any direction and to any extent.

Why the Greatness Piece?

So why bother with this additional step?

Look at people who are doing great things in their lives. It never fails that underneath the vestiges of the actual great works are qualities of greatness that seem to run the show.

Look at a woman like Oprah Winfrey. It's easy to watch her show and be in awe of some of her tremendously inspiring projects, but underneath this, some burning questions might arise: "How did she become so inspiring? So compassionate? So powerful? So wise? So caring and thoughtful?"

Aren't these qualities of greatness? We think so. Is Oprah fanning the flames of her greatness? Did these qualities and others just drop out off the sky, or is she purposeful in bringing these forth? Can you and I bring forth our qualities of greatness that form our unique version of being in the world? Can we acknowledge and inspire the very same for our children? Again—we think so.

We believe greatness is a given. It's there in all of us, right this moment. Most of us don't know it or think in these terms, but once we turn this faucet on, we really get to see how powerfully our hearts respond to these messages. Say something to a child about his greatness, and you will see that it was as if it were there all along, just waiting to bloom.

Isn't greatness what we all want to be anyway? **Would it ruin your life to wake up more great tomorrow morning? Would it ruin the life of your child or the others you know?** And if you woke up more thoughtful, considerate and compassionate, wouldn't that in a way be a spiritual experience? Wouldn't being greater in any of these ways awaken more wonderful response from the world and more wonderful aliveness in you? Wouldn't the truth be that this is a greater you? Would you rather be less great tomorrow when you awaken?

Look at all you've already done in getting to this point in this journey of transforming your child. If nothing else, you've read to this point and at least considered this information. This shows the greatness of openness. It already shows you care deeply about your child—another quality of your greatness. And if you have tried any of the strategies, you are demonstrating resolve and determination—further qualities of your greatness.

We hereby accuse you of greatness!

Our call to action is to take this to your child. Try, even now and then, adding an affirmation of the qualities of greatness to your recognitions of your child's successes. You will ignite and awaken something deep in your child's heart that will quicken her spirit and will give you all the more to cheer about.

Chapter Sixteen
Unveiling the Potential
New Horizons

VIRTUALLY ANY CHILD can be tuned to the frequency of success if you are willing to do what it takes: adopt ruthless and strategic opportunism, commitment and conscious determination. Remember that it takes more time and energy to handle problems than to take part in solutions.

Think about how grateful we feel at Thanksgiving time and how we open our hearts at other times such as the birth of a child or Christmas. **Imagine perpetuating that level of care into everyday moments.** After all, the present breath could be our last. We would be enormously grateful for this next breath if we weren't sure another would be available. If we weren't sure that another minute would be available with our child, ourselves and our other loved ones, we might well open our hearts to a wealth of everyday moments with great gratitude.

Stephen Levine, in *A Year to Live*,[5] states that "with 250,000 people dying each day, and knowing we are somewhere down the line, who has time to put life aside? We prepare for death by living every second, living life minutely, by exploring our body, mind and spirit with a merciful awareness. To be this close to the moment in which our life is unfolding," he continues, "we need to cultivate a deeper awareness through the development of a meditation practice."

A truly living meditation is an ongoing *taking notice* of all we encounter and feel. When we notice moment-to-moment fluctuations in the world around us and in our thoughts, moods, emotions and actions; and when we witness all of this with eyes and heart open and within the context of our usual everyday experiences, we are living in a meditative state. And this doesn't have to be boring, or even serious: you can choose to see the world with an amused and compassionate overlay—a kind of continuous Video Moment that embodies a healing awareness and sense of appreciation. **Just as we can cast an overlay of delight onto every thing a small child does right in a day, we can choose to do so with our perspective on the world in general.**

Life is composed of nothing but moments: this moment and each that ensues. Ten people viewing this same moment will see it in ten different ways;

---

5. Levine, Stephen, *A Year to Live: How to Live This Year as if it Were Your Last.* New York: Bell Tower, 1997, p. 39.

we are the directors and producers of the footage that comprises our lives. We get to apply our reason, humor, and perspective to each and every one of those moments. We get to tilt the camera any way that suits our tastes and sensibilities. We get to call in the voiceover to that footage. Each moment is a creative endeavor.

We can choose to hold an intention that changes every last second of existence into a sweeter reality. The way we choose to create each moment, each success, is an art form, and holding an intention that supports this endeavor instantly changes the nature and trajectory of our interactions. The way we choose to see and propel greatness is an art form that allows us to convert molecules into miracles.

When we bring this healing awareness to ourselves or others, we heighten aliveness. When we apply healing awareness to our children, we also, in effect, teach them the highest form of meditation. Taking notice becomes second nature. When children become adept at noticing how things make them feel, they become healthier and happier. It's only through denial, the opposite of taking notice, that detrimental patterns of drinking, drugging and other unhealthy activities can thrive. These are ways of turning away from life rather than toward it.

Taking notice is like creating on the inside a sun that peeks through the clouds to illuminate an awareness of something positive, any time it chooses.

Deep within the heart and mind of every child is a potential far beyond what we ordinarily see manifested, especially for the energy-challenged child. Fortunately, most devoted parents and teachers help readily accessible children tap into this incredible world of potential in a fairly straightforward way. However, devotion alone does not usually cut it in working with children who are less accessible. Devotion must be combined with skillfulness. Skillfulness will determine our approach and the way in which we strategically choose to deliver our love and energy.

As we apply skillfulness, we are going to be amazed as the very children who might have become lost souls in past generations—those intense children few knew how to handle—become the most special children in future generations. As we reach a critical mass of young people who are whole, who believe in themselves and others, who see and feel and appreciate the worth of themselves and others, who live their lives with greater clarity and resolve than ever before, who are stronger on the inside than ever before, and young people who are not afraid of their intensity, we will without doubt see a generation in which this same skillfulness is second nature. This generation will find it simple and natural to reveal the potential of one another, in the way that farming the bounty of the land was natural to past generations. It will be a generation in which the fruits of humanity are plentiful and amazing.

We are the revealers of the potential. **We get to play God by deciding what qualities we are going to energize.** We are the soil makers and the rainmakers. Plants always grow toward the sun, and we are in essence the sun for our children. Radiate your light lovingly and strategically. Go at it with a passion. Send your energy for every aspect of your child's potential you can imagine. Enjoy your imagination. *Go for the trajectory of greatness!*

Last Words and Reminders

Nurture your own heart. We all have a strong need to be noticed. How many people do we know who have developed a lifestyle based upon unfortunate ways of getting noticed? Those who do not feel successful on the inside—those who haven't developed the inner format to notice themselves for the good stuff—will tend to find a way to be noticed for aspects of themselves that lack purpose and direction.

If you believe that the only way you'll be noticed is for your outrageous remarks, appearance or strange activities, then a fair amount of your energy is going to go to fueling this pattern. If the only time you notice yourself is when you've screwed up, then you will perpetuate screwing up. That lifestyle is very prevalent and subtle. You'll see 90 percent of recreational athletes minimizing their glee over a halfway decent effort but kicking themselves into the next county for a poor outcome. This just perpetuates the pattern.

We tend to give a lot more impact and energy to our problems than we give ourselves credit for solutions or movement in the right direction. The way around this is to develop a mind-set and an assortment of techniques that *front-load* the attention you give yourself for the ordinary and everyday things that compose your life. If you sufficiently notice the simple things in yourself, you will not have to go to the trouble of having nonsense in your life in order to get excited.

A person who meditates focuses his attention to his breath or to his thoughts. We think that the enhancing effect of meditation can be greatly heightened by **practicing an internal version of the Nurtured Heart Approach. Appreciate, acknowledge and recognize yourself in detail and add pizzazz for the everyday ordinary tapestry of your life events and efforts.**

> "I like that I just spoke very respectfully to that customer. I didn't let her remark get to me and I resisted zinging her back with a snide comment. That was a great choice."

As simplistic as this may seem, thoughts like these will make a world of difference in the way you feel and see the world. If you give yourself energy for positive events, you'll feel successful and will spin off successes wherever you go. You may not need to have a medical crisis or a problem or mess up your diet or exercise routine to get your own attention.

Keep in mind how we parent ourselves internally along the lines of limit setting. Watch out for traditional consequences. If we internally chastise, lecture or debate over a problem, we wind up inadvertently energizing and rewarding the problem. We also may wind up perpetuating and reinforcing an internal pattern based on an impression that there is more response, animation and gratification to be obtained from a life of issues and failures.

You can refuse to do more of the same by having more energized and juicer self-appreciation. Take it to an even higher level by experimenting with noticing and acknowledging the qualities of greatness that you show each and every day.

Most people go a lifetime without ever being told how great they are or telling themselves about their greatness. We have such a lively ability to notice and wax poetically about even tiny increments of what is wrong, but can barely muster an under-energized "good job" for ourselves when it comes to something positive. Reflecting positives on one's self is regarded by many as self-indulgent or egotistical, but beating one's self up all day for the smallest perceived error is par for the course.

When a friend or loved one passes away we think nothing of providing glowing eulogies that reach deep into describing the far-reaching and extensive qualities of greatness that person has shown. This seems to be the case even when it has been glimmers let alone the more inspiring versions. So we know it is there, though how many people do we know who truly lay claim to their greatness while they are still alive? We are awakening and nurturing the greatness of our children. Now it is the time to awaken and nurture ours as well.

This will not only propel you further in what you are accomplishing in using this approach with your children and others, but also wait until you experience how it impacts your life.

Your greatness is a given. Your having read this book speaks volumes about your greatness. You care deeply; you are determined to find answers; you are open to alternative ways of looking at things; you have an intellect that supports the endeavor of digesting new information. You want the best for your child…the list goes on and on and on. *All of these qualities are aspects of your greatness.* Being determined, caring and open are not only great qualities, but qualities of YOUR greatness, which you express in your own unique ways.

Think back to some sporting event where you cheered wildly, and then consider how you put only a fraction of that energy into cheering for your own positive events. Be willing to notice small successes and movement in the right direction. **As in the sporting event, if something problematic happens, focus on solutions and put the problem behind you as quickly as you can. Stay intent on cheering your team.**

Keep remembering Shamu. It's great to have high expectations, but if we start with the rope at 22 feet we won't have very much to cheer about. It's okay to start with the rope underwater. It's okay to put rope everywhere. Think back to how excited you were when your child took her first steps. Be that excited about her beginning efforts in all her endeavors…and in all your endeavors!

And remember that success has a life of its own. In having become your child's therapist and in having shifted the way in which she switches her intensity from failures to successes, you have set a new life style in motion. Success will become second nature to your child, like breathing, and she will both attract successes from the outside and generate successes from the inside everywhere she goes.

Keep nurturing successes everywhere and you will see the fruits of a nurtured heart.

About the Authors

Howard Glasser is the founder of the Children's Success Foundation and creator of The Nurtured Heart Approach (NHA). Howard is dedicated to nurturing greatness in all children, especially the difficult or intense ones. Howard's set of core methodologies have been designed to help all children channel their intensity in successful ways. Using NHA, hundreds of thousands of parents, educators, and child-advocacy agencies around the world have awakened children to their own inner wealth.

Howard is the author of *Transforming the Difficult Child,* currently the top-selling book on ADHD; *Notching Up the Nurtured Heart Approach: The New Inner Wealth Initiative*, a leading book on school interventions; and *All Children Flourishing,* on using the Approach with all children, difficult or not. Four of his eight books are in the top one percent of all books on Amazon, confirming the need and relevance of his message and methodology at this moment in time.

Howard has been a featured guest on CNN, a consultant for 48 Hours, and has consulted for numerous psychiatric, judicial, and educational programs. He currently teaches the Nurtured Heart Approach through live presentations and internet-based courses via the Nurtured Heart Online University.

Although he has done extensive study in Clinical Psychology and Educational Leadership, Howard feels his own years as a difficult child contributed most to his understanding of the needs of challenging children. Without his experience and intuition, Howard believes the Approach would never have found such tremendous success.

Howard has been called one of the most influential living persons working to prevent children's reliance on psychiatric medications. His work also supports children in developing the inner strength to resist addictive substances.

Though the Nurtured Heart Approach began as a means for helping difficult or challenging children, Howard believes all parents and educators, even those with well-behaved children, can benefit from learning how to inspire thriving relationships with the people in their lives. He welcomes you to the Nurtured Heart Approach and in finding a new path to greatness.

Jennifer Easley, M.A., is a child mental health specialist and nationally certified counselor who has worked with difficult children and their families for over 30 years in community mental health settings. She has consulted in Seattle and Tucson school districts and believes that both parent and teacher support are instrumental in creating healthier children. She has worked with Howard Glasser in Tucson and is now living and practicing on Vashon Island in Washington. Her primary focus is on sharing non-conventional healing techniques with others. This is her first book.

Special Thanks

MANY OF THE STORIES contained in this book were taken directly from the lives and experiences of parents and children the authors have worked with at the Center for the Difficult Child. Names and unique identifying factors have been changed to protect privacy. Many parents the authors have worked with asked them to write this book. It is intended to guide and support them, as well as to affirm the incredible efforts expended and transformations accomplished by families who have used these strategies.

In many ways we owe the most appreciation to the children with whom we have worked. As you know, difficult children are usually not the recipients of thanks or gratitude. Children with severe behavior problems rarely have the opportunity to be successful enough to gain appreciation or recognition. In our case, however, it is they who have moved us to search for new answers, new methods and ultimately solutions such as this model. It is also to them, and those who care and work with them, that we dedicate this book—in hopes that their lives can be touched in positive ways through this approach.

Special Thanks

Final Notes

HOWARD GLASSER HAS WRITTEN THIS BOOK because he knows that sharing this successful model with parents can have a bigger impact on children and families who might otherwise be lost to a maze of frustration, anger and failure within the current culture of care. Contemporary supports for the difficult child and the family have been increasingly "capitated"—cut or pared down to having fewer counseling sessions covered by most insurance and public assistance programs, and leading to a more intolerant view of the intense child within school and community settings. Many parents adamantly pleaded that we write this book, not only as a resource of ongoing support for them as they use the model, but also for other parents who are undertaking the demanding task of raising a challenging child without effective support.

Jennifer's participation was prompted by her former experience as a therapist using conventional treatment approaches in a community mental health setting. Not only were the approaches she previously learned failing many children and their families, she was ready to leave the field due to her own sense of failing to help as a counselor.

"It took years for me to acknowledge that conventional treatment was not producing visible results—often prolonging a family's dependence upon a therapist instead of empowering them to become the true healers of their own families. After settling in Tucson, I heard about Howie's work in the community. I learned his model, and with rather dazzled amazement witnessed the power and speed of the transformations. Time and time again I saw the changes, the healing, and the amazing strength of parents as they emerged with new tools to help their children. I became convinced, for the first time that short-term treatment was not only more ethical and realistic for most families, it was more effective. Seeing the positive evolution of families with this model made writing this book a necessary challenge."

—Jennifer Easley, M.A.

221

THE CHILDREN'S SUCCESS FOUNDATION, founded in 1996, is a nonprofit organization devoted to the purpose of introducing this model into existing educational institutions and making the model available to parents at each school where it is being used.

If this book has helped you transform your child to a new life of success, become an ambassador. Teach a friend, neighbor or acquaintance what you have learned. The Children's Success Foundation would be delighted to accept your tax-free donations of any size to help fund future use of this approach in schools and in community initiatives. We would also value your correspondence. Please send your stories and outcomes and any other helpful strategies that you would like to share to:

THE CHILDREN'S SUCCESS FOUNDATION
4165 West Ironwood Hills Drive
Tucson, Arizona 85745

You can find out more about the Nurtured Heart Approach at the website and learning center that supports this approach:

www.ChildrensSuccessFoundation.com

Resources

Nurtured Heart Approach Support Information

Two websites are available to those who seek further information about the Nurtured Heart Approach: **www.ChildrensSuccessFoundation.com** and **www.DifficultChild.com**

The Children's Success Foundation website is the online learning center for the Nurtured Heart Approach. It is a website where parents, educators, coaches and therapists can gain acquisition of the approach, the techniques and then continually hone their expertise through innovative learning modules, discussion forums, web courses as well as feature articles, products and services supporting the approach.

The Difficult Child website is also fully in support of learning the Nurtured Heart Approach and providing an array of resources.

Books on the Nurtured Heart Approach

Those listed below are available in most libraries and bookstores and from online sources.

They can also be ordered online at the Nurtured Heart Approach Bookstore, which can be accessed at either **www.ChildrensSuccessFoundation.com** and **www.DifficultChild.com**

Phone Orders can be made toll free by calling our fulfillment center – SPExpress - **800-311-3132**

Transforming the Difficult Child: The Nurtured Heart Approach (Revised 2013) by Howard Glasser and Jennifer Easley

All Children Flourishing – Igniting the Greatness of Our Children (2008) by Howard Glasser with Melissa Lynn Block

Transforming the Difficult Child WORKBOOK – An Interactive Guide to the Nurtured Heart Approach (2013) by Howard Glasser, Joann Bowdidge and Lisa Bravo.

ADHD Without Drugs – A Guide to the Natural Care of Children with ADHD (2010) by Sanford Newmark, MD

Transforming the Difficult Child: True Stories of Triumph (2008) by Howard Glasser and Jennifer Easley

Notching Up the Nurtured Heart Approach – The New Inner Wealth Initiative for Educators (2011) Howard Glasser and Melissa Lynn Block

Notching Up the Nurtured Heart Approach WORKBOOK – The New Inner Wealth Initiative for Educators (2011) Howard Glasser and Melissa Lynn Block

Audio Visual Resources

Transforming the Difficult Child DVD – (2004) 6 Hours based on an actual filmed one-day seminar – with video clip illustrations.

Transforming the Difficult Child DVD – (2004) 4 Hours based on an abbreviated version of the above.

Transforming the Difficult Child CD – (2011) 3.5 Hours recorded from a live seminar.

Transforming the Difficult Child: The Nurtured Heart Approach – Audio Book (2012) – by Howard Glasser and Jennifer Easley – Read by Howard Glasser.